C000115837

797,885 Books

are available to read at

www.ForgottenBooks.com

Forgotten Books' App
Available for mobile, tablet & eReader

ISBN 978-1-333-38457-9
PIBN 10496980

This book is a reproduction of an important historical work. Forgotten Books uses state-of-the-art technology to digitally reconstruct the work, preserving the original format whilst repairing imperfections present in the aged copy. In rare cases, an imperfection in the original, such as a blemish or missing page, may be replicated in our edition. We do, however, repair the vast majority of imperfections successfully; any imperfections that remain are intentionally left to preserve the state of such historical works.

Forgotten Books is a registered trademark of FB &c Ltd.
Copyright © 2017 FB &c Ltd.
FB &c Ltd, Dalton House, 60 Windsor Avenue, London, SW19 2RR.
Company number 08720141. Registered in England and Wales.

For support please visit www.forgottenbooks.com

1 MONTH OF
FREE
READING

at

www.ForgottenBooks.com

By purchasing this book you are eligible for one month membership to ForgottenBooks.com, giving you unlimited access to our entire collection of over 700,000 titles via our web site and mobile apps.

To claim your free month visit:

www.forgottenbooks.com/free496980

* Offer is valid for 45 days from date of purchase. Terms and conditions apply.

English
Français
Deutsche
Italiano
Español
Português

www.forgottenbooks.com

Mythology Photography **Fiction**
Fishing Christianity **Art** Cooking
Essays Buddhism Freemasonry
Medicine **Biology** Music **Ancient**
Egypt Evolution Carpentry Physics
Dance Geology **Mathematics** Fitness
Shakespeare **Folklore** Yoga Marketing
Confidence Immortality Biographies
Poetry **Psychology** Witchcraft
Electronics Chemistry History **Law**
Accounting **Philosophy** Anthropology
Alchemy Drama Quantum Mechanics
Atheism Sexual Health **Ancient History**
Entrepreneurship Languages Sport
Paleontology Needlework Islam
Metaphysics Investment Archaeology
Parenting Statistics Criminology
Motivational

A History of
The French War

By

ROSSITER JOHNSON

New York

Dodd, Mead and Company

Publishers

Can 290 . 7

Francis Parkman fund

COPYRIGHT, 1882,

BY

DODD, MEAD & COMPANY.

PREFACE.

THE history of the struggle between the Gaul and the Briton for possession of North America, though in form a straggling story, stretching over two centuries, offers one of the most interesting studies of national character and destiny. To treat it exhaustively in a volume like this was impossible, if not undesirable ; but it is hoped that enough has been told to give the reader a clear idea of the character and sequence of all the significant events, and to suggest something of the philosophy of the long contest. A knowledge of this is absolutely necessary to any intelligent study of the subsequent history of our country.

The part played by the red man should not be overlooked. Bloody and terrible it was to the vanquished soldier, thrice bloody and hideous to the settler and his little family ; but though it prolonged and embittered the struggle, it had no real effect upon the result. In the earlier wars on this continent, the tomahawk and scalping-knife were enlisted mainly in the service of the French against the British ; but the Briton conquered the Frenchman nevertheless. In later wars, the same savage weapons in savage hands were wielded for the English against the Americans ; but the American conquered the Englishman. There is no more important lesson to teach the youth who must be our future soldiers and commanders than this, that in the warfare of nations the exercise of cruelty has never secured the ultimate victory. The power that only tortures and murders cannot become even a balance of power when two races are in conflict for precedence, or two opposite ideas for survival. Civilization must fight out its own battles.

An account of Pontiac's conspiracy, the final grand effort of the Indian to drive off the encroaching Saxon from American soil, would have formed an interesting sequel to the narrative of the French war ; but the limits of space forbade. I am indebted to my sister, Mrs. Joseph O'Connor, for valuable assistance in the preparation of this volume.

R. J.

NEW YORK, September 13, 1882.

CONTENTS.

A HISTORY OF THE FRENCH WAR.

CHAPTER I.

EARLY VOYAGES.

Claims of European Nations to American Territory—Contests of the English and French—The Indians in War—The Cabots—Cortereal—Spanish Explorers—Decree of Alexander VI.—Verrazzano—Cartier—Stadaconé—Hochelaga—Donnacona.

FOR more than a hundred years after the discovery of the continent of America, at the close of the fifteenth century, no permanent settlement was made by Europeans in its northern portion. The New World was looked upon mainly as a land of adventure and discovery, a land holding the possibility of unimagined wonders and undreamed-of riches, waiting only for the hand brave enough and adventurous enough to seize them and carry them back in triumph to the Old World. The sailor and the merchant looked to it for the realization of their brightest visions, and crowned heads confidently expected its wealth to replenish their exhausted treasuries ; but not till the latter part of the sixteenth century was it sought as a refuge and a home by the persecuted adherents of the new religion, and as a missionary field by the reawakened zeal of the older Christian Church.

The claims of European nations to American territory were vast and vague. When an adventurer touched a strip of sandy shore, he at once planted upon it the flag of his nation, and took possession of the whole continent in the name of his sovereign. These indefinite claims—in some instances strengthened by colonization or confirmed by Indian grants —were afterward used as a pretext whenever individual interests or religious hatred or European wars excited any of the feeble American colonies to make themselves and their neighbors still feebler by intercolonial hostilities.

The most successful explorers were Italians ; but they were all in the service of countries other than their own — in that of Spain, England, or France. The Spaniards made no attempt to establish colonies, or seriously to assert their claims, north of Florida ; and there they came somewhat into collision with the English and French. To those two nations was left the great struggle for the possession of the northern coast and the interior.

The worst feature of their contests was the participation of the red men, with their savage and indiscriminate modes of warfare. That most of their peculiar atrocities were committed in the interest of France was not wholly due to greater depravity on the part of the French ; for in later wars the English showed themselves quite willing to employ the same barbarous and irresponsible allies, knowing that their outrages would be perpetrated, not upon the hereditary foes of England, but upon Englishmen themselves. Many of the leaders on both sides would have been glad to have their savage friends conform to the usages of civilized warfare ; but when the Indian's zeal was once awakened and his thirst for blood aroused, it was impossible to hold him to a code which he did not recognize, and which to him seemed weak and cowardly. His own laws of war knew no mercy for the conquered. When he failed, he expected none ; and when he was victorious, he deemed himself defrauded if he were forced to let prisoners go untortured and unharmed. Hence the horrible massacres that followed some of the French victories.

That the Indians fought more frequently and zealously on the side of the French, was due to the superior tact and skill of the French in dealing with them, and to the fact that they earlier saw the advantage of gaining and holding the friendship of the natives. The British at first adopted the policy of avoiding them as much as possible, of driving them

back into the interior ; they regarded them as incapable of civilization, and scarcely looked upon
them as subjects for the influences of Christianity.
The French, on the other hand, tried from the first
to Christianize, if not to civilize them.   They drew
them when they could into missionary villages near
their own settlements, and sought to bind them to
themselves by the bonds of a common religion. The
wild life of the savages attracted many adventurous
spirits from the French colonies, who lived among
them as *coureurs de bois*, or wood-rangers, adopting
their mode of life and gaining an influence which
told largely for France in times of war.

Almost the only Indians who stood by the English
were the Iroquois, or Five Nations, whose home
was in New York.   Even their friendship often
wavered ; and it might be said that their adhesion
to the English was not because they loved them
more, but because they loved the French less.
Their enmity may have been caused by the fact
that the French, in the early days of their settlement
in the country, joined against the Iroquois with their
enemies, the Algonquins of the St. Lawrence.

When the English woke to the importance of
taking advantage of the distrust of the Iroquois
toward the French, they were never successful in
rousing them to the zeal in their cause which the

Indians of Maine and New Brunswick displayed in the cause of the French. Yet, though the English colonies availed themselves, as far as they could, of the help of the savages, it must be admitted that the record of the French in America is stained with many more atrocities not justifiable by any rules of civilized warfare—descents on unarmed laborers in the fields, and midnight attacks on peaceful settlements, with all the horrors of indiscriminate massacre, which were incited and often led by Frenchmen, and even in some cases by the ministers of religion, and in periods of nominal peace.

The contests between the English and the French for the possession of American territory were not ended until the close of the Seven Years' War in 1763. It is a curious fact that while the colonies which England had settled with her own sons, and which helped her to conquer New France, had revolted and become an independent nation in twenty years, those then wrested from France, French in their origin and devotedly loyal to the French Crown, have contentedly remained under British rule for more than a century.

The English claims were based on the discoveries of John and Sebastian Cabot, Venetians living in England, who, in 1497–'8, examined the coast from Labrador to Virginia. The Portuguese, in 1500, sent out Gaspar Cortereal, who explored the coast northward, and stole some of the natives, whom he took home for slaves. The Portuguese merchants therefore called the place *Terra de Labrador*, " land of laborers."

The best known explorers sent out by Spain, after Columbus, are Juan Ponce de Leon, who discovered and named Florida in 1512 ; Hernan Cortes, the conqueror of Mexico ; Pamphilo de Narvaez, who discovered the land of the Appalaches ; and Hernando De Soto, who found the Mississippi in 1541, and was buried in its waters the following year. Under the name of Florida, Spain claimed a vast country extending from the Atlantic to the Rocky Mountains, and from the Gulf of Mexico to the Arctic Ocean. This claim, based on the right of discovery, was further confirmed to Spain by a bull of Pope Alexander VI., making the Spaniards exclusive masters of all America. The decree of the Pope, however, was not powerful enough to prevent Francis I. of France from attempting to gain some share in the glory and profits of discovery.

The first explorer sent out by the French Government was John Verrazzano, an Italian ; though French sailors, in common with those of other nations, had resorted to the coasts of Newfoundland for years to fish for cod, some as early, at least, as

1504. Newfoundland and Labrador, or parts of them, were indefinitely called Baccalaos, a word said to mean codfish in the dialect of the Basque provinces. The sailors had a tradition that two islands north of Newfoundland were haunted by demons, whose clamor filled the air with confused sounds which were heard by ships venturing' near the unholy coast. They were called the Isles of Demons, and were represented on maps of the time with their infernal inhabitants dancing about in wings, horns, and tails.

Verrazzano set out in 1523 with four ships, but encountered a storm, and finally crossed the ocean with only one, the *Dauphine,* carrying fifty men and provisions for eight months.* He first saw the continent near where Wilmington, North Carolina, now stands ; but, as the shores were thickly lined with savages, he did not dare to land. The Indians made signs urging the sailors to come on shore, and one, more daring than the rest, took some presents

---

* The authenticity of this story, which rests upon a letter attributed to Verrazzano and published by Ramusio in 1556, has recently been called in question and, if not disproved, at least shown to be doubt ful. I have thought best, however, to let the reader see it, with this warning as to its character. It was first disputed by T. Buckingham Smith, in 1864. J. Carson Brevoort defends the story, in his "Ver- razzano the Navigator" (New York, 1874), and Henry C. Murphy re. jects it, in his "Voyage of Verrazzano" (New York, 1875).

and swam for the beach ; but, losing his courage
when near the land, he threw all he had to them and
started to return.   A breaker, however, tossed him
back upon the beach, and the Indians, running to
his aid, took him ashore, and built a great fire.
The terrified sailor, and his companions who were
looking on from the boat, had no doubt that they
were going to make a meal of him, or offer him in
sacrifice to the sun.   But he soon found that the fire
was to warm him and dry his clothes.   The Indians
gathered about him, admired his white skin, caressed
him, and took him down to the beach when he
wanted to return to the boat, dismissing him with
most affectionate embraces.

The *Dauphine* proceeded northward along the
coast, carrying away an Indian child stolen from its
mother in Virginia, explored New York Bay and
Long Island Sound, and stopped in the harbor of
Newport, where the white men were most cordially
treated by the Indians.   Having gone as far north
as Newfoundland, Verrazzano returned to France,
and wrote for the King the first known description
of the Atlantic coast of the United States.

   The most illustrious navigator sent out by France
in the sixteenth century was Jacques Cartier, of the
seaport town of St. Malo, in the northwestern part
of the kingdom.   He was sent at the suggestion of

Philip Chabot, Seigneur de Brion, Admiral of France, a favorite of the King, who induced his master to make another attempt to gain a footing in the country which had given so much wealth to the Spaniards. Cartier sailed on the 20th of April, 1534, with two ships of sixty tons, and one hundred and twenty-two men.

The voyage was so prosperous that Cartier reached Cape Bonavista in Newfoundland on the 10th of May. Finding the land still covered with snow and ice, he turned to the southeast, and landed at a port which he named St. Catharine. Then turning north again, he named some small islands Bird Islands. He was surprised, he says, to see a white bear as large as a cow on one of these islands, to which it had swum from the mainland, a distance of fourteen leagues. As soon as it saw the boats, it took to the water, and Cartier killed and took it the next day near Newfoundland. He sailed nearly around the island, which he described as the most wretched country to be found, with " nothing but frightful rocks and barren lands covered with scanty moss — but inhabited, notwithstanding, by men well-made, who wore their hair tied on the top of the head, like a bundle of hay, with birds' feathers irregularly inserted, which had a most curious effect.''

Crossing to the mainland, he entered a deep bay, which he named the Bay of Chaleurs, on account of the heat.   There is a tradition that it had before been entered by Spaniards, who, finding no signs of mineral wealth there, exclaimed, *Acá   nada !* "Nothing there !"— an expression which the Indians caught up and repeated to the French, who supposed it to be the name of the country, whence the word Canada.   It is more probable, however, that Canada is the Iroquois word *Kannata*, a village.

Having explored a large part of the bay, Cartier landed at Gaspé and took possession in the name of the King of France, raising a cross thirty feet high, on which was hung a shield with the arms of the country and the words, *Vive le Roy !* "Long live the King !"   After discovering Anticosti, he returned to France, taking with him two Indians, who picked up a little French and served as interpreters the following year.

The reports of Cartier's voyage convinced the court of Francis I. that it was desirable to found a colony, both for the purpose of establishing a profitable trade and for saving the heathen, not only from their heathenism, but from the heresies that might be imported among them by the Protestant peoples of Europe.   The Vice-Admiral Charles de Mouy obtained a fuller commission for Cartier, with

three well-equipped vessels ; and all the sailors assembled at the Cathedral on Whitsunday, by Cartier's directions, and received the bishop's bene-
diction.

They embarked on the 19th of May, in fine
weather, but a furious storm arose the next day,
and the scattered ships were tossed about for more
than a month, but at last met in the gulf or Great
Bay on the 26th of July. On the 10th of August,
Cartier gave to a small bay in the mainland, north of
Anticosti, the name of St. Lawrence, in honor of
the saint whose day it was. This name was afterward extended to the whole gulf, and to the river
also, which had before been known as the River of
Canada, or River of the Great Bay, and by Cartier
called the River of Hochelaga. Hochelaga was the
chief Indian town on its banks, and stood on the
site of Montreal.

They ascended the river, entered the Saguenay
on September 1st, examined the mouth of that river,
and then pursued their voyage up the great stream.
The large island just below Quebec, now known as
the Isle of Orleans, was so covered with grape-vines
that Cartier named it Bacchus Island. He stopped
next in the St. Charles, just north of Quebec, near
its mouth. On the site of the present city of
Quebec—between Fabrique Street and the Coteau

de Sainte Geneviève, it is thought—was an Indian town called Stadaconé. Here he received a visit from a chief, named Donnacona, who talked with Cartier by the aid of the two Indians who had been to France.

Cartier had heard of the much larger town farther up the river, called Hochelaga, and resolved to push on to it. The Indians of Stadaconé, who were of a different nation from those of Hochelaga, tried to dissuade him, representing that the way was long and beset with difficulties. When this failed to change his purpose, they pretended to have received a message from one of their gods threatening the French with storm and tempest, if they should ascend the river. Cartier sent back word to the god that he was a fool, and set out with one of the ships, the *Great Hermine*, and two long-boats. The anxiety of Donnacona and his people was probably caused by the fear that a rival nation might take from them the advantages of trade and alliance with this strange new people, from whose unknown abilities and resources they hoped not only gain, but an easy victory over their enemies.

The voyagers were obliged to leave their ships at Lake St. Peter, having missed the channel and run aground, and went on with only the two boats, reaching Hochelaga the 2d of October. The town

was round, and enclosed by three rows of trees.
The middle row stood upright, and the other two
were inclined and crossed above it. Then the sides
of the pyramidal wall were covered with logs well
fastened together. There was but one gate ; and
along the inside of the enclosing wall or palisade
was a gallery reached by ladders, and stored with
stones for the defence of the fortress. Inside of the
town were fifty cabins, each over fifty paces long
and fourteen or fifteen paces wide. These cabins
were tunnel-shaped, made of saplings bent together,
and covered with bark. Each was occupied by a
large number of families.

The Hochelagans received the French with courtesy, feasted them, and gave them gifts. They
looked with great admiration at the dress of the
strangers, their armor and weapons, their trumpets,
their fair skins and bearded faces. Cartier has left
a description of a peculiar kind of service held
among them. One day the warriors formed a circle,
on the outside of which were the women and children, and in the centre the Frenchmen, all the savages gazing at them '' as if they were going to play
a mystery.'' Then the chief advanced, pointed at
his decrepit limbs, and made signs that the French
should heal him. His example was followed by all
the sick, the halt, and the lame, who came them-

selves, or were brought to the supposed healer.
Cartier was perplexed, but seized the opportunity
to make a religious impression on their minds.   He
recited the beginning of the Gospel of St. John,
made the sign of the cross on the sick, and gave
presents of knives to the men, beads to the women,
and little tin lambs to the children.   Then he
prayed and recited aloud the passion of the Saviour,
and the ceremony was concluded by a mighty blast
from the trumpets, which set the savages nearly
beside themselves with wonder and delight.

The same day Cartier climbed the mountain, and
gave it the name which is now borne by the city and
the island, Mount Royal—Montreal.   Looking from
its summit over the vast extent of wooded country,
with the great river rolling by and the dark waters
of the Ottawa descending to meet it from the
unknown wilderness, he thought no better site for
a city could be found, and hoped, no doubt, himself
to lay there the foundations of a French empire in
the West.

On taking leave of the friendly savages, the
French returned to the St. Charles, called by them
the St. Croix, where they had left the greater part
of the men.   They found that barracks had been
built during their absence and surrounded by a kind
of intrenchment, sufficient to protect them from a

surprise. The Indians, however, continued friend-ly. But the sailors were attacked by scurvy, and twenty-five of them died. Cartier himself fell sick, and all of them might have perished, had they not learned by accident of the Indian remedy for the disease—a decoction made from the leaves and bark of a tree called by the Indians *Anneda*, which is thought to have been the white pine. A week after they began using it, the sick were all restored.

In the spring Cartier set sail for France. Having got Donnacona and some of his principal men into his hands, he carried them with him ; a piece of treachery which he excused by saying that the savages were making hostile preparations and at-tempting to get hold of Cartier himself. The Indians he took away were all baptized in France, and died there. Donnacona lived four or five years after his capture.

CHAPTER II.

DESTRUCTION OF FRENCH SETTLEMENTS.

Roberval and Cartier—Civil Wars in France—De la Roche—Pontgravé and Champlain—De Monts—Poutrincourt and Lescarbot—The Micmacs—The Jesuits—Madame de Guercheville—Colony of St. Saviour—Destruction of St. Saviour and Port Royal.

EITHER Cartier's report of his second voyage disappointed the hopes which had awaited the result of his enterprise, or the war in France drove the subject from the minds of those who had power to push on the undertaking ; for nothing further was done till 1540, when a gentleman of Picardy, Francis de la Roque, Seigneur de Roberval, received a patent, declaring him Lord of Norumbega, the King's Viceroy and Lieutenant-General in Canada, Hochelaga, Saguenay, Newfoundland, Belleisle, Carpon, Labrador, Great Bay, and Baccalaos. This flourishing and pompous beginning had a most contemptible outcome.

The next year Roberval went to the St. Lawrence, sending Cartier, who was to be his pilot, in advance. The Indians at Stadaconé crowded about Cartier's ship, asking for Donnacona and their other countrymen who had been taken away, and Cartier told them Donnacona was dead, but the others were living in France in great state, and were not willing to return to their own country. The Indians received the story with distrust, and when Cartier, after building a fort at the mouth of Cape Rouge River above Stadaconé, left most of his men there, and went up the river to Hochelaga, they killed two of those who were left. On Cartier's return, the men at the fort, which was called Charlesbourg Royal, discouraged both at the hostility of the Indians and the failure of Roberval to arrive from France, whither he had gone for supplies, clamored to go home, and Cartier yielded. Near Newfoundland they met Roberval, who ordered them back; but Cartier stole away with his ship in the night. In 1543 he went out again, and brought back the remnant of Roberval's colony, much reduced by disease and executions for mutiny.

Roberval seems to have been stern and vindictive, uncompromising and impolitic in his management, and ill adapted to be the head of a colony where he had to rule a lawless band of adventurers and convicts within, and keep the peace with suspicious and crafty savages without. Under his rule, men were hanged for theft and insubordination, and the whipping-post was in frequent requisition. In one case several men were banished to an island and kept there for some time in fetters.

Cartier, after the inglorious ending of his career as a navigator, which had begun so brilliantly, settled down to a quiet life at his country-house in the suburbs of St. Malo, which was still standing a few years ago.

More than half a century passed before the project of settling colonies in North America was revived. France had been torn by dissensions between the Catholics and Protestants ; eight civil wars were waged during the reigns of Charles IX. and Henry III., a period of twenty-eight years. But the rule of the moderate and tolerant Henry IV. restored tranquillity to the kingdom ; and the spirit of adventure and discovery revived. During the interval, the fisheries and the fur-trade had been carried on in the vicinity of Newfoundland by Frenchmen and sailors of other nations, and had grown to large proportions.

In 1598 the Marquis de la Roche received a grant from the King to colonize New France, with substantially the same title which had been conferred on Roberval. By the terms of this grant he was made an almost absolute monarch, having sole power to raise troops, make war, build towns, give laws, impose punishments, and grant pardons ; but he was required to keep in view the establishment of the Roman Catholic faith. The gains and profits of the first voyage were to be divided into thirds, one for him, one to be distributed among his companions, and one applied to the expenses of war, fortification, and other common charges.

For the purpose of establishing this magnificent transatlantic feudal viceroyalty, the Marquis gathered a company from the prisons, and under the guidance of a skilful pilot named Chedotel, landed at Sable Island, a desolate spot south of Cape Breton. Here De la Roche put ashore forty of his convicts, and went on to explore the coasts of Acadia, intending to call for the men on his way back ; but contrary winds prevented a landing, and the wretched men were left alone on the sandy and barren island.

When they found themselves deserted, and the last hope of the vessel's return had died away, they built cabins of the wrecks of Spanish vessels. A few sheep and cattle were roaming about the island, sprung from some that had been on board the wrecked ships, or left there in a forgotten enterprise by the Baron de Lery ; and these, with the fish they caught, furnished a living. When their clothes were gone, they dressed in sealskin. So they lived for seven years. Various misfortunes had assailed De la Roche when he returned to France, and he had been unable to do anything toward their release ; but at last the King heard of them, and sent Chedotel to bring them back. The forty men were reduced to twelve, whom Chedotel took to France and presented before the King in the same dress in which he found them, " covered with sealskin, their hair and beards of a length that made them resemble the pretended river-gods, and so disfigured as to inspire horror. The King gave them fifty crowns apiece, and sent them home released from all process of law."

After the death of De la Roche, patents were granted to others, who used them mainly to enrich themselves by trade. But in 1603, the Sieur de Pontgravé, a merchant of St. Malo, having received permission from the King to continue discoveries in the region of the St. Lawrence and make settlements there, associated with himself Samuel de Champlain.

This great man was destined to become the real founder of New France. He was born at Brouage, in Saintonge, a department of Western France, in 1567. After serving in the army of Henry IV., he had gone to the West Indies as a captain in the Spanish service, and kept a journal, which he called " A Brief Discourse of the Most Remarkable Things

Seen by Samuel Champlain of Brouage, in the West Indies." He drew his own illustrations for it — maps of the coasts, pictures of strange animals, and Indians burned for rejecting the gospel or whipped for not going to mass. This manuscript is still preserved at Dieppe, and has been published in an English translation. The accounts which he afterward gave of his adventures in the French colonies, under the title, " Voyages in New France," are an important source of information regarding the early history of those colonies.

Pontgravé and Champlain ascended the river to find Cartier's town of Hochelaga ; but it was gone, probably destroyed in some Indian war. The rapids prevented them from going farther, and they returned to France, to find that a new commission had been given to Pierre du Guast, Sieur de Monts, of Saintonge. This gentleman was a Protestant, but agreed to establish the Roman Catholic religion among the Indians, while his own sect was to enjoy full freedom of worship. He went out with four ships, taking in his own some Catholic priests and some Huguenot ministers, who edified the crew with their disputes, even " falling to with their fists on questions of faith." A Franciscan friar who wrote a history of Canada says the crew buried in one grave a priest and a minister, who happened to die at about the same time, to see if they would lie peaceably together.

De Monts went to Acadia, and landed his men on the southern shore of what is now Nova Scotia, and then sent out Champlain to explore the coast and find a place for a settlement. He entered and named the harbor of Port Royal, where Annapolis now stands, a place which holds an important position in the early history of America. Crossing the Baye Françoise, now the Bay of Fundy, they entered the St. John's, naming it in honor of the saint whose feast fell on that day, and selected for the site of their colony an island in St. Croix River, called by them Isle St. Croix, and now known as Doucett's Island. The St. Croix they called River of the Etchemins, from the tribe of Indians living there.

During the winter Champlain explored the coast as far as Cape Malabar, taking possession of the country in the name of the King of France. Finding that the island selected had been chosen unwisely, De Monts moved his colony in the spring to Port Royal. A settlement had already been begun there by his lieutenant, De Poutrincourt, who had taken a fancy to the place, wished to bring his family and live there, and had therefore obtained a grant of Port Royal and the vicinity from De Monts.

The next year Poutrincourt brought from France with him Mark Lescarbot, an advocate from Paris, who proved a great acquisition to the colony, being quick and fertile in invention of schemes, and able to inspire the men with enthusiasm for carrying them out. He induced them to plant fields and construct roads, showed them how to make fire-bricks, and build a furnace for clarifying the gum of the fir and making pitch ; and under his direction they built a watermill to take the place of the hand-mills they had been using. The priests had all died, and Lescarbot undertook to read and expound the Scriptures on Sundays. The supplies were abundant, and the winter passed with plenty of good cheer and fun, led by Lescarbot and Champlain. Lescarbot afterward wrote a history of New France.

To their feasts the Micmacs, or Souriquois Indians of Acadia, were made welcome. These Indians were firm and serviceable allies of the French during all the time of their occupation of the country ; and their chief, an old man named Mambertou, became a great favorite with the settlers. Lescarbot wrote a poem commemorating a victory he gained over the tribe of the Armouchiquois.

De Monts, who had lost the privilege given him

of carrying on the fur-trade to the exclusion of all others, succeeded in getting it restored, on condition that he plant a settlement on the St. Lawrence. He therefore removed his men and supplies, and Champlain went with him, leaving Port Royal to Poutrincourt, who had obtained a confirmation of his grant of the place from the King. At the same time the King notified him that something must now be done for the conversion of the Indians ; and the King's confessor, Father Cotton, being directed to choose some Jesuit fathers to go over and begin the work, selected two, Pierre Biard and Enemond Masse.

But Poutrincourt was unwilling to take the fathers over. Some historians have supposed that both he and Lescarbot were secretly Protestants ; but it is more probable that they merely shared the prejudice against the Jesuits as extremists in the Church and secret friends of Spain, which was not uncommon among good Catholics in France at the time. Poutrincourt gave Father Cotton to understand that he should soon embark at Bordeaux. Thither Father Biard repaired, and waited a whole year, but there were no signs of departure. The Jesuits complained to the King, and the King sharply rebuked Poutrincourt, who promised to go at once, and made his preparations ; but at the last moment he begged Father Cotton to let the missionaries wait until another year, that the colony might be in a better condition to receive them. Father Cotton let the matter go ; and Poutrincourt sailed. When he arrived at Port Royal, wishing to show the King that America could be Christianized without the Jesuits, he began to gather in the Indians for religious instruction ; he had with him a priest named La Fleche. Old Mambertou was the first convert, and others followed so rapidly that in a few weeks Poutrincourt was ready to send over to the King a list of twenty-five Indians who had been baptized into the Church. Mambertou received in baptism the name of the King, members of his household were called after the royal family, and the lesser Indians after other titled personages at the French Court.

The list was taken over by Poutrincourt's son, Biencourt. But Henry IV. had fallen by the knife of an assassin, and Biencourt gave it to the Queen regent, supposing the matter of sending the Jesuits would not be pressed any farther. But they had succeeded in interesting in their favor the Marchioness de Guercheville, a woman of great energy, enthusiasm, and devotion to the Church, who assumed the rôle of patroness of the mission to the Indians, and collected money for building and furnishing a chapel.

Two Huguenots who were associated with **Bien-court** refused to let the Jesuits go ; but **Madame de Guercheville** raised money at court and bought them out. Then she purchased from De Monts all of his claim under the grant of Henry IV., which had now been revoked, intending to get it renewed ; and she did afterward receive a royal patent for all of North America from the St. Lawrence **to** Florida, excepting Port Royal, which had been given to Poutrincourt. She made a contract with Biencourt by which the missionaries were to be supported from the proceeds of the fisheries and **the** fur-trade.

The missionaries at length reached Port Royal, in June, 1611 ; but there was never a very good understanding between them and Poutrincourt, who resented the Jesuits' interference with what he considered his own province. Lescarbot reports him as saying to Biard, '' I with my sword, Father, have hopes of Paradise, and you with your breviary. Show me my way to heaven, and I will show you yours on earth.''

The missionaries were anxious to learn the Indian language ; but those of the French who could have helped them would not. Old Mambertou, however, came to them for instruction in Christian doctrine, and helped them to some knowledge of his language, though he did not live long after their arrival. Biard, to show how the Indians had been taught by Father La Fleche, reported that when he was teaching him the Lord's Prayer, Mambertou objected to the petition for daily bread, saying, " If I only ask for bread, I shall get no fish nor moosemeat."

The story of Mambertou's death is interesting. Father Masse took him to his own house when he fell ill ; but care and remedies were of no avail. Mambertou saw that he must die, called for the last sacraments, and exacted a promise from Biencourt that he should be buried with his own people. Father Biard said it could not be allowed ; for to bury the chief in heathen ground would be a stumbling-block to the Indians. Biencourt urged his promise, and said the father had only to bless the spot where the chief should be laid. The missionary replied that this could not be done unless all the pagan bodies were first removed ; and that, of course, was out of the question. But Mambertou was obstinate, and Biard declared he would have nothing to do with the funeral. The terrors of the world to come and the firmness of the Jesuit at last prevailed ; Mambertou gave way, died with the consolations of the Church, and received Christian burial.

The Jesuits made some farther attempts to bring the savages into the fold of the Church. Biard went to visit the Kinibequi, or Kennebecs, and other Indians in what is now the State of Maine, in company with Biencourt; and Father Masse made an expedition with Louis, the son of Mambertou, from which he came back worn with sickness and hardship. But the commandant and his son treated their Jesuits grudgingly; the colony was growing feeble, depending on supplies from France and help from the Indians, and neglecting the care of the soil.

On the other hand, the Jesuits, in concert with Madame de Guercheville, made it uncomfortable for Poutrincourt in France. His funds were running low, and the colony was a constant drain upon them. He was forced to admit Madame de Guercheville as a partner, in order to get aid for Port Royal. She sent over another Jesuit, a lay-brother, Gilbert Du Thet. But quarrels ensued at the colony; Du Thet was sent back; and Madame de Guercheville, who by this time had received her grant of the greater part of North America, determined to begin a new settlement.

She therefore sent out a vessel in the spring of 1613, under the command of the Sieur de la Saussaye, who, stopping at Port Royal, took on board the two Jesuits, and sailing on began a settlement on Mount Desert Island, which was named St. Saviour.

But the colony was destined to be short lived. Samuel Argall, a piratical adventurer of Virginia, set out for a fishing excursion off the coast of Maine. On his way, he heard of the new settlement from the Indians, and resolved to drive away the French, on the strength of patents from the English King giving to the London and Plymouth Company the control of North America up to latitude 45° N. After a short engagement, in which Brother Du Thet valiantly fired off a cannon which he forgot to aim, and soon after fell mortally wounded, La Saussaye surrendered.

Argall took possession, cut down the cross the Jesuits had raised, and, searching the baggage of La Saussaye, found and stole his commission. The next day he asked Saussaye to show his commission, saying that he should respect the authority of the French King, although the country belonged to the English. La Saussaye, of course, could not find the commission ; whereupon Argall denounced him as a pirate, and gave up the French ship and the houses of St. Saviour to be plundered by his men.

After this he treated the colonists more mildly. He offered them a small bark to take them home to

France ; but it would not hold them all. Fifteen embarked in it, including the commandant and Father Enemond Masse, who went to look after their spiritual interests. At first they had no pilot ; but in a day or two, as they were coasting along, they found their pilot, who had fled from the English to the woods, and took him in. Near Port de la Hêve, on the southern shore of Acadia, they met two French ships, which took them safely to St. Malo.

The rest of the French prisoners were induced by Argall to go with him to Virginia. He promised that they should be treated well, allowed the free exercise of their religion, and be sent to France in a year if they cared to go. But when they reached Jamestown, where Sir Thomas Dale was acting as Governor, Dale declared that they should all be hanged as pirates. Argall tried to protect them, pleading the terms of the surrender and the promises by which he had induced them to come to Virginia ; but Dale would not relent ; he said they had been trespassing on English territory without authority, and they deserved the fate of pirates. Seeing no other way of saving them, Argall was obliged to produce the stolen commission of La Saussaye and confess his baseness. Sir Thomas was compelled to give up at sight of the commission from the

French King, but he declared that the French should be driven out of Acadia.

This he at once made preparations to do, though that part of the continent was included in the grant made by the English King to the Plymouth Company, while Virginia was under the control of the London Company; so that the Virginians had no claim whatever to interfere with the French in Acadia. He fitted out three ships, and gave the command to Argall. Biard and Quentin, the Jesuits who had gone with Argall to Virginia, went with them, as did several others of the Frenchmen. They sailed first to St. Saviour, and destroyed all they had left at their previous visit. Next they went to the island of St. Croix, where De Monts had had his colony, and razed the deserted buildings. Then they crossed the Bay of Fundy to Port Royal, guided, it is supposed, by Father Biard, who saw an opportunity to be revenged on Poutrincourt's colony.

Biencourt, who was in command, was absent among the Indians. But supplies had lately been sent from France, and these the invaders had the satisfaction of seizing or destroying by fire. "And please God," says Biard, in his story of it, "that the sins committed there may have been also consumed." They cut off the arms of France and the

names of the founders of the colony, which had
been cut in a large stone standing in the fort, and
left the fort itself in ruins.   Sailing up the river,
they saw the fields and mills where the men were at
work.   Biard, it is said, tried to induce some of
them to leave Biencourt and serve under Argall.
But they rejected the treacherous suggestion with
scorn, and one of them threatened to split the holy
father's head open with a hatchet if he dared to
make another of the kind.

. Biencourt tried to make an agreement with Argall
to divide the trade of the country ; but Argall refused to consider him in any light but that of an in-
truder on the territory of King James.   Biencourt
also asked the surrender of Biard, to whose treachery he attributed all the misfortunes of Port Royal ;
and the Jesuit, who was looked on with almost as
much distrust by the English, was in a dangerous
position.   His own account says he was saved by
his display of humanity and his forgiving spirit.
" He put himself on his knees before the captain at
two different times and on two occasions, to pray
for pity toward the French at Port Royal, to persuade him to leave them some provisions, their
sloop, and some other means of passing the winter.
And see what contrasting petitions were made to
the captain ; for at the same time when Father Biard

was thus interceding for the French, a Frenchman was crying out from afar, with abuse and accusation, that the Father ought to be butchered. Now Argall, who has a noble heart, seeing the Jesuit's sincere affection, and the beastly inhumanity of that Frenchman, refused to listen to the accusations.''

After the destruction of Port Royal, the French colonists were scattered. Some went to the settlements on the St. Lawrence ; but most of them spent a miserable winter, roaming in the woods and getting what help they could from the savages. Poutrincourt gave up all hope of the colony ; and in 1615 he was killed in a civil conflict in his own country. His son, with some few companions, among whom was Charles de la Tour, spent his life in Acadia and made efforts to rebuild Port Royal.

Argall sailed again for Virginia, taking back with him the Frenchmen of St. Saviour. But he encountered a storm at the very beginning of the voyage, and one of the three ships was lost ; Argall's own reached Jamestown in safety, but the one having the Jesuits on board was driven northward and then to the Azores, where it put into port at Fayal. It was a fortunate storm for Father Biard ; the ship carried a formal accusation from the Port Royal men to Sir Thomas Dale, against the Jesuit ; and the Governor, as Biard says, '' was waiting to cut

off his voyages by showing him the end of the world
from the top of the gallows.''

The ship, which was the one taken from La
Saussaye in Argall's first expedition, and was now
commanded by Turnell, the lieutenant of Argall,
was in some danger from the Portuguese at Fayal,
where it came to port ; the officers were at the
mercy of the Jesuits, who had only to accuse them
as pirates. But Biard and Quentin promised the
master of the ship that they would lie hidden while
in port, a promise which Biard claims great credit
for keeping.

When the ship arrived in England, Turnell was
put into prison on suspicion of being a pirate. He
had no papers to explain his position, and appear-
ances were against him ; he was in possession of a
French ship ; and he was only released on the testi-
mony of the Jesuits. After spending some time in
England, Fathers Biard and Quentin were claimed
by the French ambassador and sent home. La
Saussaye and his companions were at length shipped
from Virginia to England, and in the end reached
their own country. Madame de Guercheville sent
La Saussaye to demand reparation in London ; but
she seems to have succeeded only in getting her ship
restored. This was the end of the first serious
attempt at French settlement in Canada.

CHAPTER III.

QUEBEC FOUNDED, AND TAKEN BY THE ENGLISH.

Founding of Quebec—Friendship with the Algonquins—Expeditions against the Iroquois—Story of De Vignan—Introduction of Priests—Hostile Attempt of the Iroquois—Grant of Acadia to Sir William Alexander—Religious Troubles in France—Capture of Quebec by Kirk—The La Tours in Acadia—Treaty of Germain-en-Laye—Death of Champlain.

ACCORDING to the terms of his grant, which required him to make a settlement on the St. Lawrence, De Monts sent Champlain to select a site and begin the work of building a town. Arriving at the spot where Cartier, more than seventy years before, had found Stadaconé, the capital of Donnacona, Champlain selected the same site for his settlement, and resolved to build a town on the promontory just where the Indian town had stood. All traces of Stadaconé had now disappeared. The Indians called this part of the river Quebec, signifying "a narrowing in," or a strait, the river here being only about three quarters of a mile in width.

The history of Quebec has justified the sagacity of Champlain's choice. Rising three hundred feet above the river, the steep wall of rock forms a natural stronghold and commands the stream below.

Here, in July, 1608, Champlain began preparations for the oldest permanent settlement in North America, except the one at Jamestown, Virginia, which dates from 1607. Having first put up some rude barracks for temporary shelter, the men made an embankment along the present line of Mountain Street. Then they built a wooden wall with openings for defence, and within the wall three houses. Outside the wall they dug a moat.

During the winter Champlain took care to gain the friendship of the neighboring Indians. The supplies at the fort were abundant, and were freely divided with the famishing savages, who were accustomed to make very slight provision for winter. The Indians of the St. Lawrence belonged to the great family of the Algonquins, whose various tribes were scattered over Canada, New Brunswick, Nova Scotia, the New England and Middle States, except New York, and parts of Virginia, Michigan, Wisconsin, Illinois, Indiana, and Kentucky.

Their deadly enemies were the Iroquois, or Five Nations, including the Mohawks, Oneidas, Onondagas, Cayugas, and Senecas, who lived in New York. In 1715 the league of the Iroquois was joined by the Tuscaroras of Carolina, and hence they are often mentioned in history as the Six Nations. The Hurons and Eries lay near the lakes which bear their names. At this time the Hurons were in league against their kindred, the Iroquois, with the Algon-quins of the St. Lawrence.

These Indians had great hopes of the alliance of the French in their warfare against the powerful league of the Iroquois; and in the spring of 1609 they asked Champlain to join them in an expedition to the Mohawk country. Satisfied that his best policy lay in the alliance with the Algonquin tribes, and anxious to penetrate farther into the ~·eat un-known region at the west, in the hope of finding some clue to the passage to the East Indies, which was the dream of all the early voyagers, Champlain joined them with eleven other Frenchmen. This began an enmity between the French and those fierce and powerful tribes, which lasted for more than a century and a half.

The Indians assured Champlain that there was no obstruction along the water route they intended to take, and he therefore embarked in a shallop, while they took to their canoes. They ascended the St. Lawrence and the Sorel or Richelieu, which they called the River of the Iroquois. Hearing at length the noise of rushing water, Champlain left some of his men in charge of the shallop and, pushing on through the woods, came to the Chambly Rapid. Unwilling to abandon the undertaking, he told the Indians that, notwithstanding their deception, he would keep his promise and go on with them. He sent back the shallop with all his men but two, who refused to leave him ; and the Indians shouldered their light canoes, walked through the woods past the rapid, and embarked on the stream above.

At night they made an encampment, protecting themselves on the land side by a strong abatis of trees, and arranging the canoes so that in case of a surprise they could embark with ease and celerity. Then they all went to sleep without sentinels, answering Champlain's remonstrances by saying that those who labored all day needed rest at night.

Proceeding up the river, they entered the lake of which it is the outlet. To the east and southeast lay the rolling summits of the Green Mountains ; to the west rose the Adirondacks, covered with silent woods, but suggestive of lurking and stealthy warriors of the dreaded nations. To the beautiful sheet of water, Champlain, first of white men to look upon it, gave his own name. The islands abounded in deer, and the beavers worked in peace, for hunters were afraid to pursue their game so near the haunts of the terrible Iroquois. The Algonquins dared no longer advance by day ; they paddled their canoes at night, and rested hidden while the sun was up.

They had told Champlain of another rapid beyond

the lake, and another lake beyond that rapid—Lake George now—and they intended to go to it. But one evening when they were paddling silently up the lake at about ten o'clock, another silent fleet of canoes suddenly appeared on the water in front of them. It was the Iroquois. Both parties took to the shore and began to fortify themselves. Then the Algonquins sent to ask the Iroquois whether they would fight immediately. The answer was that it was too dark ; and they all danced and sang and shouted boasts and threats at each other through the night.

In the morning they prepared for battle. The Iroquois, about two hundred strong, marched through the forest under command of three chiefs, distinguished by the height of the birds' feathers they wore. Some had shields of wood or leather, and some had coats of mail made of woven twigs and cords. The Algonquins and Hurons issued from their defences and ran forward two hundred paces. When they were before the enemy they halted and separated into two divisions, leaving a space in the centre for the three Frenchmen. The Iroquois looked in wonder at the strange figure of Champlain, clad in glittering steel, surmounted by a plumed helmet. Then they moved to begin the attack. He aimed his arquebuse, into which he had loaded four balls, and fired ; two of the chiefs fell dead, and the third was dangerously wounded.   Then the allies raised a deafening cry and followed up the charge with a shower of arrows.

The Iroquois stood firm at first and returned th￢ charge ; but as Champlain was loading to fire again, his companions discharged their pieces, by which the frightened Iroquois were thrown into a panic, and fled in disorder.   The allies pursued them a short distance, took some prisoners, and brought away the supplies of the enemy, of which they were sadly in need.   On their way back they halted and brought out one of the prisoners for torture.   Disgusted with their horrible ingenuity, Champlain remonstrated, for some time without effect ; but at length he got leave to end the sufferings of the poor wretch by a shot from his arquebuse.

One of the Indians dreamed the following night that the Iroquois were in pursuit.   Not doubting the omen, the allies took to flight, only halting when they reached the islands above Lake St. Peter, where they hid themselves for the night.   At Quebec they separated, assuring Champlain that they should want his help in future wars.

When he returned from France the next spring, they were waiting for him.   Another journey up the St. Lawrence to the Sorel, another wild engagement, in which Champlain was slightly wounded by an arrow, another defeat of the Iroquois, through their fright at the strange and deadly weapons of the white men, and Champlain was again a hero with the Algonquins.   They gave him one of their prisoners, and the Hurons consented to take home with them a Frenchman that he might learn their language, on condition that Champlain should take with him to France a young Huron, who should bring back to them a trustworthy account of the country of their white allies, as seen through Huron eyes.

In 1611 Champlain attempted to establish a trading-post at Montreal, and had a site cleared ; but the settlement did not thrive.   In 1613, he went there, accompanied by a young man named Nicholas de Vignan, who had drawn considerable attention to himself in France, by stories of his adventures.   He professed to have ascended the Ottawa River to a great lake from which it flowed ; having crossed the lake, he said, he discovered another river leading to the North Sea ; at the mouth of that river he saw the wreck of an English vessel, whose crew had been killed by the Indians.   All this was told with so much detail and apparent honesty, that Champlain was deceived—the more easily as rumor said that Hendrick Hudson, during the voyage in which he discovered the bay that bears his name, had been put into a boat with eight others, and abandoned by his mutinous crew. Not doubting that the wreck was Hudson's vessel, Champlain resolved to ascend the Ottawa without delay, believing that he should find the long-sought northwest passage.

With Nicholas de Vignan, three other Frenchmen, and an Indian, he toiled up the river, in canoes, which had to be carried past the rapids and falls through the tangled forest, until they reached the Isle des Allumettes. Here was the home of the Ottawas, many of whom had been down to Montreal for trade and war, and were known to Champlain. They received him with kindness; but when he asked for help to continue his journey to Lake Nipissing, they told dreadful stories of the meanness, treachery, and sorceries of the tribe of the Nipissings.

Champlain said his companion, De Vignan, had been there, and had come back in safety. The Indians were greatly astonished at this, and plumply called Nicholas a liar.

"Nicholas," said the chief, "is it true that you said you had been to the Nipissings?"

Nicholas was silent for a time, then said in their language, of which he had some knowledge, "Yes, I have been there."

"You are an impudent liar," said the chief. "You know very well that you went to bed here every night with my children and got up every morning ; if you went to those people, it must have been in your sleep."

Champlain took Nicholas aside, and conjured him to tell the truth. Nicholas swore that all he had said was true. Champlain then told the Indians De Vignan's whole story—of the lake, and the river to the North Sea, and the wrecked ship—all of which the Indians insisted were outright lies. In great perplexity Champlain took De Vignan aside again, and promised if he would now tell the truth to forgive what was past ; but threatened that if he should be found out in a deception, he should be hanged without delay.

Nicholas thought it over, and then confessed. He had not expected that Champlain would have the perseverance to go so far as to discover the truth ; and he was anxious to enjoy the glory of the discovery. Champlain was so enraged he could scarcely endure the sight of him ; but he kept his word, protected De Vignan from the Indians, who officiously offered to despatch the liar for him, and let him return to Montreal and go on his way.

On his next visit to France, Champlain, who was a

man of sincere piety, and is recorded to have frequently said that the salvation of one soul was of more value than the conquest of an empire, obtained four Recollect missionaries to return with him, for the spiritual welfare of the colony and the conversion of the Indians. One of them, Father le Caron, who was assigned to the mission among the Hurons, went to Montreal with Champlain. There they found the Indians assembled for the fur-trade, and anxious to get the help of the French in another expedition against the Iroquois. Champlain promised it, and went to Quebec to get ready. The Indians, impatient of the delay, set out for their homes to collect their warriors, and Le Caron and twelve other Frenchmen went with them.

Finding them gone, on his return to Montreal, Champlain set out to follow them. Passing up the Ottawa and the Mattawan, he crossed to Lake Nipissing, which he traversed, and entering the French River reached the Georgian Bay. He coasted along its eastern shore southward, and thence went overland to the Huron villages. In one of them he found the zealous Recollect, whose ardor had been kindled by the sight of so many heathen, and who wrote to a friend, " Alas, when one sees such a vast number of infidels, needing but a drop of water to make them children of God, what zeal he feels to work for their conversion and to sacrifice for it his repose and his life !''

The Indians had built him a chapel of bark, and the priest had raised within it an altar with the sacred images and the candles ; and after Champlain's arrival, the first mass was said in the little chapel, and the missionary work among the Hurons was begun.

When the war parties of the Indians were all gathered, they made their journey to the southeast, by way of Lake Simcoe, the Talbot River, Balsam Lake, and the rivers Otonabec and Trent, to Lake Ontario, and crossed to New York, landing somewhere near the site of Sackett's Harbor. Concealing their canoes, they struck southward, were soon among the Iroquois, and attacked some small parties whom they found in the woods and fields.   The Iroquois took refuge in a fortified town, probably in the neighborhood of Lake Onondaga.

The defences consisted of a kind of fort surrounded by an abatis of trees thirty feet high, which supported a gallery where great quantities of stones were kept, to be hurled down on assailants.   The Hurons were repelled at their first attempt to take the fort.   Then they set fire to the abatis ; but the Iroquois had provided against fire by conducting water within the walls from a pond outside, and the flame was soon extinguished. Unable to control the Hurons, Champlain was obliged to let them carry on the attack in their own way ; and after three hours of fighting they retired discomfited. Champlain, although wounded, favored renewing the attack ; but the Indians insisted on waiting for some promised reënforcements. As these did not arrive, the Hurons retreated after five days, and returned to their own country. Their confidence in Champlain was lost ; they had supposed that his presence and the use of the fire-arms would always give them an easy victory. Sulky and disappointed, they refused to keep their agreement to send him back to Quebec ; and he was obliged to spend the winter among the Hurons.

In 1622, the Iroquois attempted to exterminate the French, in retaliation for the help given to the Algonquins. One party attacked some Frenchmen who were at the passage of the St. Louis Sault, or Rapid, and were repelled with loss. Another party went down to Quebec and besieged the convent which had been built for the Recollect Fathers on the St. Charles. But the fathers had a little fort ; and, by means of prayers within and balls without, they succeeded in driving off their assailants. The Iroquois were forced to content themselves with some Hurons whom they found not far away, and made prisoners.

After various changes in the management of the affairs of the colony, which were not prosperous, they had been placed under the control of two Huguenots, William de Caen and his nephew Emeric. The colony had been carefully kept free from Protestants, who would have settled in New France in great numbers if they could have been allowed to do so and to enjoy the free exercise of their religion. De Caen was ordered to take over some Jesuits; but when they arrived he would not permit them to stay at the fort or Chateau St. Louis, a building which Champlain had begun in 1620 for the citadel. The jealousies between the Jesuits and the authorities, and between the Jesuits and the other orders, proved a fruitful source of trouble in Quebec for years afterward. On account of the complaints of the Jesuits that Emeric de Caen obliged Catholic sailors to join in the prayers of his Huguenots, De Caen was ordered to stop all Protestants from praying or singing psalms on the St. Lawrence. But the sailors remonstrated, and a compromise was finally agreed upon, by which the prayers were allowed and the psalm-singing only forbidden.

In 1627, Cardinal Richelieu deposed the De Caens

and put the control of New France into the hands
of the "Company of One Hundred Associates."

After the devastation of Acadia by Argall, the
country, though claimed by both England and
France, was neglected by both. Biencourt inherited a claim to Port Royal from his father, Poutrincourt—who held it in right of a grant from the
French King—and lived in the country with his
friend, Charles St. Etienne de la Tour, who had
come to Acadia in boyhood with his father, Claude
de la Tour, a French Huguenot. In 1623, Biencourt died, having bequeathed his interest in Port
Royal and the surrounding country to Charles de la
Tour.

Meantime, the King of England, James I., had
granted the whole tract of land now forming New
Brunswick and Nova Scotia, together with the
peninsula between the mouth of the St. Lawrence
and the Bay of Chaleurs, to Sir William Alexander,
afterward Earl of Stirling, a now forgotten poet
and dramatist. The entire territory was called
Nova Scotia ; and the limits of Nova Scotia and
Acadia were long afterward a fruitful subject of
dispute and bloodshed between the English and the
French. In 1622, Alexander made an unsuccessful
attempt to plant a colony, and three years later an
order of Baronets of Nova Scotia was created.

Each baronet was to receive a tract of land six miles by three, and in return was to help in the work of colonizing the country.

In 1626, war broke ˙out in France between the Catholics and Protestants. Rochelle, the stronghold of the Huguenots, was held by the rebels, and Richelieu was besieging it, determined to put an end to the Protestant power in the kingdom. The city was making a desperate resistance, and Charles I. of England sent a fleet to the help of the rebels. Charles de la Tour, who had built a fort near Cape Sable, sent to France for arms and ammunition to prepare him for defence, in case the English should take advantage of the troubles in Europe to attack Acadia. The message was taken by his father, who came back bringing the supplies, in company with one De Roquemont, who had charge of cannon, ammunition, and stores for Quebec.

When hostilities opened between England and France, an expedition was fitted out under the auspices of Sir William Alexander to attack the French in America, and the command was given to Sir David Kirk, a Huguenot of Dieppe, who had fled from religious persecution in France.

Stopping at Tadoussac with his ships, Kirk sent a party to destroy the settlement at Cape Tourmente, and another to summon Quebec to surrender.

Champlain answered that he should hold his position
to the last, and, putting his poor defences in the
best possible order, waited anxiously for the expected supplies from France. But Roquemont's
ships were intercepted by Kirk, who took some of
them and sank the rest in the river. Supposing,
from Champlain's answer to his summons, that
Quebec was strongly fortified and garrisoned, he
made no further attempt at the time to take it.
But the following year he sent his brother Louis
to besiege it. The loss of Roquemont's supplies,
and the wrecking of another vessel which had been
sent over with food, had reduced the people of
Quebec almost to starvation, and they took to the
woods, where they dug roots and picked up acorns
for food. Many of them wandered off to the
Indians ;. some made their way to the sea-coast in
the hope of getting a passage to France in fishing-
boats. Champlain had only sixteen men left to
defend the fort, and as Kirk offered favorable
terms, he surrendered without resistance. The
soldiers were to march out with their arms and
baggage and a beaver robe apiece ; the friars with
their clothing and books ; everything else was to be
left in the fort. The French were to be furnished
with a vessel to take them to France. Louis Kirk
took possession of Quebec, July 20th, 1629, and the

banner of St. George waved on its heights for the first time, just one hundred and thirty years before the victory of Wolfe.

The elder La Tour, who was with Roquemont's fleet, was taken prisoner and carried to England. There he was presented at court and received with great favor. Moved, perhaps, by the treatment of Protestants in France, he renounced his allegiance to his own country, married one of the maids of honor of the Queen of England, was created a baronet of Nova Scotia, and received a grant of land there from Sir William Alexander. His son was invested with the same title and was to share the territory with him. In return, La Tour agreed to plant a Scotch colony and convey to the English his son's fort at Cape Sable.

In 1630, he went over with his colonists in two ships; but his son received the proposal to throw off allegiance to France with great indignation, much to the discomfiture of his father, who had had no doubts of success. After several attempts to persuade his son to a change of mind, he landed his men and assaulted the fort, but failed to capture it, and then took his Scotch colonists to Port Royal. When it became probable that Acadia would be given up to France by England, his son invited him to Cape Sable, and built a house for him outside the walls of the fort, stipulating that neither he nor his wife should ever set foot within them.

Champlain urged upon the French Government the policy of insisting on the restoration of New France when the treaty of peace should be made. The question was seriously debated whether it was worth while to keep and colonize Canada. All attempts so far had involved large outlays, with small returns. There was no mineral wealth, such as the Spaniards and Portuguese had brought from their colonies ; and Spain and Portugal, with all the treasure from Mexico and Peru, had declined rather than grown stronger.

On the other hand, it was argued that the right means had not yet been taken ; that the monopolies granted to individuals had interfered with colonization ; that New France might be peopled with the overflow of population at home ; that mines might still be discovered there ; that the fur-trade and fisheries, properly conducted, might be a great source of wealth ; and, above all, that France owed a religious duty to the heathen of the western wilds.

The restoration of New France was finally made one of the conditions in the treaty between the two powers which was signed at St. Germain-en-Laye, March 29th, 1632, when Canada, Acadia, and Cape

Breton came once more under the dominion of France.

Champlain died in the fort at Quebec, December 25th, 1635, and was buried in a sepulchre built by the colonists, the site of which is not very definitely indicated in the accounts of the time. About the year 1866, the Abbé Laverdière found traces of the tomb on the site of the Recollect Chapel in Champlain Street. The ground had been broken up the year before for the laying of water-pipes; but a vault was found containing a coffin and human bones, apparently those of some distinguished person, and near by were the remains of three others. On a wall of the vault which was still standing was found a part of the name, SAMVEL DE CHAMPLAIN.

Champlain's adventurous and courageous spirit, combined with his pure and disinterested motives, and his remarkably clear and far-sighted judgment, make him one of the most attractive and heroic characters in the early history of America. Though an enthusiast in the work to which he gave his life, he was forbearing toward the cowardice, the avarice, and the half-heartedness of colleagues, even when they retarded and almost ruined his work. Though faithful to his creed, narrow in the interpretation of it, as was the fashion of his age, and zealous in spreading it, he never appears as a persecutor.

CHAPTER IV.

THE FRENCH IN THE WEST.

The Iroquois—Fate of the Hurons—Fight at the Long Sault—Forts on the Richelieu—Montreal—The Jesuits—Discoveries in the Mississippi Valley—La Salle—La Chine—Iberville on the Gulf of Mexico.

THE history of Canada for many years after the death of Champlain is little more than the history of the Jesuit missions and the fierce battles of the Algonquins and Iroquois, in which the French suffered with their Indian allies. The Mohawks had not only recovered from their superstitious fear of fire-arms, but had supplied themselves with them from Dutch traders in the New Netherlands. Determined to exterminate the Hurons and Algonquins, they descended the St. Lawrence in war parties, and surprised their foes on the way down to the French settlements with their loads of bear and beaver skins for the summer trade.

The Governor of Quebec built a fort at the mouth of the Richelieu to intercept them ; but they easily avoided its guns by shouldering their birchen canoes at a point above and carrying them northeastward through the woods, to be launched on the St.

Lawrence below, while the garrison would not discover that they had passed.

By 1650, the Hurons were almost annihilated. Their principal towns had been· burned, and the inhabitants slaughtered, dispersed, or carried away. A remnant was taken to Quebec by the missionaries, and settled in several places successively in the vicinity of the city. Some of them are said to be · still living at the last place to which they were removed, called New Lorette. Some settled among their conquerors in Central New York, where they clung to the religion taught them by the Jesuits, and many good Catholics were found among them by missionaries in 1668.· That part called the Tobacco Nation wandered from place to place through the Northwest, driven by the Iroquois and the tribes among which they attempted to settle. They rested successively on the Island of Michilimackinac, the western shore of Lake Michigan, the banks of the Mississippi, the western shore of Lake Superior, the Strait of Mackinaw . once more, and at last at the western end of Lake Erie, where they were known as Wyandots. Under this name they fought with the French against the English.

In 1660, when a large party of the Iroquois were on their way to attack Quebec, a company of seventeen men, all between twenty-one and thirty-one years of age, under Adam Dollard, Sieur des Ormeaux, asked leave of the commandant of Montreal, in whose garrison they were, to go out and attack them.   It was almost certain death ; but their enthusiasm would take no denial, and the commandant gave a reluctant consent.

They were joined by a party of forty Hurons and four Algonquins, and at the foot of the Long Sault took possession of an old palisaded fort, built long before by the Algonquins.   The Iroquois came, and a desperate fight ensued.   The assailants were repeatedly repelled, and the French party, though suffering for want of water, held out bravely ; but after four or five days they were deserted by all the Hurons except their chief, Etienne Annahotaha, persuaded by some of their countrymen who had been adopted by the Iroquois, and who told them that a large reenforcement was on the way.

The reënforcement came, but the fort held out three days longer.   All the Frenchmen fell but one, and he, badly wounded, was carried away by the victors.   The Hurons who deserted were treated as prisoners.   But the Iroquois, although victorious, were discouraged and demoralized by the bravery of the heroes of the Long Sault, and returned to their own country.

In 1665, the Marquis de Tracy was sent over with two hundred soldiers to subdue the Iroquois. A fort was built, under command of an officer named Chambly, at the rapids in the Richelieu which bear his name, and another was erected on the site of the old Fort Richelieu, which had been built at the mouth of the river in 1642. The new fort was in charge of an officer named Sorel, whose name is preserved in that of the town and river. Salières, the Colonel, built a third fort above Chambly, called St. Theresa. The three western of the Five Nations were now at peace with the French, but the Mohawks and Oneidas continued hostile.

Courcelle, the Governor of Canada, and Tracy marched their men into the Mohawk country, and took their five important towns, the Indians flying at their approach without striking a blow. In 1667 the Mohawks asked for French mechanics and missionaries to be sent among them. The request was granted, and the French had almost unbroken peace with them for twenty years.

According to the authorities, the founding of Montreal was brought about in a wholly supernatural way. A gentleman of moderate fortune, named Dauversière, living at La Flèche in Anjou, was directed by a mysterious inward voice to establish a hospital-convent on the island of Montreal, in the

St. Lawrence; and about the same time a priest named John James Olier de Verneuil was also directed by an inward voice to send priests to the island of Montreal, to bring the American Indians into the true church. It is said that neither knew anything of the place; particulars regarding New France were published every year by the Jesuits, but these men saw the island in visions.

At length they chanced to meet, knew each other at once, and understood their common design. They formed a plan for establishing religious communities on the island, and for raising a colony to accompany them, and were soon joined by others, obtained a title to the island, raised some money, and resolved to send out forty men to begin a settlement under Paul de Chomedey, Sieur de Maisonneuve, who took charge in the same spirit of pious zeal which actuated the founders.

More associates were soon added to the company, many of them women of wealth, and another miracle supplied a leader for the nuns. Mademoiselle Jeanne Mance felt herself called to labor in Canada, and her spiritual director assured her that the call was doubtless divine. Chancing to go into a church at Rochelle, after she had determined to go, she met Dauversière, when the two instantly knew each other and understood each other's secret intentions

as had happened before with Dauversière and Olier.
Mademoiselle Mance went with Maisonneuve and his
colony, in 1641, and in 1642 they laid the foundations of Montreal, which they called Villemarie—
the town of Mary.

During all these years the missionaries were per-
forming wonders of courage and devotion among
the ungrateful and treacherous savages. Father
Nicholas Viel, a Recollect, on his way home from
among the Hurons to spend a time in retirement at
Quebec, was drowned by the treacherous Indians
who were bringing him in a canoe down the rapid of
the River of the Prairies, back of Montreal ; and the
rapid is still called the "Sault au Recollect."
Fathers Garneau and Mesnard were murdered by the
Ottawas.

The Jesuits were ready to enter every dangerous
field, and even to rush to martyrdom ; they established missions among the Hurons, notably that of
Sainte Marie on the River Wye ; they even attempted the conversion of the Iroquois. Father
Isaac Jogues, taken prisoner by them as he was returning from the Huron mission, might have escaped,
but thought it his duty to remain with his captive converts and prepare them for death. With
two lay associates of his order, Goupil and Couture,
he was carried to the Mohawk country and made to

suffer every torture that savage ingenuity could devise. Goupil was murdered on suspicion of having bewitched children with the sign of the cross.

Jogues suffered not only from his wounds, but from hunger; for he would not eat meat that had been offered to heathen gods. But he thought himself sufficiently rewarded by the opportunity of baptizing a few children and dying Indians. The following summer, going with a fishing-party to a place near Fort Orange, now Albany, he was assisted to escape by a Dutch trader; and the Dutch afterward paid a ransom for him, of the value of three hundred livres. He and his companions were the first white men to look on Lake George. At his next visit, three years later, he named it Lake St. Sacrament.

He went to France from New York, but returned to Canada in 1644, and volunteered to establish a mission in the Iroquois country in 1645. Undeterred by the recollection of the horrors of his former visit, he went back; but a sickness that prevailed among them during the summer, and the destruction of their harvest by caterpillars, were laid to the evil spell of a box of papers which he had left among them during a short absence. Jogues was seized on his return, and after being beaten,

hacked, and treated with the utmost cruelty and
indignity, was killed by a blow from a hatchet.
His companion, Father Lalande, shared his fate,
and their heads were set up on the palisades of the
town.

Father de Noué, a Huron missionary, was found
kneeling and frozen in the snow, in a midwinter
journey to Fort Richelieu.   Father Daniel was in
the Huron town of St. Joseph when it was assailed
by the Iroquois, and busied himself among the
panic-stricken inhabitants, baptizing and absolving.
When the assailants forced an entrance, he directed
those near him where to fly, and went to meet the
enemy to gain time for them.   A shower of arrows
was sent at him ; but the undaunted priest threatened
the assailants with the vengeance of God, at the same
time assuring them tnat repentance would gain his
favor.   A shot pierced his heart, he fell dead, and
was burned in his church, where his body was thrown
by the victors.

Charles Garnier and Noel Chabanel fell, the first
by the Iroquois at St. Jean, the other by a renegade
Huron convert who fancied the Christian religion
had been the destruction of the Huron nation.
Jacques Buteux was slain by the Iroquois on a toil-
some winter journey to the nation of the White
Fish, whose country was north of Three Rivers.

Jean de Brébeuf and Gabriel Lalemant were taken
at the Huron town of St. Louis when it was destroyed by the Iroquois, and slain after horrible tortures. The skull of Brébeuf—whose body, together
with that of Lalemant, was found on the scene of
his martyrdom—is still preserved at the Hôtel-Dieu
in Quebec, together with a silver bust of him which
his relatives sent over from France.

In the pursuit of their calling, the Jesuits pene-
trated far beyond the frontiers of the colonies, and
discovered lands and waters never before seen by
Europeans. It was due in part to their explorations
that the French laid claim to the Mississippi Valley
and the region of the Great Lakes, and that they
gained the alliance of so many of the tribes that inhabited the West, by whose help they came so near
establishing their claim. Father Claude Allouez, a
missionary to the Ottawas, explored the southern
shore of Lake Superior in 1667, and in 1670, with
Father Dablon, he explored the regions about the
Upper Wisconsin. In 1673, Father Marquette, with
Louis Joliet, discovered the Mississippi, and descended as far as the mouth of the Arkansas. Father
Hennepin accompanied La Salle down the Illinois
and up the Mississippi, and wrote descriptions of
his voyages.

One of the most renowned of French explorers of

the interior of the continent was Robert Cavelier de la Salle. Hearing of the great rivers at the west, he collected a party to go in search of them in 1669. The party numbered twenty-two, and included a priest, Dollier de Casson, noted for his great size and strength. It was said of him that when in his full strength, he could stretch out his arms and hold a man on each hand. The party set out from La Salle's seigniory on the St. Lawrence, which he called St. Sulpice. It was near the La Chine rapids, eight or nine miles from Montreal. They gave out that they were going to find a western passage to China. In Western New York they met Joliet, and learned something of his discoveries. For some reason, La Salle and others of the party returned to the St. Lawrence ; and on this account, it is said, his place was called in derision, La Chine (China), a name which it still retains and which is now applied to the rapid. De Casson and some of his companions went on, and were the first to sail through Lakes Erie and St. Clair.

In 1678, La Salle, having received a monopoly of the trade in buffalo-skins for five years, and permission to establish forts and trading-posts at the West, set out again. He built Fort Miami at the mouth of the St. Joseph, and Fort Crevecœur on the site of Peoria, Illinois. In 1682, he descended

the Mississippi to its mouth, and took possession
for France.   In 1684, he brought a colony of two
hundred and eighty persons to form a settlement on
the Mississippi ; but they missed the mouth of the
river and, going on to the shores of Texas, landed at
Matagorda Bay.   One of their four ships, the store-
ship, was wrecked, and two were taken away by the
naval officer in charge.   A fort called St. Louis was
built ; but the colony languished, and in 1687 not
more than one seventh remained.   La Salle started
northward by land with several companions ; but
some of them formed a conspiracy and assassinated
him near a branch of Trinity River, while the
survivors of his colony were nearly all murdered by
the Indians.

In 1699, D'Iberville and his brother De Bienville,
planted a French Colony on the Bay of Biloxi, the
first in the present state of Mississippi.   French
Protestants asked leave to settle on the lower Mississippi, but were told that the King had not driven
Huguenots from France to form a republic of them
in America.   In 1702 a fort was built on the Mobile
River by the colonists of Biloxi—the first settlement
in Alabama—and another was placed at the mouth
of the Mississippi.

The French had now a chain of forts and trading-
posts from the St. Lawrence to the Gulf of Mexico.

The oldest settlement in the Mississippi Valley is Kaskaskia, originally a Jesuit mission ; and besides the stations at St. Joseph and Peoria, there were posts at Detroit, Chicago. Vincennes, and other places on the line of the great lakes and rivers.

CHAPTER V.

ACADIA.

Destruction of English Trading-Stations—Feud between Charnisay and La Tour—Capture of Acadia by the English—Restoration to France by the Treaty of Breda—St. Castine at Penobscot—Attack by Andros—Hostilities by Indians—War between England and France.

AFTER the restoration of Acadia to France by the treaty of 1632, grants were made to Frenchmen in the country, and some colonists were sent out. There was room for a variety of interpretations of the treaty in regard to the territory near the Penobscot and Kennebec Rivers, according to the understanding of the limits of Acadia. The English trading-stations at Penobscot and Machias were broken up by parties of Frenchmen and the traders were plundered of their goods. The Plymouth colony attempted to re-take Penobscot ; but the French had strengthened the place and continued to hold it, warning the English to encroach no farther than Pemaquid.

The principal grants of territory in Acadia were made to Nicholas Denys, Isaac de Razillay, and Charles La Tour. De Razillay's rights passed into

the possession of D'Aulnay de Charnisay ; and the
story of a strange feud between him and La Tour is
the history of Acadia for years. La Tour's fort
and trading-station was at the mouth of the St.
John, Charnisay's at Port Royal. Disputes and
jealousies arose between them as early as 1635 ; and
Charnisay attempted to dislodge his enemy by
means of his influence at court.

He laid before the King and the Prime Minister
accusations of treason and other crimes against La
Tour ; and in 1641 an order was sent to the accused
to appear and make answer to the charges. At the
same time Charnisay was ordered to seize him and
take control of his fort, if he should refuse to obey
the order. La Tour refused, on the ground that the
order was based on misrepresentations. The vessel
sent to take him to France carried back letters from
Charnisay giving accounts of La Tour's defiance,
and before the end of the year he himself went to
France for help against his rival.

La Tour put his defences in the best possible
order, and sent a messenger to Boston, a Huguenot
from Rochelle, to propose an alliance. Though La
Tour himself had been a Protestant, he had professed
the Catholic faith ; but his wife was still a Protestant, and Charnisay used that fact to excite
prejudice against them at the French court. The

authorities at Boston readily accepted La Tour's proposal for free trade between his colony and theirs ; but they were more wary when it came to the question of furnishing him aid against Charnisay, and promised nothing. The next year La Tour sent his lieutenant to Boston with fourteen men and letters to John Winthrop, again asking assistance.

The people of Boston treated La Tour's men with great consideration, and were edified at their respectful attendance at the Puritan meetings, though they were Catholics. The lieutenant accepted with thanks, from one of the elders, a Testament in French, with notes by a Protestant minister, and promised to read it. He induced some of the merchants to fit out a ship and send it at once to open the trade.

On its way back, this ship stopped at Pemaquid, where it happened to meet Charnisay. He showed the officers an order from France for the arrest of La Tour, and gave them notice that he would seize any vessel he should find trading with the rebel. By giving mortgages on his lands to one Le Borgne, he had raised a large amount of money, with which he bought five vessels and hired five hundred men to serve against La Tour.

Failing of support from New England, La Tour sent to Rochelle in France, and a large armed ves-

sel, carrying one hundred and forty men, was sent
to him from that city. When this ship, the
Clement, reached St. John, she found the harbor
blockaded by Charnisay, who had come with two
ships, several small vessels, and five hundred men,
to assault the fort. Failing to take it, he established a blockade, hoping to starve the garrison
into surrender. La Tour and his wife now stole
out of the fort one night, reached the *Clement* in a
small boat, and sailed directly to Boston, where La
Tour with some of his men landed at Winthrop's
garden on Governor's Island.

The Governor called a meeting of the magistrates
for the next day, and the captain of the *Clement*, to
authenticate his mission, laid before them letters
from the Vice-Admiral of France and the agent of
the Company of New France, authorizing him to
carry supplies to La Tour, who was called the King's
Lieutenant-General in Acadia. The fact that these
papers were issued when an order for La Tour's
arrest was in the hands of Charnisay, is explained by
the confusion in the administration of the government, caused by the recent death of Richelieu, and
the expected death of the King, Louis XIII., who
died in May, 1643, before the *Clement* reached the
St. John.

On the evidence of these documents, the authorities of Boston gave him permission to hire men and vessels with which to relieve his fort. The merchants of Boston were anxious to see La Tour reinstated, not only from friendship toward him, but for the interests of trade ; for Charnisay was unfriendly and would have no commerce with them. Two of them let to La Tour four vessels, with fifty-two men and thirty-eight pieces of ordnance ; and he raised a force of ninety-two soldiers and armed them for service. The agreement was, that these vessels should accompany La Tour to St. John and aid the French ship in his defence in case Charnisay's forces should attempt to interfere with him. The owners of the ships sent an agent authorized to determine how far La Tour should be allowed to use them in the operations against his enemy. The New England soldiers were commanded by Captain Hawkins.

Not until the five ships appeared in sight of the harbor of St. John did Charnisay suspect that La Tour was not shut up with his men inside the fort. Not daring to cope with the force brought against him, he ordered his vessels to set sail at once for Port Royal. La Tour's fleet gave chase, and Charnisay ran his ships aground opposite the mill of Port Royal, and his men went to work to strengthen the defences. Captain Hawkins sent Charnisay a letter from Governor Winthrop, explaining the attitude of his government in the matter, and proposing a reconciliation between him and La Tour; but Charnisay would not open the letter, because the address did not give him his title of Lieutenant-General, and he sent the captain a copy of the order for La Tour's arrest.

As the messenger reported that Charnisay's men seemed confused and frightened, La Tour wanted to make an attack at once, and Hawkins gave his men permission to follow him if they chose to do so. About thirty of them joined in the attack, and Charnisay's men were driven from the mill, three being killed and one taken prisoner. The New Englanders escaped without loss. La Tour lost three men. On the way back to his fort the ships took a pinnace of Charnisay's, loaded with a great quantity of moose and beaver-skins, which were divided between La Tour and the crews and owners of the Boston ships. Much uneasiness was felt in Boston about the seizure of Charnisay's pinnace, from fear that it would involve them in a quarrel with that enterprising and dangerous rascal.

Charnisay built a new fort at Port Royal, and then sailed for France to get more help to crush La Tour; while soon after his arrival there, La Tour's wife reached Rochelle, in search of aid for her husband. Charnisay, by his influence at court, obtained an

order for her arrest on the same ground as that for
the arrest of her husband—that she was a traitor and
a rebel.   Hearing of it in time, she fled to England · and finding friends there, she set sail for
Acadia, in a ship loaded with supplies and munitions of war.   The ship carried as a passenger Roger
Williams, famous in the history of New England.

The master of the vessel spent so much time in
trading on the way, that it was six months before
they reached Acadia, and on the coast they fell in
with a vessel sent out by Charnisay to watch for
them.   The master concealed Lady La Tour and her
party, and gave out that he was on the way to Boston ; by which means they escaped, but the ship
was obliged to go on to its pretended destination.
When they reached that port, Lady La Tour
brought suit against the owners of the ship for the
damage she had sustained by the delay, and was
awarded two thousand pounds.   In satisfaction of
this judgment, she seized the cargo of the ship,
valued at eleven hundred pounds, and hired some
Boston vessels to take her home with her supplies.

Before she was ready to sail for St. John, a messenger from Charnisay, Monsieur Marie, accompanied by ten Frenchmen, arrived in Boston with
orders for the arrest of La Tour and his wife, and
asked that the people of New England should help

Charnisay to carry out the King's commands, or at least should refrain from giving any further aid to the rebel.

The magistrates explained their neutral position and their desire to effect a reconciliation between the rivals. Marie said La Tour should be assured of life and liberty if he would voluntarily surrender, but if taken in his rebellion he would be sure to lose his head ; and Charnisay was determined to capture his wife on her way home, believing her to be the cause of her husband's obstinate rebellion. At length the magistrates agreed to sign a treaty of peace with Charnisay ; but they reserved for their people the right to trade with whomsoever they chose. Having obtained this agreement, Marie hurried away before Madame La Tour set sail, in the hope of giving information to Charnisay in time for him to take her prisoner on her way, but he was too late ; and Madame La Tour reached St. John in safety.

Charnisay soon had an opportunity for retaliation. La Tour went to Boston and sent back a small vessel laden with stores. Charnisay captured it and turned the crew, all English, out on a desolate island covered with snow, and kept them there ten days without fire and with no shelter but a ruinous cabin. Then he sent them home in an old shallop, without a compass ; but they managed to get safely to Boston.

As Charnisay's ship was sailing away, it was hailed by two monks on the coast of the mainland, who wished to be taken on board. They had been sent out from the fort by Madame La Tour, on the discovery that they were secretly plotting in favor of Charnisay. They told him the fort could be easily taken ; La Tour was away, and the place was poorly supplied with men and munitions. Charnisay therefore pressed on for another attack. But Madame La Tour was not disposed to surrender ; she directed a fire against the ship, which killed twenty men and wounded thirteen, and Charnisay then retired in disappointment and wrath.

Two months later he returned to the attack once more. He had kept La Tour from reaching his fort by the vessels watching in the Bay of Fundy. La Tour's wife, however, withstood the siege three days, compelling Charnisay at that time to draw off his forces ; and had it not been for the treachery of a sentry, who betrayed the fort for a bribe, she might have been finally successful. The traitor allowed the enemy to scale the walls while the garrison were at prayers. Even then the lady put herself at the head of the men, and made a spirited resistance. Charnisay at length offered to grant life and liberty to the garrison if the fort were surrendered ; and knowing that she must yield at last, and anxious to save the lives of her men, the lady accepted the terms.

No sooner was Charnisay in possession, than, disregarding his compact entirely, he hanged all the garrison but one man, saving him only on the condition that he should act as the hangman. He compelled the lady to witness the execution with a rope around her neck, to signify that she deserved the same fate. Broken by the horrible scene, and the dangers and excitements of the siege, Madame La Tour lived only three weeks after the surrender of the fort, while her husband remained in Boston, ruined in fortune and homeless.

The next year Charnisay concluded a treaty of peace with New England. He claimed eight thousand pounds damages for the attack on his mill by the men under Hawkins in 1643 ; but his commissioners finally agreed to accept a small present by way of acknowledgment that the New Englanders were in the wrong in that affair. Governor Winthrop had an elegant sedan chair which had been on its way from the Viceroy of Mexico to his sister in Spain in a Spanish ship, when the ship was seized by an English adventurer, who gave it to Winthrop. This chair was frugally devoted to the work of repairing the friendship with Charnisay; and his commissioners departed with it and the treaty of peace.

In the following year Charnisay received a commission making him Governor and Lieutenant-General for the King in Acadia, and giving him the exclusive right to the fur-trade and the products of the mines. It remained for him to drive out Nicholas Denys, who was established in the eastern part of the peninsula, but this was accomplished much more easily and speedily than the expulsion of La Tour. The forts of Denys were taken, his fishing stations broken up, and himself and his family sent into exile.

Charnisay was now supreme in Acadia, and high in royal favor. His commission gave him the credit of having upheld the royal authority against armed rebels, of having built a seminary, provided friars to bring the Indians to a knowledge of the true religion, and driven foreigners from the King's dominions at the mouth of the Penobscot. But he did not long enjoy his triumph. In 1650 he was drowned in the river of Port Royal.

After the capture of his fort and the death of his wife, La Tour went to Newfoundland to get help from the Governor. Failing in this, he spent the following years in Boston and Quebec, until news

reached him of the death of Charnisay. He then
went at once to France, received an acquittal from
all the charges against him, and a commission as
Governor and Lieutenant-General for the King in
Acadia, and returned to take possession of his old
fort. Charnisay's widow and children were still
living in Acadia. Madame de Charnisay made an
agreement with the Duke de Vendôme, by which
he was to help her to recover the rights granted to
her husband, and to share with her and her children
in the possessions to be recovered. But before anything had been done toward dislodging La Tour and
Denys, who had also returned to his forts, La Tour
entered into a compact with Madame de Charnisay
which superseded the agreement with the Duke,
consolidated the claims, and restored peace between
the families. This was no less than a contract of
marriage between La Tour and Madame de Charnisay, signed in February, 1653.

At this time a new claimant appeared in the person of Le Borgne, to whom Charnisay had mort-
gaged his possessions. He was proceeding to dis-
possess La Tour and Denys, when he was interrupted by an enemy from without. Four vessels had
been sent from England for operations against the
Dutch colonies, and men were enlisted in Massachusetts ; but news arrived of peace between England

and Holland, and the force was turned against the French in Acadia. La Tour surrendered at the first summons, being without provisions or stores for defence, and Le Borgne gave up Port Royal after a slight resistance. Acadia was now once more in the hands of the English, and garrisons of New England men were placed in the forts; but the French settlers and missionaries were allowed to remain.

La Tour, with his usual activity and fertility in resources, sailed to England and appealed to Cromwell to confirm to him the grant made to him and his father jointly by Sir William Alexander in 1630. The success which seemed always to attend him when he pleaded his cause in person, attended him here. Cromwell granted to him, in connection with two of his own faithful followers—Thomas Temple and William Crowne—an immense tract of land, including the whole coast of the Bay of Fundy to a distance of one hundred leagues inland, all of the peninsula, and a large part of the present State of Maine. A small rent was to be paid in beaver-skins, and only Protestants were to be allowed to settle in the country, but the French Catholic settlers already there were not to be disturbed. La Tour soon sold out his rights to Temple, and retired from public affairs. Temple made great improve-

ments, and began to receive large returns in trade
for his outlay, when the subject of the restoration
of Acadia to France was again brought forward.

In 1667, by the treaty of Breda, which closed the
war that England had been waging for two years
with Holland and France, France gave back to England half of the Island of St. Christopher, which she
had taken, and received Acadia.

The disputed post of Penobscot, or Pentagoet,
was now occupied by the Baron de St. Castin, who
carried on a large trade there. He had lived a long
time among the savages, married an Indian wife,
and had great influence over all the tribes of that
region, belonging to the family of the Abenaquis.
In the spring of 1688, Edmund Andros, Governor
of New England, attacked St. Castin, on the ground
that the land was included in a grant made to the
Duke of York, at this time James II., King of England. St. Castin and his family fled to the woods,
and Andros plundered his dwelling. The result of
this was, that the Indians became restless, incited,
it was supposed, by St. Castin ; but the Revolution
in England by which James II. lost the throne
brought on a war between France and England, and
the colonies in America prepared for hostilities.

CHAPTER VI.

KING WILLIAM'S WAR.

Iroquois Attack on Montreal—Plan of the French—Capture of English Posts at Hudson Bay—Massacres at Dover, Saco, and Pemaquid—Three Expeditions Planned by Frontenac—The Schenectady Massacre—Salmon Falls Destroyed—Attack on Casco—Expedition Planned by the English—Sir William Phips—Capture of Port Royal—Schuyler at La Prairie—Phips at Quebec.

AT the opening of this war, the French had the post at Fort Frontenac, where Kingston, Canada, now stands, and one at Niagara, besides those on the western lakes and in the Mississippi Valley. In July, 1689, a thousand Iroquois attacked Montreal, massacred men, women, and children, burned houses, laid waste the fields, and carried away prisoners and plunder. The garrison at Fort Frontenac, panic-stricken, destroyed the fort and fled down the river in canoes, many of them losing their lives in shooting the rapids. After this disaster, the Governor, Denonville, was superseded by the former Governor, Count de Frontenac, one of the most efficient officers and one of the most striking and picturesque characters in the whole history of Canada.

Frontenac was instructed to carry out a plan laid

before the Government by Callières, commandant
at Montreal. Callières was to ascend Lake Champlain under pretence of marching against the Iroquois, then surprise and take Albany, descend the
Hudson, and seize New York, thus giving the French
the finest harbor on the coast, and cut off the Iroquois from receiving arms and ammunition from
the English. Callières was then to be appointed
Governor of Albany and New York. He was instructed to allow only French Catholics in the province ; the French Huguenots already there were
to be sent to France, and all other Protestants banished to other colonies. A fleet was sent over to
attack New York while Callières was engaged in
land operations, and Frontenac came over in one of
the vessels, as did also some Iroquois whom Denonville had treacherously seized two years before, and
sent over to work in the galleys. The fierce revenge
taken by their nation forced him to ask that they
should be sent back. Frontenac had the tact to
make a firm friend of their chief on the passage, and
the friendship was afterward of service to him.

The first news he received on his arrival was that
of the massacre at Montreal, the loss of Fort Frontenac, and the abandonment of Niagara. On the
other hand, the English posts at Hudson Bay had
been attacked by two brothers of the Le Moyne

family, Sainte Hélène and Iberville, and all but one
had been taken. At the same time, the Abenaquis
in Maine had been making havoc among English
settlements. Their first attack was on Dover, or
Cocheco, in New Hampshire, in June, and was in
satisfaction of revenge that had been nursed for
thirteen years.

In 1676, near the close of King Philip's War,
Major Waldron, of the Dover militia, had treacherously seized over two hundred Indians with whom
he had just made peace, hanged several, and sold
the rest into slavery. In retaliation, the Indians
selected Dover for the first assault. They sent two
squaws to Waldron's house, who begged for a
night's lodging, and were allowed to sleep on the
floor. In the night they opened the gates, and the
warriors rushed in. Waldron, who was eighty years
old, seized his sword, with the exclamation, " What
now? what now?" and defended himself bravely,
till he was felled by the blow of a hatchet. Then
they placed him in a chair, and cried, " Judge
Indians now ! Judge Indians now !" Some who
were in debt to him cut great gashes in his breast
with their knives, exclaiming, " So I cross out my
account !" The old man fainted under the tortures,
and was killed with his own sword.

At Saco several men were killed in July by

Indians, who in August attacked Fort Pemaquid, garrisoned by fifteen men under Captain Weems. The one hundred assailants were all converted Indians, and were accompanied by their priest, a Jesuit named Thury. The fort surrendered the second day on condition of life and liberty to the garrison, a promise which was kept to Weems and a few others, while the rest were killed as they were leaving the fort, or carried away prisoners. Father Thury said it was due to his exhortations that the Indians refrained from torturing the prisoners, and "immediately killed those whom they wished to kill." These and other similar attacks broke up the settlements in Maine east of Casco Bay.

Frontenac now planned three expeditions against the English colonies—one from Montreal to devastate New York, one from Three Rivers to destroy the New Hampshire towns, and one from Quebec to make a descent on Maine.

The Montreal party of two hundred and ten was about half Frenchmen, bush-rangers largely, and the other half-converted Iroquois who had settled near Montreal. They were reluctant allies against their heathen kindred, but more than willing to fight the English. The party was led by Mantet and Sainte Hélène, and accompanied by Iberville.

They marched in the dead of winter through the

forests and up the frozen streams, drawing their provisions on sledges. When they reached Lake Champlain, the Indians asked where they were going. "To Albany." The Indians laughed at the idea of attempting Albany with such a force, and advised a descent on Schenectady, or Corlaer, as the French called it, from Anthony Van Curler, its founder. The leaders assented, and after a slow and painful march, the party reached the Mohawk River near the village.

There were dissensions in New York at this time between the followers of Leisler and the opposing party, and Schenectady was divided by the feud. The chief magistrate, John Alexander Glen, often called Captain Sander, and Lieutenant Talmage, who was in command of a small party of Connecticut militia at the block-house, were opposed to Leisler, whom most of the citizens of Schenectady favored. For this reason they laughed at the magistrate and the lieutenant, who urged them to guard against surprise and be prepared for defence. They left the gates of the city open, and set up images of snow for sentinels.

The French and Indians entered the village about eleven o'clock on the night of Feb. 8th, 1690, and formed a line within the palisades and around the houses, completely enclosing them. Then they raised

the war-whoop, the first intimation of their presence
to the villagers.   The doors of the houses were bat-
tered down, and the wretched inhabitants brained
at once with the tomahawk, or reserved for a more
horrible fate.   Sixty were killed, of whom twelve
were children.   Some fled through the eastern gate
toward Albany and found shelter, many of them
with limbs frozen by exposure to the excessive cold.

The next day a party went to the house of the
magistrate, Glen, across the river. He was prepared
for defence ; but they assured him they had orders
not to harm him or any one belonging to him.   He
had several times saved French captives by his influence with the Iroquois, and the officers in return for
this service allowed him to take all his relatives
from among the prisoners.   He naturally found a
great many—so many as to make the surly savages
grumble at the great extent of his family connection.

The village was fired, and not more than half a
dozen of the eighty houses escaped the flames.
Twenty-seven prisoners were carried away, as well
as a large number of horses and other plunder ; and
not more than one sixth of the inhabitants of Schenectady remained unhurt.   About thirty Mohawks
in the town were carefully spared by the French,
who were fully awake to the importance of appeas-

ing the Five Nations and cultivating their friendship.

The party from Three Rivers, numbering about
fifty, fell upon the town of Salmon Falls, on the
Piscataqua, March 27th. It had two forts, but neither had placed sentinels. The scenes of the Schenectady massacre were re-enacted ; thirty-four were
killed, and over fifty taken, some of whom were tortured on the retreat. The French were pursued by
a small party from Piscataqua, and after a skirmish
at a bridge over Wooster River, in which the pursuers lost a few men, went on to join the war-party
from Quebec.

This party, under an officer named Portneuf,
numbered nearly five hundred, after being joined by
some Indians under St. Castin and the men from
Three Rivers. They were on their way to the settlement at Casco Bay, near the present city of Portland.
The place was defended by a fort and four block-
houses, and had about one hundred defenders under
the command of Sylvanus Davis. Thirty of his
men went out against the enemy, contrary to his
orders, and all but four lost their lives. After a
siege of four days, Fort Loyal surrendered on condition of liberty to the garrison and a guard to the
nearest English town—all of which, according to the
account of Captain Davis, was solemnly promised

and sworn by the French leader. Nevertheless, they were given to the Indians as soon as they had laid down their arms and left the fort ; and when they protested were told they deserved no quarter, because they were rebels against their rightful king, James II. The Indians murdered some, and carried away the rest. The fort and town were burned, and the dead left unburied.

These successes of the French carried courage and enthusiasm to Canada, and aroused the English colonies to action. It was resolved, at a congress held in New York in May, that a land force should march on Montreal, while a fleet should be sent from Boston to capture Quebec.

Massachusetts had just fitted out seven vessels and seven or eight hundred men, and placed them under the command of Sir William Phips, to attack Port Royal in Acadia. It was a harbor for French vessels which roamed the waters and preyed on New England commerce, and a place of stores whence the Indians drew their supplies of arms and ammunition to carry on the border warfare.

Sir William Phips, at this time about forty years old, had had an adventurous career. Belonging to a family of twenty-six children reared in poverty and ignorance in the woods of Maine, he learned to read and write after he became a man. His boy-

hood was spent in tending sheep ; he then became
apprentice to a ship-carpenter, in whose service he
spent four years.   When he was twenty-two he went
to Boston and married a widow older than himself.
She had some property, and set him up in business ;
but he was not prosperous, and soon lost all his wife's
capital.   He was not discouraged, but began to
follow the sea, and often told his wife that she should
yet live in a " fair brick house in the Green Lane of
Boston."   The Green Lane was in the northern
part of the city, and was occupied by well-to-do
citizens.   In 1683, Phips heard of a Spanish ship
which had been wrecked near the Bahama Islands
and was supposed to have carried down with it a
great deal of gold and silver.   He thought a swift
and easy way to the possession of the " fair brick
house" would be to bring up some of this treasure
from the sea, and accordingly went there in a small
vessel, but did not get enough to pay for his outlay.
But while he was on this voyage he heard of another
Spanish galleon which had been wrecked fifty years
before somewhere on the coast of the West Indies.
There was a tradition that this ship carried down a
vast amount of treasure, but no attempt had been
made to recover it.   Undiscouraged by his first failure, he went to England, and succeeded in getting
an audience of the King, James II., who was so much

impressed by the scheme that he appointed Phips captain of a ship called the *Rose Algier*, with eighteen guns and ninety-five men. Two years were spent in the West Indies, searching for the wreck without success. The sailors were discouraged, organized a mutiny, and arming themselves with cutlasses, came to the captain and demanded that he should turn pirate. Phips, as brave as he was persevering, fell upon the leaders and used his fists so vigorously that he knocked down several of them and awed the rest into submission. It was not long before they made another attempt; and though he succeeded in quelling the second mutiny also, it would have been dangerous to keep such a crew much longer on the sea; the ship was old and leaky, and the captain thought best to go back to England. But before he went he was so fortunate as to find an old man who remembered the shipwreck, and told him it was very near Porto Plata, on the northern coast of Santo Domingo, or Hispaniola, as it was then called.

Phips returned to England to get a better vessel and crew. The King had lost all confidence in the scheme and would have nothing more to do with it; but the Duke of Albemarle and some other noblemen fitted out a ship for him, and he sailed for Porto Plata. Here he anchored, and built a large boat to go nearer the reef where the wreck was said to have taken place than the ship could venture. Taking some skilful Indian divers in the boat, a part of the crew went to the spot and examined the waters, but could see nothing. As they were about giving up the search, one of the sailors noticed through the clear water a beautiful feathery seaweed growing from a rock at the bottom. He told one of the divers to bring it up to him ; and when the diver came up with the plant he said he saw some great cannon at the bottom. This was enough. The galleon was found. The divers were sent down, and the first one that rose brought a lump of silver worth nearly two hundred pounds. The sailors rowed to the ship, and showed their prize to the captain. The crew all went to work, and brought up gold and silver and precious stones, bullion, coin, cups, and sacramental plate—to the value of three hundred thousand pounds. It is said that a captain who was with Phips lost his reason at the sight of such an amount of treasure.

The share of Captain Phips amounted to only sixteen thousand pounds. But this was enough to enable him to live in style in Boston in those days. The Duke of Albemarle sent Mrs. Phips a gold cup valued at a thousand pounds, and the King conferred upon Phips the honor of knighthood.

To Sir William Phips, then, who had become a man of importance in the colony, was entrusted the command of the expedition against Acadia, and he appeared off Port Royal on the 19th of May. The fort was in command of Meneval, the French Governor, who summoned the inhabitants by firing a cannon ; but only three of them came.

The next day Phips entered the harbor and summoned the commandant to surrender. Meneval sent Petit, a priest, to negotiate ; and it was agreed that the troops, consisting of seventy men, should be sent to Quebec or to France, that private property should be respected, that the inhabitants be left in peaceable possession of their lands and the free exercise of their religion, and that the church should not be injured.

While Meneval was on board the flag-ship arranging the terms, some of the soldiers and citizens of Port Royal broke into a storehouse and carried off a quantity of goods, which they hid in the woods ; and Phips made this a pretext for violating all, or nearly all, the terms of the capitulation. He allowed his soldiers to break into the church, cut down the cross, and shatter the ornaments of the altar. The houses of the priests were plundered ; and they, together with Meneval and fifty-nine of the soldiers, were carried to Boston and imprisoned.

The inhabitants were called together and asked to take the oath of allegiance to William and Mary ; most of them did so, and were left unmolested ; but a few refused, and their houses were pillaged. Phips organized a temporary government, with a sergeant of the garrison at the head of it, and a council of six chosen from among the inhabitants. They were instructed to govern the place for the King of England, and to allow liberty in matters of religion.

Meneval gave his money and personal effects to Phips for safe keeping ; but when he wanted them returned, Phips refused, and Meneval petitioned the Governor and Council at Boston to order Phips to restore them. They did so, but Phips paid no attention to it. Then Governor Bradstreet wrote to him, commanding him to comply immediately with the order, and Phips reluctantly gave up some of the money and some of the poorest articles of clothing, but kept the greater part of the articles, which Meneval thus enumerated : " Six silver spoons, six silver forks, one silver cup in the shape of a gondola, a pair of pistols, three new wigs, a gray vest, four pair of silk garters, two dozen shirts, six vests of dimity, four night-caps with lace edging, all my table-service of fine tin, all my table linen," etc.

Before returning to Boston, Phips sent Captain

Alden to take La Hêve and Chedabucto. He carried to Boston twenty-one pieces of ordnance, and a sum of money belonging to the King, besides the plunder taken from private individuals. Alden, who had captured the two places without much trouble, brought a large quantity of goods belonging to the fishing company.

A few days after their departure, a French ship, the *Union*, arrived at Port Royal with goods, provisions, arms, ammunition, and presents for the Indians, to ensure their continued loyalty to France. On board were some recruits for the garrison, an officer of engineers named Saccardie, and Meneval's brother, Villebon, who had been in Acadia before, and now came to lead the Indians against the English. When he found what had befallen the settlements of Acadia, Villebon determined to go to the River St. John, and occupy the fort at Gemseg, and accordingly crossed over, leaving orders for the *Union* to follow.

No sooner had he gone than two pirate ships appeared. Finding the town undefended, the crews landed, seized all they could carry away, and burned sixteen houses. They hanged two men, and taking the *Union* and her cargo, sailed off with Perrot, a trader, and Saccardie the engineer, after having tortured Perrot to make him tell where he had hidden his

money. When Villebon learned of the disaster, he
returned to Fort Gemseg, and told the Indians that
the English had stolen their presents, but that he
was going to France to get them much nicer ones,
and exhorted them to be faithful to the French, to
keep up the war, and to be ready to go with him
the following spring. He then went to Quebec to
sail for France.

When Phips returned to Boston, preparations for
an attack on Canada were already far advanced.
Aid was sought from England ; but everything there
was concentrated on the struggle in Ireland with the
adherents of James II., and the colonists were left
to fight it out alone. The plan was, to march a
land force under General Winthrop against Montreal, while a fleet was to sail from Boston for the
capture of Quebec. Thirty-four ships, the largest
of which carried forty-four guns, were made ready
and manned with two thousand two hundred sailors
and militia, under the command of Major John
Walley. The success of Phips in Acadia led to his
appointment as commander of the expedition.

The force destined for Montreal set out from
Albany much reduced by sickness and the withdrawal of the militia of the eastern colonies, made
necessary by attacks on the border settlements.
Bands of Indians from eastern New York gathered

at Albany to join the expedition, and those of the
west were to be in readiness on Lake Champlain.
But before they were prepared, the season was far
advanced ; the work of making canoes was stopped
by the want of birch-bark, and it was too late in the
season for elm-bark to be made available.   The adherents of the two factions in New York politics
quarrelled with each other and with the Connecticut
soldiers ;   the supplies were insufficient ; and the
Indians of the western tribes failed to keep their
engagement.

Captain John Schuyler was in advance with less
than two hundred men, pushing on down the lake ;
but Winthrop, finding it impossible to do anything
with the disorderly forces of the main body,
marched them back to Albany.

Frontenac had prepared for the expected attack
by strengthening the stockade forts along the Upper
St. Lawrence, and holding a great council with the
Indians who came down from the Upper Lakes to
trade.   He was now seventy years old ; but, brandishing a tomahawk about his head, he danced the
war-dance and sang the war-song, arousing the Indians to the highest pitch of excitement and enthusiasm.

Schuyler arrived just after Frontenac had gone to
protect the other settlements.   The Indians, who

formed the greater part of his band, refused to
attack.the fort ; and so the extent of the operations
was the destruction of houses, harvests, and cattle,
and the killing or capture of twenty-five settlers.
Thus the land expedition of the English was worse
than a failure.   It accomplished nothing ; it stained
their record by the use of the Indian method of attack on peaceful settlers ; and it tended to bring
them into contempt with their savage allies.

After a long delay, the fleet under Sir William
Phips was prepared to sail from Boston.   The
weather was unfavorable, the ocean voyage was
long, and Phips had no pilots acquainted with the
St. Lawrence. So slow was the progress of the fleet
that the advantage of surprise was lost.   Two small
French vessels were captured on the way ; and from
information obtained from them in regard to the
state of the defences of Quebec, Phips anticipated a
victory as easy as that at Port Royal.

But Frontenac had been employed during the
summer in building palisades on the undefended side
of the city ; and Major Prévost, who commanded in
Quebec during his absence in Montreal, receiving
timely warning of the departure of the fleet from
Boston, sent word to Montreal, and hastened to
improve the defences of the city ; the gates were
barricaded, cannon mounted, palisades and moats

placed wherever they were needed, and batteries
posted in the lower part of the town near the river.
Frontenac went down the river in a canoe as soon
as he heard of the danger to his capital, leaving
orders for all the forces at Montreal and intervening
points to gather at Quebec.

On the 5th of October the fleet arrived before
Quebec, and Phips demanded a surrender. The
messenger was blindfolded and led by two officers
in a roundabout course, followed by a tumultuous
and jeering mob. When the bandage was taken
from his eyes, he found himself in the presence of
the Governor and his superior officers. He delivered
his letter to the Governor and an interpreter trans-
lated it into French. The letter said :

" The war between the crowns of England and
France doth not only sufficiently warrant, but the
destruction made by the French and Indians, under
your command and encouragement, upon the persons and estates of their Majesties' subjects of New
England, without provocation on their part, hath
put them under the necessity of this expedition for
their own security and satisfaction. And although
the cruelties and barbarities used against them by
the French and Indians might, upon the present
opportunity, prompt unto a severe revenge, yet,
being desirous to avoid all inhumane and unchris-

tian-like actions, and to prevent shedding of blood
as much as may be,

   " I, the aforesaid William Phips, Knight, do here-
by, in the name and in the behalf of their most
excellent Majesties, William and Mary, King and
Queen of England, Scotland, France, and Ireland,
Defenders of the Faith, and by order of their said
Majesties' government of the Massachusetts-colony
in New England, demand a present surrender of your
forts and castles, undemolished, and the King's and
other stores, unimbezzled, with a seasonable delivery
of all captives, together with a surrender of all your
persons and estates to my dispose : upon the doing
whereof you may expect mercy from me, as a Christian, according to what shall be found for their Majesties' service and the subjects' security. Which
if you refuse forthwith to do, I am come provided,
and am resolved, by the help of God, in whom I
trust, by force of arms to revenge all wrongs and injuries offered, and bring you under subjection to the
crown of England, and when too late make you wish
you had accepted of the favour tendered.

   " Your answer positive in an hour, returned by
your own trumpet, with the return of mine, is required upon the peril that will ensue."

   When the reading of the letter was finished, the
messenger reminded Frontenac that it was ten

o'clock, and his answer must be given by eleven. The French officers exclaimed at the impudence of the demand, and some of them said Frontenac ought to hang the messenger of such a pirate as Phips had shown himself to be. Frontenac told the messenger that he need not wait so long for his answer ; that he did not acknowledge William of Orange as King of England, knowing no King of England but King James ; that the King of France was about to restore King James to his throne ; and that his subjects in Canada were prepared to make war on the English colonists, who were rebels against their lawful sovereign. He alluded to the violation by Phips of his agreement at Port Royal, and said, " I will answer your master only by the mouths of my cannon, and he shall learn that I am not to be summoned in this way to surrender."

The officer was led back blindfolded, as he had come, and when Frontenac's answer was received, Phips held a council, at which it was decided to make a combined attack by land and sea. Major Walley, with a force of militia, was to be landed above the St. Charles at Beauport, to ford the river, and climb to the rear of the town by the heights of St. Geneviève. Several of the smaller vessels were to support the land soldiers by ascending the St. Charles with provisions and ammunition, and assist

in the attack with their guns. Then the larger
vessels were to assail the city from the St. Lawrence
side, and land a part of the troops to storm the defences.

Two days passed before it seemed best to the
English to begin carrying out the plan. While they
were waiting, the forces which Frontenac had ordered from Montreal arrived, under the command of
Callières, so that the number of troops reached about
three thousand. The city was full, the inhabitants
of the Lower Town having taken shelter in the convent, the hospital, and the seminary of the Upper
Town. Provisions were low, and there was danger
of famine if the siege should be long continued.
Masses were constantly offered, a picture of the
Holy Family was hung on the cathedral spire, and
the nuns kept up an unbroken stream of prayer to
the Virgin and all the saints for the deliverance of
the city.

At length on the 8th, at noon, boats were sent
out to Beauport, below the St. Charles, carrying
Major Walley with about twelve hundred men.
Having landed, they began their march, but had
not gone far when they were assailed from the woods
and thickets by a band of French and Indians under
Sainte Hélène. Walley's men charged bravely or
them, and they retreated, but kept up a continual

fire from behind the rocks and trees as they went, sending confusion into the ranks of the English. Walley drew his forces together and encamped, in expectation of the ships which were to support him.

Without waiting till Walley was in full readiness to climb the heights in the rear and co-operate with the attack from the fleet, Phips rushed on with his larger ships and drew them up before the town. He was greeted by a shot from the Château St. Louis, and at once opened with all his cannon. A rapid firing ensued on both sides, which was kept up until nightfall. Comparatively little damage was done by the English ; their guns were not charged heavily enough with powder to give the balls much effect, and their gunnery was poor. Many of the balls struck the wall of rock, and many of those that reached the town had spent their force and failed to pierce the walls. The fire from the town was more effective ; but Phips only waited till morning to renew the attack.

The next day the troops in the town were reën-forced by the detachment which had been sent out against Walley's party ; and under the direction of Sainte Hélène the guns of the batteries in the Lower Town were aimed against the fleet with good effect. All the ships were before the town ; for those that should have gone to the aid of Walley were afraid to expose themselves to the danger ; and there was no central command strong enough to enforce obedience--if, indeed, anything was thought of at the head of the fleet except the business immediately in hand.   A few pieces of cannon and a little powder and food were sent to the shore, but Walley received no other assistance.

The ships were at length disabled by the fire and were drawn off beyond the reach of the guns of the town.   The attack by water had proved a miserable failure ; and Walley was too poorly supported to effect anything by land.   On the morning of the 10th, the day after the repulse of the fleet, he went to consult with Sir William Phips. During his absence his men advanced to cross the St. Charles and make an attack, but were met by a party under Sainte Hélène and driven back with loss.   Walley returned with orders to take them to the fleet, and boats were sent in the night, in which they were to embark the following night.

During the 11th, another skirmish took place, with about the same result.   Walley's troops fought courageously, but were too poorly disciplined to fight with advantage ; while the French and Indians fired from behind rocks and trees and farm-houses. Walley withdrew, and as soon as darkness came on embarked his troops in the boats and joined the fleet.   As the ships were disabled, and the stock of ammunition low, the undertaking was now abandoned, and the fleet dropped down below the Island of Orleans, where it stopped for repairs.   After an exchange of prisoners, the vessels made their way slowly homeward.

While Phips was on his way down the river, three ships arrived from France bringing money and stores to Quebec, and ran up the Saguenay.   Phips attempted to capture them, but failed.   He reached Boston in five or six weeks ; some of his vessels were more than three months on the way, and several— as many as nine, by some accounts—were wrecked.

This miserable outcome of an expedition from which so much had been hoped, carried dismay and foreboding to the New England colonies.   In Quebec there was great rejoicing when the fleet disappeared down the river, marred only by the fear that the ships from France might be surprised on the way and captured.   When they arrived in safety, the general joy knew no bounds.   If the siege had been prolonged, the city would have suffered from famine and perhaps been forced at last to surrender ; for the warning had not been long enough to give time for providing food for the great number that were gathered in the capital, and the supplies from France had not arrived.

A procession was formed, which carried the image of the Virgin to every church and chapel in turn, with appropriate ceremonies ; *Te Deum* was sung in the cathedral ; and the banner bearing the cross of St. George, which had waved at the mast-head of Phips's vessel, and was shot away by one of Sainte Hélène's cannon, was picked up from the river where it had fallen, and carried to the cathedral, where it hung for years. Frontenac sent the news to France, urging the Government at the same time to provide troops for the complete conquest of New York and New England ; and a medal in honor of the victory was struck in Paris.

CHAPTER VII.

CLOSE OF KING WILLIAM'S WAR.

THE English made no attempt to secure their conquest in Acadia, and Villebon was appointed Governor by the French Government and instructed to lavish presents on the Indians and keep them and the French constantly engaged in war. All supplies would be sent from France, so that none of the men need be kept at home for the cultivation of the soil.

The vessel which took Villebon to Acadia cap tured Colonel Edward Tyng, who had been sent from Massachusetts as Governor of Port Royal, and John Nelson, who was going with him. Nelson inherited a claim to Acadia, from his uncle, Sir Thomas Temple, to whom Cromwell had made a large grant, and he was well acquainted with the country and the

language of the Indians.   He and Tyng were taken
to Quebec.

Villebon took possession of Port Royal without
opposition, and administered to the colonists the
oath of allegiance to the sovereign of France.   He
established himself at Fort Gemseg on the St. John,
and set about the work of inciting the Indians to
war.   A chief named Moxus had already attacked
Wells with two hundred Indians, and had been repelled by the garrison under Captain Converse.
Seconded by the priest Thury, Villebon persuaded
the Indians to form a great war-party, though some
who had signed a truce with the English were reluctant.

They set out in January, 1692, and marched a
month over icy streams and through bare forests to
southwestern Maine.   On the night of Feb. 4th, they
encamped at the foot of Mount Agamenticus, and
in the morning moved cautiously to the village
of York.   They caught a boy cutting wood in a
forest, forced information from him, murdered him,
and pushed on.   Dividing into two parties, they
began their work at a signal.   There were five fortified houses, having projecting upper stories with
loop-holes for guns.   One was taken at the first assault.   The unprotected dwellings were attacked,
and all their inmates who did not escape to the for-

tified houses were slain or taken captive. The minister, Mr. Dummer, was shot at his own door as he was about to mount his horse to visit a parishioner. After unsuccessfully attacking the other four fortified houses, the party withdrew with eighty prisoners, having killed nearly a hundred.

In June of the same year, an attack on Wells, by about four hundred Indians, was a complete failure. The Indians attempted to fire some ships lying in the river, by means of a burning raft, but it ran aground. The French officers tried to induce them to make a regular assault on the fort ; but they carried it on in their own fashion, with a tremendous amount of noise and desultory firing. The men in the fort held out bravely ; the women loaded their guns, and some fired ; Converse answered defiantly every summons to surrender ; and the Indians were glad to draw off with one prisoner, after burning the church and the deserted houses. Villebon consoled some who lived near his fort with a prisoner to burn, an Indian ally of the English, taken near the St. John.

During the summer, Sir William Phips, now Governor of Massachusetts, having authority to rebuild the fort at Pemaquid, set out with Benjamin Church, noted for success in Indian wars, and one hundred workmen. On the way they buried the dead left at Casco in 1690, and carried the cannon of Fort Loyal with them. Phips laid the founda- tions for a strong fortress of stone, and left the men to finish it. When done, it was the best fort the English had in America ; the front wall was twenty- two feet high, and the great round tower at the southwestern corner twenty-nine feet high. Eigh- teen guns were mounted, and sixty men placed in it as a garrison. Phips named it Fort William Henry.

Madockawando, the Indian father-in-law of the Baron de St. Castin, had gone to Quebec to carry to Frontenac the news of the building of this fort, and Frontenac resolved to drive the English away at once before it should be completed. He had two ships of war, and arranged that they should sail with about four hundred men, take in as many more as they could get at Villebon's fort and Pentagoet, and then capture Pemaquid and destroy the settlements along the coast of the present States of Maine and New Hampshire.

John Nelson was still a prisoner in Quebec when Madockawando came with his intelligence, but was treated as a guest by Frontenac, and had apart- ments at the Château St. Louis. He discovered that an expedition was on foot, and, through his knowledge of the Indian language spoken by the chief, and in other ways, he managed to get some information as to the details. He bribed two French soldiers to desert, and carry a letter to Boston. A ship of war was at once sent from Boston to the defence of Pemaquid, which was not yet finished, and when the French vessels arrived, and found the place thus defended, they gave up the enterprise without attempting to strike a blow. Iberville, who commanded the expedition, was censured severely by Frontenac, and the Indians were so indignant that they threatened to break their alliance with the French.

The colonists, harassed continually by the Indians, their border settlements broken up, their harvests and cattle destroyed by these sly and faithless hordes, whom no treaties could hold, made repeated applications to England for help ; and at length a plan was formed. A fleet under Sir Francis Wheeler was to be sent to Martinique, and after service there was to go to Boston, take on as many troops as the colonies should have been able to raise, and proceed to Quebec ; the troops to be under the command of Sir William Phips. But the attack on Martinique was a failure. Six hundred of the men were killed, and three hundred taken prisoners. Half of the sailors and three fourths of the soldiers died of yellow fever before the fleet reached Boston, and the epidemic was carried into the city.

The design of an attack on Quebec was then necessarily abandoned.

The English made a treaty with the eastern Indians, supposing that all the tribes were represented ; but Villebon, who had built a fort on the St.
John nearly opposite the site of Fredericton, Fort
Naxouat, took measures to stir them up to break
the treaty.   Taxus, a chief friendly to the French,
was honored and feasted at the fort, and Villebon
gave him his best coat.   He sent presents and ammunition to be distributed among the various tribes ;
and, what was of vastly greater importance to the
French cause, he set on the Jesuits—Vincent Bigot
on the Kennebec and Pierre Thury on the Penobscot—to incite their converts to the work.

Their plans were nearly defeated by tidings that
the English were going to exchange prisoners at
Pemaquid, according to the treaty ; for the French
had told them the English were trying to entrap
them.   Had it not been for the cunning of Thury,
the Indians, or a large part of them, would have
gone to their homes from the Penobscot, where they
had been gathered by St. Castin and Villieu who
had been appointed to lead them.   But Thury pri-
vately told those chiefs who had not been present at
the conference with the English, that Madockawando and the others had taken altogether too much

on themselves, and assumed too much importance in making a treaty without their concurrence. This was enough ; their jealousy was aroused, they were all for war, and Madockawando and some of his followers who still held out were at length persuaded, at a dog-feast given by Villieu, by means of the presents of the French and the jeers of their savage companions.

About two hundred and fifty of them set out in canoes for Piscataqua. At Pemaquid, Villieu, disguised as an Indian, landed with a few savages and went to the fort, carrying some furs to trade to the soldiers. Leaving the Indians to make the bargain, he walked away unobserved, studied the plan of the fort, and made a drawing of it.

At the village of Oyster River, now Durham, in New Hampshire, the Indians took five of the twelve fortified houses ; three families escaped, but two were slaughtered. The seven other houses were resolutely defended. The owner of one of these, Thomas Bickford, placed his family in a boat and sent them down the stream ; then he went back to his house, and by keeping up a constant firing, now from one point and now from another, shouting orders as if to his garrison, and giving the assailants glimpses of him in different clothing at different parts of the house, he defended the place successfully alone, and saved his house and his whole family. About one hundred persons were killed, and twenty-seven carried away. After mass had been said by Thury, the Indians took to their canoes. Some of them wanted to go home ; but Taxus with a large party remained to work what havoc they could on neighboring settlements. They divided into small bands, and killed some of the inhabitants of Groton, York, Kittery, and other places. Villieu on his return set out for Quebec to warn the Governor of a rumored expedition against that city, taking with him some Indians, and a string of thirteen English scalps, which were presented to Frontenac.

During these years the Iroquois, incited by the New York colonists, went down the St. Lawrence and fell upon the least protected settlements from time to time, killing, burning, and capturing. A large party of them, encamped near the mouth of the Ottawa, sallied out in bands, and kept the frontier in terror. Over one hundred men were marched against them under Vaudreuil, and routed a band of about forty near Repentigny ; and when men and supplies arrived from France, a large force was sent against them, and their camp was broken up. After this defeat, they refused to keep up hostilities unaided by the English, and an expedition was then organized under Major Peter Schuyler.

About two hundred and fifty men were gathered at Albany, half of them Indians. They descended Lake Champlain and the Richelieu in canoes, and debarked a few miles above Fort Chambly, whence they marched to attack the French at La Prairie, opposite Montreal. Callières, who was now Governor of Montreal, had been warned, and had gone over to La Prairie with seven hundred men, but he was too ill to command during the attack, which took place early in the morning of the 11th of August. The camp was broken up, the soldiers driven into the fort, and great loss inflicted on the French, and then Schuyler drew off his men, destroying the growing crops as he went.

On the way back he was met by a force of French soldiers and Canadian Indians from Fort Chambly, under an officer named Valrenne, who, knowing of their attack on La Prairie, had come out to cut off their retreat. A fierce combat followed. Some of the Indians ran away ; but the English and the French fought with desperation, and the Mohawks remained steadfast. The force at La Prairie did not come up till the fighting was over. Schuyler's men at length succeeded in breaking through the centre of the enemy's rank, and then faced about and drove the French before them, forcing them to retreat. This is according to Schuyler's own account. The

French also claimed the victory, and Valrenne was highly commended for having repelled the English.

As the Iroquois continued their raids on the French, it was resolved to invade the Mohawk country. A force of nearly seven hundred French and Indians set out from Montreal in the middle of January, 1693. After a weary march on snow-shoes they passed Schenectady early in February, went on to the first Mohawk castle, or town, and took a few prisoners without resistance. The second was taken quite as easily ; but at the third the Mohawks, who had gathered there for a feast and a war-dance, fought desperately, though they were at last overpowered. The invaders lost thirty men, and the Mohawks about the same number. The Canadian Indians had promised to put their captives to death in accordance with the command of Frontenac that no quarter should be given ; and as many of these Canadian Indians were converted Iroquois, it was hoped that such a proceeding on their part would preclude any reconciliation from ever taking place between them and the Iroquois of New York. But they refused to keep their promise, and the French turned homeward with about three hundred prisoners.

Warning had been given at Albany of the French invasion, by a young man who had been carried away from Schenectady at the burning of that town in

1690. He was taken with the invading expedition, and ran away when he reached the neighborhood of his old home. Schuyler hastily gathered two hundred men and, joined by three or four hundred Indians, marched against the French. Some Mohawks caught up with the French, and told them Schuyler was coming to parley with them, as peace had been declared in Europe. The Canadian Indians said they would wait ; the French were distrustful, and anxious to push on their retreat. The Indians prevailed, and a fort was built of felled trees.

When Schuyler came up, instead of seeking a parley, he began to build a similar fort, or rather his Indians did. The French attacked it, and were defeated in three attempts ; then they quietly packed their baggage and moved off in the night during a heavy snow-storm.

The Acadians were anxious that the fort at Pemaquid should be reduced. Not only was it a standing assertion of the English claim to disputed territory, but it kept them in constant fear of English influence over their unstable allies. There was need also of protection for the fisheries and the fur-trade, which were seriously encroached upon by the English, who offered much better terms to the Indians, both in Acadia and New York, than the French would. A pestilence had weakened the Indians of

the east, who were hungry and needy, and disposed
to seek the best market for their furs, regardless of
their friendships or preferences.

They were still anxious to exchange prisoners
with the English ; but when they were at last summoned to Pemaquid, they were told that nothing
could be done till they should bring in all they had
taken.   As the English had not brought their men,
they thought this was asking too much, and refused
to treat further.   In 1696 the Governor of Massachusetts sent them another summons.   The Penobscot tribe, the only one that answered, took five prisoners to give for five of their tribe who had been
taken by the English, and arrived at Pemaquid in
February, 1696.   The fort was commanded by Captain Pascho Chubb, who received the Indians cordially, took back the prisoners they brought, and
promised to give them some presents, and to send
at once to Boston for their men, whom they desired
in exchange.   He then proposed a conference near
the fort, where nine of his men were to meet nine of
the Indians, all unarmed.   The Indians accepted,
but the liquor which was freely given them rendered
them less wary than usual, and they did not notice
a party of soldiers who had come out from the fort
and stood ready for action at a short distance from
the scene of the conference.   Chubb's men carried

concealed weapons, and at a signal fell upon the Indians and killed several of them, of whom two were chiefs. The Indians fought savagely, and several of the soldiers also fell. According to French accounts, the Indians themselves were treacherously disposed, but none the less this treachery of Captain Chubb roused their hatred of the English to new fury, and did more service to the French cause than all the persuasions and presents which Villebon had lavished upon his reluctant allies.

That officer had long been urging upon the Government at Quebec the necessity of another attack upon Pemaquid ; and now that the folly of its commander had made the Indians eager to take revenge, preparations for the expedition were pushed on with vigor. In the summer of 1696 the Acadians and Indians assembled on the Penobscot and the St. John, and waited for two ships of war under Iberville and Bonaventure, which were to come from Quebec. While they were waiting, two British ships and a tender from Massachusetts were hanging about the coast, and the crews made several attempts to land.

When at length the French ships, which had taken on board thirty Micmac Indians at Cape Breton, arrived at the St. John, a sharp engagement took place. One of the English vessels, the *New-*

port, was captured ; but a fog enabled the *Sorling* and the tender to escape. The victorious vessels took on fifty more of the Micmacs and their priest, Father Simon, who were waiting at the mouth of the St. John, and proceeded to Pentagoet. Here were Villieu, and St. Castin, and the faithful Father Thury with twenty-five French soldiers and three hundred Abenaquis. Attended by a fleet of Abenaqui canoes, the ships set out for Pemaquid, arriving there August 14th, 1696.

The Abenaquis, under the lead of St. Castin, were put ashore for the land attack, while Iberville summoned Chubb to surrender. Chubb replied that he would not give up the fort, " if the sea were covered with French ships, and the land with Indians." The attack began ; the French and Indian marksmen surrounded the fort, hiding in places where they were sheltered from its cannon, and kept up a constant fire. During the night the heavy guns were loaded, and the batteries made ready for use by the next afternoon. Before they were fired, St. Castin sent word to Chubb that if he and his soldiers held out until the fort should be carried by assault, they would get no quarter from the Indians, who remembered his former treachery. The letter was followed by five bomb-shells.

Chubb immediately sounded a parley and offered

to surrender, on condition that he and all his men should be protected from the Indians, and sent to Boston to be exchanged for French and Indian prisoners. Iberville sent them to an island in the bay, and despatched Villieu to take possession of the fort. One of the Indians whom Chubb had taken in February was found in irons in the fort, nearly dead with hunger and long confinement, and his countrymen were so incensed that they would have made short work with the garrison if Iberville had not taken the precaution to send them away.

The cannon of the fort were carried to the ships, and then the walls were blown up and the ruins fired. Notwithstanding the money and labor expended on the fort, and its apparent strength, it was not well planned. There were no casemates, and a shower of bomb-shells would have made havoc with the garrison. When Chubb reached Boston he was thrown into prison on a charge of cowardice. He was liberated after several months and returned to his home in Andover ; but Indian vengeance was on his track, and the next year he and his wife were killed by a party of savages.

Massachusetts had a force ready to send against the French, under Benjamin Church, when news of the capture of Pemaquid reached Boston, and Church started immediately with about five hundred men, partly Indians, embarked in sloops and whaling vessels. After doing a small amount of damage at Penobscot, he went on to Chignecto at the head of the Bay of Fundy, where he landed and took possession of the place without meeting any resistance from the twenty or thirty men in the settlement. The inhabitants saved their lives by producing a certificate that they had taken the oath of allegiance to the British Crown ; but the soldiers plundered without restraint, and then burned the town.

After this easy triumph, Church sailed for the St. John. An officer named Chevalier was stationed with a few soldiers at the mouth of the river, while Villebon's fort of Naxouat was situated farther up. These soldiers were taken by the Indians of Church's force, and Chevalier was killed. One of the captured Frenchmen told Church where to find the cannon of the old fort, which were buried in the sand, and the New Englanders dug them up and put them on board. On the way back to Boston they met three ships from Massachusetts, with two hundred men under Colonel Hathorn. Hathorn deprived Church of his command for having conducted the expedition in such a manner, and turned the force back to attack Fort Naxouat. But, warned by the arrival of Church, Villebon had been strengthening his fort and gathering into it a force of settlers and Indians.

The attack began on the 18th of October, and continued two days without success. During the night of the 19th the English quietly embarked and sailed away, having had eight men killed and seventeen wounded, while only three of the French suffered injury. This was the end of hostilities between the British and French colonists during what is known as King William's War. But the Indians kept up a petty warfare, ravaging the borders of settlements and butchering defenceless families.

In the spring of 1697, a band of Indians reached the village of Haverhill, raised the war-cry, and began their horrid work. A man named Dustin was at work in the field, having with him his seven children, while his wife with the baby, one week old, and Mary Neff, a neighbor, were in the house. As soon as he became aware of the presence of the Indians, Dustin started for the house; but, seeing he was too late to be of any use there, he escaped to the woods with the children that were in the field with him. The savages killed the infant, set fire to the house, and took Hannah Dustin and Mary Neff to the woods with the other prisoners they had taken. Some of these were killed, and the rest were divided among the Indians, who separated and returned to their homes.

The two women fell to the lot of two families, who, taking a leisurely march northward, were on their way to some Indian village. They encamped one night in the forest, on a small island in the Merrimack, near the present city of Concord, N. H. The Indians went to sleep about their camp-fire, after having counted on their beads the prayers taught them by some Jesuit enthusiast at their mission station. Hannah Dustin had planned an escape and inspired Mary Neff and Samuel Leonardson, a boy captured at Worcester, to take part in it. When all the Indians were still, the three rose quietly, took each a tomahawk, and at a signal all struck together on the heads of the sleeping savages. They struck with such nerve and skill that the two men of the party, two of the three squaws, and six of the seven children were instantly killed. A little boy was spared ; and he and a wounded squaw who ran with him into the woods were the only survivors. In the morning Hannah Dustin took the ten scalps, together with the gun and tomahawk of the Indian that killed her child, and a canoe carried her and her companions down the Merrimack to their home. They received a bounty of five pounds apiece for the scalps, and a present was sent to them by the Governor of Maryland.

In the same year, 1697, a squadron of fifteen ships

was sent out from France, under the command of the Marquis de Nesmond. It was to go to Newfoundland, capture any English ships that might be there, then sail to the Penobscot and take on board as many Indians and French soldiers as could be collected. It was expected that Canada would send fifteen hundred. This force was destined to take possession of Boston. One part was to land at Dorchester and enter the town from the south by way of the Neck; another was to land at Noddle's Island, take boats to Charlestown, capture it, and enter Boston from the north; while still another portion of the forces was to land directly in the town near Long Wharf. Boston once taken, the forces were to march northward along the coast, and, with the assistance of the fleet, take all the settlements. The towns were to be burned after everything of value that could be removed had been taken out.

Frontenac prepared his forces, and made ready to command them in person. But the fleet was detained by contrary winds until it was too late for the plan to be carried out that season. In September a treaty of peace between France and England was signed at Ryswick, and thus the scheme for destroying the New England settlements came to nothing.

But before peace was declared, the French had met with unqualified success in the north. As soon as Iberville had destroyed Pemaquid, he took charge of an expedition for the conquest of Newfoundland. The island was claimed by the English, by virtue of the discoveries of the Cabots and Sir Humphrey Gilbert, and the fishing settlements planted by Englishmen on the coast. The French, however, asserted that fishermen from Brittany, Normandy, and the Basque Provinces had fished on the coast long before, and that through them France had a prior claim.

At this time the French had a town and a fort at Placentia Bay, which gave them control of the southern coast. The eastern coast was occupied by a long line of small English settlements, the principal of which was St. John. Expeditions had been planned by each nation during the hostilities, for driving the other out ; but all of them had fallen through.

When Iberville arrived, the Governor of Placentia was already at St. John with a fleet of privateers, attempting to take the place. Iberville joined him, and St. John was soon reduced to ashes. Then the ships were withdrawn, and Iberville with his soldiers and Indians marched along the eastern coast, attacking and destroying every town in turn. It was in the depth of winter ; the ground was covered with snow and ice ; and the soldiers went stumbling along the unbroken paths, tripping against rocks and logs concealed under the snow, but merry with the excitement of the march, and elated with their success ; for the villagers surrendered without the slightest resistance, and the soldiers plundered without restraint. Nothing was left to the English but Bonavista and Isle Carbonnière.

In the spring, Iberville and his brother Serigny were sent to re-take Fort Nelson on Hudson Bay, which, after being taken by them in 1694, had fallen again into the hands of the English in 1696. The French called it Fort Bourbon. It was of great importance, being in the midst of a vast region abounding in valuable furs. The brothers set out with four ships of war and a transport. Although it was July when they entered Hudson Bay, the water was filled with floating ice, and the supply-ship was crushed. Iberville's ship, the *Pelican*, was in great danger, and when at last she got free and sailed into the unobstructed waters of the open bay, nothing was to be seen of the other three ; they were still struggling amid the ice.

Iberville and his men sailed on alone to begin the attack ; but before they reached the fort, they were overtaken by three armed English ships. There was a close and desperate engagement. One of the English ships sank under the heavy broadsides of the *Pelican*, with all on board ; another surrendered, and the third sailed away and escaped. The *Pelican* was badly injured ; and a fierce storm arising, she was stranded and split amidships by the fury of the wind and waves. The crew escaped to the shore, but they were in danger of starvation, and were about to make an attack on the fort as the only hope of saving themselves, when the three ships appeared. Fort Nelson, which was occupied by the traders of the Hudson Bay Company, was incapable of resisting an attack by mortars, and it soon surrendered.

In the summer of 1695, Frontenac rebuilt the fort at the head of the St. Lawrence, on the site of the present city of Kingston, which was sometimes known as Fort Catarocouay, but named by him now, as before under the French, Fort Frontenac. He was determined either to conquer the Iroquois, or to bring them over to alliance with the French, or rather, perhaps, to bring them over by conquering them, if they should refuse to make a permanent treaty of peace.

In the summer of 1696, he commanded in person an expedition against the Indians of New York, and with twenty-two hundred men crossed Lake Ontario to Oswego. The Onondagas, when they heard of the advance of the French, set fire to their principal village, and fled. One old man of the tribe was found hidden in a hollow tree, and was dragged out. The Indians who were with the French wanted to torture and burn him, while Frontenac was anxious to save him ; but the Indians were so clamorous, that it was finally decided to be the better policy to give him up. During the horrible tortures inflicted on him he never quailed, but taunted his tormentors to the last. When at length a mortal thrust was made, he said, '' I thank you ; but you should have finished me by fire. Learn, dogs of Frenchmen, how to suffer, and you Indians, their allies, who are dogs of dogs, remember what you should do when you stand where I stand now.''

A party was sent out to destroy the corn in the fields of the Oneidas, most of whom had fled, though thirty-five had staid to defend their town and were taken prisoners.

It was proposed that the army should next march against the Cayugas. But as it was of no use to march an army through the wilderness to take possession of a cluster of deserted wigwams, Frontenac decided to return home. In his despatches to the King, he represented the expedition as a brilliant triumph, which, indeed, would have been still more brilliant if the savages had made a stand, and given the French army a chance to overwhelm and defeat them completely, but which, nevertheless, would be of vast advantage to the French interest, in preventing an alliance between the Iroquois and the Indian allies of the French.   He took care, also, to say that the triumph could not have been effected had it not been for the rebuilding of Fort Frontenac, a proceeding in which he had gone contrary to the wishes of the King, and eluded his express orders. For this exploit he was rewarded with the cross of the Military Order of St. Louis.

Early in 1698, tidings of the peace which had been proclaimed at Ryswick, September 20th, 1697, reached Montreal, and in July official notice was sent with a letter from the King ordering *Te Deum* to be sung in the cathedral of Quebec.   An exchange of prisoners was proposed between the colonies of the two nations in America ; but a dispute arose between Frontenac and the Earl of Bellomont, Governor of New York, as to the exchange of the French prisoners in the hands of the Iroquois for the Iroquois in the hands of the French.   Bellomont proposed to negotiate the exchange.   Frontenac refused to treat with the Iroquois through the English, which would have been an admission that the Iroquois were English subjects, whereas he chose to regard them as rebellious subjects of France.

The death of Frontenac interrupted the quarrel. That able and intrepid officer had exercised a powerful influence on the fortunes of the French in America. Much less pure and disinterested than ·Champlain, exacting and quarrelsome, he continually exasperated his associates in times of peace ; but when danger threatened the colony, they instinctively felt that in his leadership was almost certain victory. He died in November, 1698, at the age of seventy-eight.

He was succeeded by Callières, upon whom devolved the settlement of the dispute about the Iroquois, who declined to allow the English to negotiate for them, asserting their independence of both the foreign powers. After many councils, and many wampum belts, and much eloquence, the exchange was effected ; but the question of the sovereignty of the west, and even of New York, still remained undecided. In the following year, 1700, the French in Acadia lost their efficient leader Villebon.

CHAPTER VIII.

QUEEN ANNE'S WAR.

The Spanish Succession—The Pretender—Attacks on Wells, Saco, Casco, Deerfield, and Lancaster—Church in Acadia—Destruction of English Towns in Newfoundland—Sieges of Port Royal—Attack on Haverhill—Final Capture of Port Royal by the English—Insurrection of the Acadians—Attempted Conquest of Canada by Admiral Walker—Attack of the Foxes on Detroit—Treaty of Utrecht—Louisbourg—Father Rasles—Expeditions of Harmon, Westbrooke, Winslow, and Lovewell—Indian Treaty—Forts at Niagara, Oswego, and Crown Point.

BUT a few years of peace succeeded the treaty of Ryswick. First came the contest in Europe over the Spanish succession—that is, the succession to the Spanish crown, which was bestowed upon one of the Bourbons, the reigning family of France. This threatened to give a great preponderance of power and influence to France, and William III. though he was old and sick, resolved to fight against a dangerous accession to the power of England's ancient enemy. But another cause of war soon arose. James II., the dethroned King of England, died at St. Germain in September, 1701 ; and before he died he received a promise from Louis XIV., King of France, that he would recognize as King of

England his son, James Stuart, often called " the Pretender"—or, in later years, after his son, Charles Edward, had also made a claim to the throne of his fathers, " the Old Pretender."

This recognition was, of course, a challenge to England, and preparations were made for war. William III. died in March, 1702, and was succeeded by Anne, the sister of his wife, and daughter of James II. War was declared by England against France, May 15th, 1702. The contest that followed is known in European history as the War of the Spanish Succession ; in American history, it is usually called Queen Anne's War ; or the Second Intercolonial War. On the one side were France, Spain, and Bavaria ; on the other, England, Holland, Savoy, Austria, Prussia, Portugal, and Denmark. It was in this war that the Duke of Marlborough won his fame.

To the people of New England, war between France and England meant the hideous midnight war-whoop, the tomahawk and scalping-knife, burning hamlets, and horrible captivity. To provide against it, a conference was called to meet at Falmouth, on Casco Bay, in June, 1703, when Governor Dudley, of Massachusetts, met many of the chiefs of the Abenaquis. The Indians, professing to have no thought of war, promised peace and friendship by

their accustomed tokens, and it was believed in New
England that they were sincere, and would be neutral during any hostilities that might arise between
the English and French colonies.

But, as usual, only a part of the tribes had been
brought into the alliance, those on and west of the
Penobscot ; and a party of lawless plunderers, by
attacking and pillaging St. Castin's place, roused
the resentment of the tribe on that river and disposed them to listen to the insinuations of their
ancient allies. French persuasions were successful,
and by August five hundred French and Indians
were assembled, ready for incursions into the New
England settlements.

They divided into several bands and fell upon a
number of places at the same time. Wells, Saco,
and Casco were again among the doomed villages,
but the fort at Casco was not taken, owing to the
arrival of an armed vessel under Captain Southwick.
About one hundred and fifty persons were killed or
captured in these attacks. In a night of February,
1704, a large party under Hertel de Rouville reached
the town of Deerfield, Massachusetts, and hid themselves in a pine forest until morning. The people
had received information from Colonel Schuyler that
they were in danger of attack, and twenty soldiers
were sent to them as a guard. On this night, how-

ever, the watch went to sleep two hours before day-break. The town was surrounded with palisades ; but huge drifts of snow were piled up against them, and they were no defence. The invaders entered undiscovered, and in a few hours forty-seven of the inhabitants were killed, the town was in flames, and one hundred and twelve prisoners were on their way to Canada. The journey to Quebec was long and painful, and two of the men starved on the way, for the party had to depend on hunting for support. Most of the prisoners were in time redeemed.

On the 30th of July, the town of Lancaster was assailed, and a few people were killed, seven build-ings burned, and much property destroyed. These and other depredations of war-parties along the coasts filled New England with consternation. The governments of Massachusetts and New Hampshire offered a bounty of twenty pounds for every Indian prisoner under ten years, and forty for every one above that age, or for the scalp of one. Yet but few were taken, even at that price. It was then resolved to fit out an expedition for retaliation, and as usual the people of Acadia were selected to expi-ate the sins of the Indians and Canadians.

Colonel Benjamin Church was put in command of five hundred and fifty men, fourteen transports, and thirty-six whale-boats, convoyed by three ships of

war.   Sailing from Boston in May, 1704, he stopped
at Penobscot, and killed and took captive a few
French and Indians, among them a daughter and
several grandchildren of St. Castin.   At Passama-
quoddy he met with similar success, and then sailed
on to the Bay of Fundy.   The ships of war were
sent to Port Royal, where they did nothing but wait
for him to come back.   Church himself went on with
the other vessels to Minas, farther up the bay.   This
place was built on marsh lands, enclosed by dykes.
The soldiers cut the dykes, plundered and burned
the dwellings, and took some prisoners.

Returning to Port Royal, Church discreetly refrained from attacking a fortified place, and the
officers signed a declaration that their force was insufficient for an assault.   Chignecto was next visit-
ed, twenty houses were burned, large numbers of
cattle killed, and the whole settlement ravaged.
The only thing that can be said in excuse for this
kind of warfare is, that it was less cruel than the
barbarous attacks for which it was intended to re-
taliate.

In 1705, four hundred and fifty men under Subercase—soldiers, Canadian peasants, adventurers, and
Indians, well armed, and with rations for twenty
days, blankets, and tents—set out to destroy the
English settlements in Newfoundland, marching on

snow-shoes. They took Petit Havre and St. John's, and devastated all the little settlements along the eastern coast, and the English trade was for the time completely broken up.

Subercase was made Governor of Acadia in 1706. The following spring New England sent Colonel March to Port Royal with two regiments, but he returned without assaulting the fort. Governor Dudley forbade the troops to land when they came back to Boston, and ordered them to go again. Colonel March was ill, and Colonel Wainwright took command ; but after a pretence of besieging the fort for eleven days, he retired with small loss, the expedition having cost Massachusetts two thousand two hundred pounds.

In 1708 a council at Montreal decided to send a large number of Canadians and Indians to devastate New England. But after a long march through the almost impassable mountain region of northern New Hampshire, a murderous attack on Haverhill, in which thirty or forty were killed, was the only result. Thirty of the assailants were killed by a pursuing party from neighboring settlements, under Samuel Ayer, and some of the prisoners were rescued. Ayer himself fell a victim to his brave effort in behalf of his neighbors.

In 1709 a plan was formed in England for the capture of New France by a fleet and five regiments of British soldiers aided by the colonists. But a defeat in Portugal called away the ships destined for America, and a force gathered at Lake Champlain under Colonel Nicholson for a land attack was so reduced by sickness—said to have resulted from the poisoning of a spring by Indians—that they burned their canoes and retreated.

The next year, Nicholson was furnished with six ships of war, thirty transports, and one British and four New England regiments, for the capture of Port Royal. Subercase had only two hundred and sixty men and an insufficient supply of provisions. His soldiers were disaffected, and as soon as the ships appeared they began deserting, complaining that they had been neglected and abandoned by their own country. Subercase had to order the canoes removed to prevent a general desertion.

Nicholson sent a summons to surrender, after three days' waiting, landed his troops after three days more, and bombarded the fort after another week. The inhabitants of the town petitioned Subercase to surrender. Nothing else could be done, and on the 16th of October the starving and ragged garrison marched out to be sent to France. For the last time the French flag was hauled down from the fort, and Port Royal was henceforth an English for-

tress, which was re-named Annapolis Royal, in honor
of Queen Anne.

Subercase sent St. Castin to Quebec to carry the
news, and Nicholson despatched a letter to Vaudreuil, the Governor, by Major Livingstone, threatening reprisals on the people of Acadia, if the barbarities of French and Indians in New England were
continued.   Vaudreuil replied that the French were
able to avenge anything he might do ; that they
were not responsible for the acts of the Indians ;
that they had not treated prisoners with inhumanity ; and that a truce might long ago have put a
stop to hostilities if the English had been willing.
He appointed St. Castin his lieutenant in Acadia,
and directed him and the missionaries to keep alive
the loyalty of the French and preserve the friendship
of the Indians.

They were so successful that the next year, when
the garrison of Port Royal was weakened by disease,
death, and even desertion, the inhabitants refused
to obey the commandant's order to bring in timber
for repairing the fort.   Sixty men sent out to seize
a band of Indians and Acadians fell into an ambuscade ; half were killed, and the remainder taken prisoners.   The people of the town then sent word to
the commandant, that since he, as they thought,
had violated the terms of the surrender, they deemed

themselves absolved from their agreement not to
bear arms, and one of the priests went to Placentia
for arms, ammunition, and an officer to lead the insurgents.   But by this time news of the uprising had
reached Boston, and two hundred men from there
soon reduced the insurgents, captured the supplies,
and forced St. Castin to fly to Quebec.

Immediately after his victory, Nicholson went to
England to secure a force for the conquest of
Canada ; and about the same time Colonel Schuyler
of New York went there for the same purpose, taking with him five Iroquois sachems to awaken interest in the cause, and to insure the fidelity of the
tribes to the English alliance.   The chiefs caused a
great sensation throughout the kingdom.   The court
was in mourning, and the sachems were therefore
dressed in black suits, but over them they wore
mantles of scarlet cloth bordered with gold.   They
were taken in coaches to an audience with the
Queen ; and presented her with belts of wampum,
while one of them made a speech, saying : " We
were greatly rejoiced when we heard that our great
Queen had resolved to send an army against
Canada.   We hung up the kettle, and took down
the hatchet.   But while we were getting ready we
were told that our great Queen could not send the
army.   We were very sorrowful.   We cannot hunt

in freedom if Canada is not taken. So that if our great Queen does not remember us, we must take our families and forsake our country, or stand neutral while the French are fighting our friends."

The Secretary of State, St. John, afterward Viscount Bolingbroke, planned the expedition. Fifteen ships of war and forty transports, placed under the command of Sir Hovenden Walker, carried seven regiments of veterans from the Duke of Marlborough's army, and a battalion of marines under the command of Brigadier-General Hill. They arrived in Boston on the 25th of June, and encamped on Noddle's Island, now East Boston. A great crowd of people gathered to witness the review of the troops. "They made a very fine appearance," wrote the Admiral, "such as had never before been in these parts of the world."

New England and New York had raised two regiments to join the fleet ; and on the 30th of July sixty-eight vessels, carrying six thousand five hundred soldiers, set sail for Quebec. New York, New Jersey, and Connecticut collected about four thousand men, including a thousand Indians, to march against Montreal, under Colonels Schuyler, Whiting, and Ingoldsby, while Nicholson had the general care of the expedition. It was expected, also, that the Indian tribe called Foxes, in Wisconsin, whose alliance had been secured through the Iroquois, would begin hostilities against the French in the stations on the lakes.

When Vaudreuil learned that a hostile fleet was on its way to Quebec and an army marching toward Montreal, he first gathered the Onondaga and Seneca deputies and persuaded them to remain neutral. Then he gave a great festival, at which the war-song was sung and the hatchet raised. There were the Christian Indians of the settlements near Montreal, called the Sault and the Mountain ; there were the Indians of the various mission stations of the Jesuits ; there were Algonquin chiefs from the banks of the St. Lawrence, Ottawas, and Hurons, and Chippewas from beyond the lakes. The raising of the hatchet by the Hurons decided these remoter tribes ; and when the festival ended, they were all declared allies of the French. Quebec was strengthened, and the settlements along the banks below were guarded sufficiently to prevent the landing of the hostile troops. Three thousand men were placed at Chambly to meet the army from Albany on its way to Montreal.

But the fleet was destined never to see Quebec. Admiral Sir Hovenden Walker was busy with ingenious plans for taking care of his vessels at Quebec during the winter after he should have taken the

place.   He said, "the ice in the river, freezing to
the bottom, would bilge them as much as if they
were to be squeezed between rocks," and concluded
that the better way would be to "secure them on
the dry ground in frames and cradles, till the thaw."
Meantime he remained in complete ignorance of the
real difficulties and dangers that lay in his path.
He had with him a French seaman of experience
named Paradis, and by following his advice might
have navigated the river in safety.   But, refusing
all counsel, he gave orders according to his own no-
tions, and the fleet approached during a fog very
near a small island ; a sudden wind from the southeast drove the ships toward it, eight of them were
wrecked, and eight hundred and eighty-four men
were drowned.

After this disaster, the Admiral ordered his fleet
about and bore off to the coast of Cape Breton,
where he held a council of officers.   All agreed that
it was not advisable to go on ; there was but ten
weeks' provision for the men, and a supply could
hardly arrive in time from New England.   In re-
porting it, Walker philosophized thus : "Had we
arrived safe at Quebec, ten or twelve thousand men
must have been left to perish of cold and hunger ;
thus by the loss of a part, Providence saved all the
rest !"   The Admiral's ships sailed for England and

the provincial vessels carried home the New England troops. Nicholson, who had reached Lake George when he heard of the issue of the attack on Quebec, returned home and abandoned his undertaking also.

In the following year, the French were assailed by a new enemy, the Foxes, or Ottagamies, whom the Iroquois had drawn into an alliance against them. A party of their warriors set out to burn Detroit, which was defended by only twenty men under Du Buisson. But, having timely warning, Du Buisson sent swift messages to the Jesuit stations to have the Indian allies of the French sent to his relief. They poured in from every side and surrounded the Foxes, who soon found themselves the besieged instead of the besiegers. They held out with desperate bravery, but were at last compelled to surrender. The warriors of the party were slain at once, and the rest divided as slaves among the conquerors. But the French had gained an implacable foe ; and for a long time the Foxes and some more numerous tribes with which they were leagued continued to harass the French posts at the West.

Negotiations for peace began in Europe in 1712, but were not concluded till the following year. The power of France had been humbled ; and not only did the policy of England prevail in the settlement

of questions regarding European territory, but England also gained large tracts of land in America
which had been claimed by her enemy. Although
France was left in possession of Louisiana, England
gained Newfoundland, Hudson Bay and Straits with
the land adjoining, the Island of St. Christopher,
and Nova Scotia or Acadia, according to its ancient
boundaries. The Iroquois, or Five Nations, were
recognized as being under the dominion of the English, and it was stipulated that France should nevel
molest them. The treaty of peace was signed al
Utrecht, April 11th, 1713.

But there was still abundant room for future mis-
understandings and disputes. The limits of the
territory of the Five Nations were indefinite, the
French applied the name Louisiana to the entire
valley of the Mississippi and the Ohio, and the
boundaries of Acadia had long been a subject of dispute. The French claimed that only the southern
portion of the peninsula of Nova Scotia was properly included in Acadia ; while the English applied the
name to a great territory bounded by the St. Lawrence, the ocean and gulf, and a line drawn from
the mouth of the Kennebec to Quebec, and including the islands of Cape Breton and St. John, now
Prince Edward Island.

Large numbers of the Acadians, restive under

British rule, removed to the provinces still under the
control of the French, many of them to Cape Breton
Island.   A large settlement was formed at Louisburg on the southeastern shore of the island.   Here
was a fine harbor, half a mile broad, and here in
time arose the strongest fortress in America, protecting the French fisheries and forming a refuge
for privateers in time of war.

The Abenaquis, seeing with jealousy the growth
of the English settlements in their territory, sent an
embassy to the Governor of Canada, asking if the
French had really given up their country to the
English.   Vaudreuil answered that nothing was said
about their country in the treaty ; and the Indians,
resolved to undertake their own defence, attacked
the English fishermen at Canso, killing several and
robbing them of all they had, and committing other
similar depredations.

The New England people had long been suspicious of the influence of a Jesuit missionary, Sebastian Rasles, at Norridgewock, on the Kennebec.   He
had been at the Jesuit mission on the Chaudière,
had travelled through the west in pursuit of his calling, and was familiar with many of the Indian languages.   For twenty-five years he had been on
the Kennebec, where he had gathered a flourishing congregation of savages, and built a church

which he had decorated with pictures painted by his own hand, and whose glittering altar was looked on with reverent awe by savage eyes. His altar-boys were little Indians, gorgeous in red and white ; and their chanting processions were a favorite bid for the admiration of the natives. The old man shared the journeys and the dangers of his flock, and his influence over them was unbounded. This influence, there was every reason to believe, was used to incite them to depredations on the English settlements ; he was said to keep a flag on which was a cross surrounded by bows and arrows, which he used to raise on a pole in front of the church when he gave them absolution before they set out on their warlike enterprises.

Father Rasles was therefore marked for destruction. On occasion of the Abenaquis threatening reprisals if some of their chiefs who were held by the Massachusetts Government as hostages were not released, a party of men under Colonel Westbrook was sent in December, 1721, to capture the priest. The hunters were away on the chase, and there was no one to protect him ; but, warned of Westbrook's approach, he fled to the woods in haste, leaving his papers behind. Among them was his correspondence with the Governor of Canada, which proved that the suspicions against him were not unfounded.

There was also a dictionary in manuscript of the
Abenaquis language, which has been preserved, and
was printed by the American Academy of Arts and
Sciences in 1833. At about the same time the
young Baron de St. Castin was also seized, as dangerous to the peace of the settlements in the east,
and taken to Boston.

Exasperated by these attempts on their leaders,
the Indians determined on war. They invited all
the tribes of their own nation not only, but those
near Quebec, to unite with them. The first blow
was struck at Merry Meeting Bay, near the junction
of the Androscoggin with the Kennebec, where
Brunswick now stands. A party of sixty Indians
captured nine families, but they afterward released
all but five men, whom they kept as security for
their hostages in the hands of the English. Two
attacks on the fort at the River St. George were unsuccessful, as were nearly all Indian attempts on
fortified places ; but many fishing and trading vessels fell into their hands, and with these they cruised
about the coast, compelling the captured seamen to
serve as their crews. Two armed vessels sent out
by the Governor of Nova Scotia re-took all the vessels, numbering more than twenty, and put a stop
to the piracies for the time.

Parties sent out the next year, under Captain

Harmon and Colonel Westbrook, made some reprisals on the savages. Harmon pursued a party of
thirty-four, and killed fifteen of them as they lay by
their camp-fires. Westbrook took a large party of
men to a village on the Penobscot, supposed to have
been above Bangor at Old Town ; it was deserted,
and they set fire to it, and all the buildings in it,
including a well-built stockade fort, a chapel, and
the residence of the priests, were laid in ashes.
During this year the Indians were comparatively
quiet, but in 1724 they broke out afresh. Men
working in the fields, or for any reason away from
the settlements, were liable to death or capture at
any moment. At Kennebunk a sloop was taken,
and every man on it was put to death.

Captain Josiah Winslow and sixteen men who
were with him were surprised on the St. George, and
every one of them was killed. Annapolis was attacked, and a party sent out from the fort was defeated. The priest of Annapolis, who was at Minas when the Indians gathered there, and might
have given warning of the intended attack, was ex-
pelled from the colony and sent to Louisburg ; another priest, who did send a warning, although it
arrived too late, was thanked and promoted by the
English ; but the church authorities afterward superseded him, placing in Minas, where the English

had stationed him, one more faithful to the French interest.

The same year another expedition was planned to seize the hated Father Rasles.   He had been urged to fly to Canada ; but, though he knew the danger, he would not leave his post.   '' God has given this flock into my care,'' he said, '' and I shall not leave it.''   This time the assailants succeeded in taking Norridgewock by surprise.   The Indians made little resistance ; all who could get away fled to the river, crossed it, and escaped to the forest.   Father Rasles, who was in his wigwam, went forward to help his flock to escape by drawing the attention of the assailants to himself, and was struck down at once, killed, scalped, and trodden under foot.   After pillaging the church and the dwellings, the soldiers set them on fire and retired.   The mourning Indians buried their priest beneath the ground where his altar had stood, and now a monument to his memory marks the spot where he fell.

In the following year Captain John Lovewell, of Dunstable, impelled by patriotism, or the desire of adventure, or the bounty on scalps, led out a party of men.   Ten Indians asleep beside the Salmon Falls River were surprised and killed, and Lovewell received one thousand pounds for the ten scalps. The next expedition was not so fortunate ; it fell into an ambuscade on the Saco ; and Lovewell and half of his thirty-four men lost their lives. Lovewell's Pond, near Fryeburg, where he fell, is named for him, and the brook flowing into it is called Battle Brook.

In the summer of the same year, a conference with the Indians was held at the fort on the St. George. They seemed disposed for peace, and in November four of the chiefs were called to Boston to form a treaty. They acknowledged the title of the English to Nova Scotia and Acadia, and promised to maintain peace and deliver up their prisoners. The treaty was faithfully observed, and the eastern colonies had a season of rest from the horrors of Indian warfare.

In 1726, the French built a fort at Niagara, where they had long had a trading-post ; and in the following year, Governor Burnet, of New York, built what he called a " stone house of strength" at Oswego. The Governor of Canada remonstrated, and threatened to destroy it, but did not venture on any violence. In 1731, the French built Fort Frederick at Crown Point, thus asserting their claim to north-eastern New York.

CHAPTER IX.

KING GEORGE'S WAR

PEACE reigned between France and England for thirty years after the Treaty of Utrecht. Queen Anne, the last of the Stuart line of sovereigns, died in 1714, and was succeeded by George I., first English king of the House of Hanover, who inherited through his mother, the Electress Sophia of Hanover, granddaughter of James I. of England. He died in 1727, and was succeeded by his son, George II. It was during the reign of this king that England became engaged in the next war which involved the colonies of North America.

In 1740, Charles VI., Emperor of Germany, died. Many years before, he had taken measures to secure to his daughter, Maria Theresa, the succession to his hereditary dominions ; and he hoped that after his death her husband, the Duke of Tuscany, would be chosen by the electors to wear the imperial crown. To secure the inheritance to his daughter, he proclaimed a law called the " Pragmatic Sanction," regulating the succession. Many of the powers of Europe demurred ; but by ceding away parts of his dominions to the other monarchies of the continent, the Emperor at length gained their consent. After his death, however, claims were made to his dominions by several princes, on grounds having more or less color of justice in themselves, but all were set aside by the Pragmatic Sanction to which they had pledged their support.

The young queen had been carefully educated with a view to the position her father designed her to occupy. She had shared his counsels, and learned something of the art of governing. She was twenty-three years of age when her father died, and being gifted with beauty, unusual mental ability, and a high spirit, she was well fitted to attract the loyalty of her father's subjects

The first to attack the rights of the young queen was the King of Prussia, Frederick II., called the Great. Raising some pretence of a right to the possession of Silesia, which had been under Austria for more than a hundred years, he prepared an

army of thirty thousand men, and sent them into
the country, in December, 1740, without having
made any declaration of war, or any demand for the
province ; indeed, he had until then professed to be
friendly to the interests of Maria Theresa.

After filling Silesia with his forces, Frederick
sent an ambassador to the Queen, offering to aid her
against her other enemies, if she would cede to him
the duchy which .he had invaded, which she indig-
nantly refused to do.   He then overran the whole of
Lower Silesia with his troops, and Prussia was successful in the first battle with Austria, that of Moll-
witz, in April, 1741, though Frederick himself ran
away.   Then all the other claimants rushed on to
the dismemberment of the Austrian Empire. France
took the part of the Elector of Bavaria, who claimed
the throne.   Prussia, France, Spain, and Poland were
combined against the Queen.   Thus began the War
of the Austrian Succession.

Maria Theresa was obliged to yield Silesia to
Frederick, in June, 1742, but succeeded in maintaining her claim to most of her other dominions, while
the Elector of Bavaria was thoroughly humbled.
The war now became a struggle on the part of Austria to wrest Alsace and Lorraine from France, and
Naples from Spain, and to make Bavaria a part of
the Austrian dominions.   England had aided Aus-

tria by subsidies and troops, and her forces met the
army of France in the battle of Dettingen in June,
1743. But it was not until March, 1744, that war
was formally declared between France and England.

When the news of the declaration of war was sent
to Louisbourg, orders were also sent that no offen-
sive measures should be taken until reënforcements
should arrive. But it was thought that a sudden attack on the small garrisons at Annapolis and Canso,
before help could arrive from New England, could
not fail of success. Du Vivier, a great-grandson of
Charles la Tour, so prominent in the early history
of Acadia, taking command of five hundred men, of
whom two hundred were Indians, and several vessels,
attacked the block-house at Canso, in May, 1744.
Having no chance of a successful defence, the garrison of eighty men surrendered at once, and were
taken to Louisbourg, on condition that they should
be sent, at the end of a year, to England or to
Boston. The buildings were all destroyed by Du
Vivier's men.

It remained only to take Annapolis. The fort
was an earthwork in a ruinous condition, held by
one hundred and fifty men under Paul Mascarene.
Du Vivier took his prisoners to Louisbourg, and remained there some time, making preparations for
going to Annapolis. Meantime, a rumor reached

that place that five hundred French and Indians, on
the way to attack it, were already on the river above
the town.   A vessel soon arrived from Boston bringing news of the declaration of war, and the officers
and soldiers of the garrison sent their families to
Boston by the return of the galley, two other vessels being sent with it, thus greatly relieving the
place of those unable to bear arms.   The men then
went to work repairing the fortifications.

The Indians who had been with Du Vivier at
Canso grew impatient waiting for his return ; and
they were easily persuaded by Belleisle, a scion of
the St. Castin family, to march against Annapolis
under his leadership without waiting for Du Vivier.
They were accompanied by their priest, La Loutre,
who, like most of the priests in Acadia, had been
faithfully laboring to keep his flock loyal to French
interests.   If the Indians had been supported
by Du Vivier's soldiers, Annapolis would probably have fallen ; for it was not in a condition to
withstand a determined assault.   But the Indians
pursued their usual methods, picking off stragglers and firing from under cover.   The English
sent out a party of workmen and soldiers, who drove
them back and tore down all buildings that could
protect them from the guns of the fort, and they
were glad to escape with a few stolen cattle.

Reënforcements were sent from Boston to the number of one hundred men or more. Du Vivier returned with two hundred soldiers, expecting a general rising among the inhabitants; but there was only a feeble response to his summons to them to enlist under the banner of France and bring in supplies for the expedition; and the Indians were disheartened by their failure. Many of the savages, however, joined him, and late in August he began his attack. After several days of ineffectual firing, he sent in a flag of truce, saying that three ships of war were on their way to his assistance, together with a large body of soldiers, and supplies of cannon and mortars, and offering to accept a capitulation conditioned on their arrival; but Mascarene refused to have any negotiations with him. The attacks were resumed and kept up night after night, until late in September, when another reënforcement arrived from Boston.

Having learned from a prisoner that Mascarene talked of attacking his camp, Du Vivier hastily drew off to Minas, and finally returned to Louisbourg. It was not long after Du Vivier abandoned the siege, that a part of his ships arrived; but finding him gone, they withdrew, while Mascarene kept his men at work strengthening the defences during the autumn and winter, in expectation of another attack

La Loutre gathered a force of Indians again, who were joined by some Canadian troops, and in the spring they made a feeble attack on Annapolis, and prowled about the country, but with no greater success than the capture of two trading-vessels.

The soldiers taken at Canso, who had been sent to Boston on parole, gave information regarding the condition of the fortress, and in January, 1745, the question of an expedition for its capture began to be agitated. Governor Shirley of Massachusetts had written to England the preceding autumn, asking help for the protection of Nova Scotia and the capture of Louisbourg ; but as yet no answer had been received. In January he laid the project before the State Legislature in a secret session. It was at first rejected, so improbable did it seem that a provincial force could effect the capture of the strongest post in North America. But afterward, on a complaint from the merchants of Boston, Salem, and Marblehead, of the injuries to their vessels from the privateers which found refuge at Louisbourg, the project was reconsidered, and resolved on by a majority of one.

The other provinces were asked to render aid. Connecticut sent five hundred and sixteen men, New Hampshire three hundred and four ; and these, with the three thousand two hundred and fifty raised in Massachusetts, constituted the whole force. Rhode Island sent three hundred, but they arrived too late. New York gave some artillery, and Pennsylvania some provisions. The New England colonies furnished thirteen armed vessels. Commodore Warren, who was at Antigua, was solicited to send some of his ships, but declined doing so without express orders from England.

It was a question who should command this expedition. With the exception of some little irregular fighting with the Indians, peace had reigned throughout the colonies for thirty years ; and there were no officers to be had in the provinces with any knowledge of the science of regular warfare. The choice fell upon William Pepperell, of Kittery, a colonel of militia, who, as a merchant, a landholder in three of the provinces, and a man of clear judgment and weight of character, would be likely to have influence with those of his countrymen who were to be led on this great undertaking.

Immense enthusiasm attended the fitting out of the expedition. Pepperell sought advice from the celebrated preacher, George Whitefield, on the question of accepting the proffered command, and Whitefield answered that if he should fail, the responsibility for the blood of the fallen would be laid to his charge, and that if he should succeed, he

would become an object of malicious envy to his
fellow-citizens.   In spite of this dark augury, Pepperell accepted.   To the New Hampshire troops
who asked him for a motto, Whitefield gave, *Nil
desperandum, Christo Duce* —" Nothing is to be de-
spaired of, Christ being the leader."   In this spirit
of religious enthusiasm, one of the volunteers carried an axe wherewith to hew down the crosses and
images in the French churches.   All sorts of advice
and schemes for the protection of the volunteers
and the speedy capture of the fort were laid before
the officers.   One inventive enthusiast brought a
model of a flying bridge which would land the army
within the walls at a single bound.   A minister had
a scheme for avoiding the explosion of mines,
and taking Louisbourg without the loss of a life.
Another had made a complete plan of the siege,
the camp, the batteries, the intrenchments.   Governor Shirley's instructions were, that the army
should land in the night and march to surprise the
fortress before daybreak.

Late in March, 1745, the fleet set sail, carrying
the army of fishermen, farmers, mechanics, and lum-
bermen, under their citizen General, William Pepperell, Brigadier-General Waldo, and their subordinate officers, mostly chosen from among the
church deacons, justices of the peace, and other cit-

izens of respectability and consideration in their townships. Among them was the soldier, Colonel William Vaughan, who had first suggested the enterprise to Governor Shirley.

Arriving at Canso early in April, they found the coast of Cape Breton so clogged with ice that not a vessel could enter the harbors, which made it probable that no news of their intentions could have reached the fort. While they were waiting, Pepperell had a block-house built in place of the one that had been destroyed the previous year, and garrisoned it with eighty men. Their spirits were raised by the capture of a richly-loaded vessel on its way from Martinique to Louisbourg, and still more by the arrival of four ships of war under Commodore Warren, who had received instructions from England to go to the help of the colonies, just after his refusal to proceed without orders had been despatched to Boston. More ships of war soon after arrived, and in a few days Louisbourg was blockaded. Warren's ships guarded the entrance to the harbor, and the places in the vicinity from which supplies might be sent were surprised and held.

Louisbourg was fortified with a stone rampart thirty feet high and forty feet thick at the base, which swept around the town in a circuit of two miles, and was surrounded by a ditch eighty feet wide. Six bastions stood out from this great wall, and there were embrasures for a hundred and forty-eight cannon and six mortars. On an island at the entrance of the harbor was a battery of thirty pieces, and on the shore opposite the entrance was the grand or royal battery of twenty-eight forty-two pounders and two eighteen-pounders, with a moat and bastions. Near the drawbridge, giving entrance to the town on the land side, was a circular battery mounting sixteen twenty-four pounders. This fortress, which was twenty-five years in building, cost thirty millions of livres, and was called the "Dunkirk of America," is now a lonely ruin, the former military importance of the place having entirely passed away.

The appearance of the fleet in Chapeaurouge, or Gabarus Bay, southward from the city, May 30th, was the first intimation of danger the French had received. They fired cannon, rang bells, and ran about in confusion ; and a hundred and fifty soldiers, under an officer named Boulardiere, were sent out to prevent the landing. But Pepperell quietly sent a detachment farther up the Bay while Boulardiere's attention was fixed on the spot where it was supposed the attempt would be made, and Boulardiere was obliged to retire into the city again. About two thousand men were landed that day, and by the next night all were on shore. Colonel Vaughan took a party of New Hampshire men and marched past the city to the northeast harbor, where they burned a number of warehouses containing naval stores and large quantities of wine and brandy. The smoke was carried into the royal battery, a panic seized the men in charge of it, and they spiked their guns and fled.

In the morning Vaughan's men took possession of the deserted battery. Boat-loads of men from the city came to dislodge them, but Vaughan stood on the shore with thirteen men and prevented them from landing till reënforcements came. The spiked cannon were drilled out and turned on the city and the island battery, throwing a deadly fire within the walls and reaching the roof of the citadel. To a summons to surrender, on the 7th of May, Du Chambon, the commandant, returned a refusal; but his men had been so mutinous before the siege that he did not dare trust them to make a sortie, for fear of desertion.

In order to place batteries for more effective work, it was necessary to carry the guns over a morass. Sledges were made, and the men drew them by straps passed over their shoulders, sinking to their knees in the bog. This task consumed fourteen nights.

Several attempts were made by the besiegers to

take the island battery, but all without success ; one, a night attack, was a disastrous failure. The assailants, discovered before they could land, and met by a sharp fire, were glad to escape after nearly an hour's hard fighting, having lost sixty men killed and a hundred and sixteen prisoners. Despairing of taking the island battery, the Americans then placed a battery on the high cape at the light-house on the eastern side of the harbor, which com-manded the island battery, and nearly silenced it.

The siege had now lasted almost six weeks, and the city had neither been entered nor had a breach been made in the walls. Other ships of war had arrived, and it was agreed that the fleet should sail into the harbor and bombard while the land forces attempted an entrance by storm. At this time the *Vigilant*, a French ship, carrying sixty-four guns, arrived with military supplies for the garrison, and was taken by a Massachusetts frigate under the command of Captain Edward Tyng. Pepperell sent news of the capture to Du Chambon under a flag of truce, and this so discouraged the commandant that he determined to capitulate, and on the 17th of June Louisbourg was surrendered, after a siege of forty-nine days. The garrison, the crew of the *Vigilant*, and some of the inhabitants of the town were sent to France.

When the American troops entered the fortress they for the first time realized the strength of the place and the magnitude of the enterprise, the undertaking of which now seemed presumptuous, and its success little short of a miracle. With the feeling that Providence had manifestly interfered to give them the victory, they listened to the chaplain who proclaimed the gospel according to Calvin from the altar whence they had cast down the images and the tapers.

There was great rejoicing in Boston when a swift-sailing schooner brought news of the victory of which the anxious communities at home were beginning to despair. Commodore Warren had sent home two prisoners some weeks before, one the commander of a battery without the walls of Louisbourg, the other, captain of a captured ship ; and these men had given descriptions of the strength of the fortress, which made New England tremble for its little army. But now bells were rung, cannon fired, and tumultuous crowds added their voices in a general shout of rejoicing.

In England the report that such a stronghold had been taken by an untrained army of provincials could hardly be believed. Sir Peter Warren, the naval commander, acknowledged the services of the colonists but grudgingly ; and though it was the most brilliant success the English achieved during the war, English historians scarcely mention it. Voltaire, however, calls the capture of Louisbourg one of the most remarkable events of the reign of Louis XV.

General Pepperell was made a baronet for his share in the enterprise, while Governor Shirley received a commission in the regular army, and afterward held the chief military command in America. Colonel Vaughan went to England to present his claims, but failed to receive any reward for his services, and died in London in obscurity and neglect.

The capture of Louisbourg led to a project on the part of the English authorities to conquer Canada, and one by the French to recover Cape Breton and Acadia, and devastate the New England coast. Governor Shirley wrote to the British ministry, urging measures for the conquest of Canada, and in response the Secretary of State sent orders to the governors of the colonies, as far south as Virginia, to raise as many men as possible, and have them ready for action. A squadron of ships and some land forces were to be sent to Louisbourg, and there met by the New England troops, when the united force was to ascend the St. Lawrence to Quebec. At the same time the soldiers from New York and the southern colonies were to assemble at Albany for the capture of Crown Point and Montreal.

The colonial troops were readily raised, to the number of about eight thousand men, and waited for the fleet. But no fleet came. When the season was so far advanced that all hopes of its arrival were given up, it was thought best to employ the troops ordered to Albany in an attack on Crown Point ; and the Iroquois as usual were found willing to join in the undertaking. The New England troops were ordered to Acadia, on the sudden intelligence that the inhabitants were on the eve of revolt, and that Annapolis was threatened by a body of French and Indians.

During the same season a large fleet had been gathered at Brest for the capture of Louisbourg, Annapolis, and Boston ; and the Canadians and their Indian allies were to be ready to coöperate with the fleet by land. Six hundred Canadians, therefore, repaired to Acadia in June, and the Micmacs and Malicites rallied once more under the banners of France. This force was waiting at Chignecto in September for the arrival of the fleet, when the Governor of Canada, having heard that the New England forces were about to embark for Acadia, sent orders to Ramezay, their commander, to bring them back to Quebec. But as Ramezay was about to go, he learned that the French fleet had arrived in the harbor of Chebucto, now Halifax.

This intelligence, which was received by Ramezay's men with great rejoicing, and had filled New
England with consternation, was not so important
as it seemed.   The fleet which had started from
France on the 22d of June, under the command of
the Duc d'Anville, comprised forty ships of war,
with transports carrying more than three thousand
soldiers and all kinds of military stores.   It was
the largest armament that had ever been sent to
American shores.   But a tempest had scattered the
ships soon after they set sail, many of them were
compelled to return, and when the Duc d'Anville
reached Chebucto he had only three of his war-ships
and a few transports left.   An infectious fever was
rapidly disabling the soldiers that remained, and on
the 16th of September, a few days after the arrival,
D'Anville himself suddenly died, not without suspicion of poison.

More ships having arrived, the officer next in command, Vice-Admiral d'Estournelle, proposed in a
council of officers that the undertaking should be
abandoned ; for some ships which were to join them
from Hispaniola had failed, their own ships were
scattered, and twenty-four hundred of their men had
died of the fever.   Three ships from Hispaniola had
been to Chebucto, but had returned to France on
failing to find D'Anville's fleet.   The abandonment

of the expedition was violently opposed by the officers, headed by Jonquière, who had been lately appointed Governor of Canada and was next in command, and D'Estournelle, excited by the opposition, took the fever, and in a fit of delirium killed himself with his own sword.

Jonquière resolved to attack Annapolis with the forces that were left; but when they arrived off Cape Sable, another storm still further disabled the ships, and news was brought the commander that Louisbourg and Annapolis were both defended by English ships. So the French vessels could do nothing but return to Brest.

Ramezay, with his Canadian and Indian followers, went into winter quarters at Chignecto, where his presence was a constant menace to Annapolis. Mascerene, commander of the garrison there, sent to Boston for troops, and five hundred men were accordingly despatched in December, and on their arrival were stationed at Grand Pré, near the River Gaspereaux in the district of Minas.

Ramezay determined to send a force against them, and in January, 1747, about four hundred Canadians and Indians set out, under an officer named De Villiers. For two weeks they travelled on snow-shoes and dragged their supplies on sledges along the wintry coast. The New England officers had some warning of the danger ; but, supposing the enemy to be isolated by the season, they paid no attention to it.

On the 10th of February the French arrived in a dense storm of snow, which prevented them from being seen by the sentries. They had accurate information from the inhabitants of Grand Pré, and ten houses where the officers were lodged were selected for the first attack. There was a desperate resistance, but the New England soldiers were under too great disadvantage ; sixty were killed, including the chief officer, Colonel Arthur Noble, and sixty-nine were made prisoners. The French lost but seven killed and fourteen wounded. Those of the English who remained could not escape, having no snow-shoes ; a capitulation was at length agreed upon, and they returned to Annapolis under a promise not to bear arms in Minas and adjoining districts for six months.

After Jonquière returned to France, another fleet was prepared to carry troops to Canada and Nova Scotia, and placed under his command. He set sail in May, 1747, with six ships of war and some transports, accompanied by six merchant-ships and a frigate bound for the East Indies. An English fleet under Admirals Anson and Warren set out in pursuit, and a battle was fought off Cape Finisterre on the 3d of May, which resulted in a complete victory for the English. They took six ships of war and all the merchantmen, with over four thousand prisoners. The captured treasure was afterward taken to the Bank of England in twenty wagons.

The people on the western frontier had been somewhat disturbed by French and Indian bands during the progress of the war. Rumford, now Concord, New Hampshire, was unsuccessfully attacked in 1746, and Fort Massachusetts, in Williamstown, was taken by a large party in the same year. Fort Number Four on the Connecticut was assailed by a large band in 1747, but was bravely and successfully defended by a garrison under Captain Phineas. The village of Saratoga was destroyed, and the inhabitants, thirty families in all, were slaughtered.

Nothing was done in America this year by the English, though the colonists believed that a reasonable amount of aid from England would enable them to bring all Canada under British sway. It was said that English statesmen thought the colonies, if their strength were revealed to them by such a conquest, and if the fear of French inroads from the north were removed, might be tempted to assert their independence; particularly as they were growing restive under some of the exactions and restrictions imposed upon them. However that may be—whether English statesmen foresaw the events that were to occur within thirty years, or whether they had simply not awakened to the importance of their colonial possessions in America—not only was nothing done to reduce Canada, but Louisbourg was restored to France, much to the chagrin of the colonists who were so proud of its capture. The treaty of Aix-la-Chapelle, which put an end to the war, October 18, 1748, gave up Louisbourg for Madras, which the French had taken, and left the boundaries of French and English territory in America as undefined as they had been under former treaties.

Parliament agreed to pay to the colonists all the expenses they had incurred for the war, and in 1749 two hundred and fifteen chests of Spanish dollars and one hundred casks of copper coin were sent from England to Boston. This money, which amounted to about a million dollars, was carried to the treasury on twenty-seven carts and trucks.

CHAPTER X.

ACADIA AFTER THE WAR.

Failure of Negotiations for the Adjustment of Boundaries—Encroachments of the French—Settlement of Halifax—Refusal of the Acadians to Take the Oath—Attacks by Indians—Burning of Beaubassin—Fort Lawrence—Fort Beau Séjour—Colonel How's Fate—Expedition to Acadia—Fall of the French Forts—Escape of La Loutre—Exile of the Acadians.

DURING the nominal peace which followed the Treaty of Aix-la-Chapelle, the representatives of the two governments were anxiously engaged in attempting to settle by actual occupation the question of boundaries, which was still left open by that treaty. It professed to restore the boundaries as they had been before the war ; and before the war the entire basin of the Mississippi, as well as the tract between the St. Lawrence River and Gulf, the Bay of Fundy, and the Kennebec, was claimed by both nations, with some show of reason, as no convention between them had ever defined the rights of each. Names had been given to vast tracts of land whose limits were but partly defined, or at one time defined in one way, at another time in another, and when these names were mentioned in treaties

they were understood by each party according to its
own interest.   The treaty of 1748, therefore, not
only left abundant cause for future war, but left occasion for the continuance of petty border hostilities
in time of nominal peace.   Commissioners were ap
pointed, French and English, to settle the question ·
of the disputed territory, but the differences were
too wide to be adjusted by anything but conquest.

While the most important question was that of
the great extent of territory at the west, and, as
we shall hereafter see, both nations were devising
means for establishing their claims to it, Acadia, or
Nova Scotia, was the scene of a constant petty warfare.   The French were determined to restrict the
English province to the peninsula now known by
that name.   The Governor of Canada sent a few men
under Boishebert to the mouth of the St. John's to
hold that part of the territory.   A little old fort
built by the Indians had stood for fifty years on the
St. John's at the mouth of the Nerepis, and there
the men established themselves.   A larger number
was sent under La Corne to keep possession of Chignecto, on the isthmus which, according to French
claims, formed the northern boundary of English
territory.

In all the years that England had held nominal
rule in Acadia, not a single English settlement had

been formed, and apparently not a step of progress had been taken in gaining the loyalty of the inhabitants. A whole generation had grown up during the time ; but they were no less devoted to France than their fathers had been. It was said that the King of England had not one truly loyal subject in the peninsula, outside of the fort at Annapolis. When the inhabitants did not choose to obey the orders of the English authorities, they represented themselves as being under fear of the Indians ; and the Indians were constantly urged to their share in the proceedings by the persuasions and inducements of the priests and emissaries of the Canadian Government. No doubt, also, the bond of religion was the strongest influence that held the Acadians faithful to France.

Among the schemes suggested for remedying this state of affairs, was one by Governor Shirley, to place strong bands of English settlers in all the important towns, in order that the Government might have friends and influence throughout the country. Nothing came of this ; but in 1749 Parliament voted forty thousand pounds for the purpose of settling a colony. Inducements were offered to discharged soldiers and sailors, and to farmers and mechanics to join the colony. They were to be carried over free, to be furnished with farming and fishing implements, and to be maintained free of expense for one year. Grants of land were offered also, privates from the army and navy were to receive fifty acres each, and officers more, according to their rank. No quit-rents were to be required for the first ten years. Twenty-five hundred persons being ready to go in less than two months from the time of the first advertisement, the colony was entrusted to Colonel Edward Cornwallis (uncle of the Cornwallis of the Revolutionary War), and he was made Governor of Nova Scotia. Chebucto was selected as the site of the colony, and the town was named Halifax in honor of the president of the Lords of Trade and Plantations. Within four months a clearing was made, and three hundred houses were built.

In July, a council was held at Halifax, when Governor Cornwallis gave the French deputies a paper declaring what the Government would allow to the French subjects, and what would be required of them. They were to be left in peaceable possession of their property and the free exercise of their religion, provided they should take the oath of allegiance to the British Government, submit to its laws, and give all possible countenance and assistance to settlers who should be sent out under his Majesty's orders. To this the people replied by their deputies, asking that they might enjoy the privileges mentioned, under condition of taking a qualified oath, one that should exempt them from bearing arms in case of war, even in defence of their own province.   Such an oath had been allowed in certain cases twenty years before ; and the precedent was urged at this time.   They wished to stand as neutrals, and, indeed, were often called so.

Cornwallis replied that nothing less than entire allegiance would be accepted.   Then the deputies asked if they might sell their property and leave the peninsula, and were told that the Treaty of Utrecht gave them a year in which to withdraw from the province with their effects, if they preferred that to becoming subjects of Great Britain ; but that now there was no alternative but confiscation or entire allegiance.   About a month later the people sent in a declaration with a thousand signatures, stating that they had resolved not to take the oath, but were determined to leave the country.   Cornwallis took no steps to coerce them, but wrote to England for instructions.

A treaty was made between the Governor and the chiefs of the Indians in July ; but on the occasion of the building of a block-house by the English at Minas, the Indians were instigated to violate the treaty, and attacks were made by them on Canso and Minas, and some vessels in the harbor of Chig-

necto. It was supposed that the missionary priest
La Loutre was at the bottom of all the trouble with
the Indians and much of the disloyalty of the Acadians ; one means of coercion was always at his
service, the refusal of the sacraments to the disobe-
dient.

In the following year Cornwallis sent four hundred
men, under Major Lawrence, to Chignecto to build
a block-house. A little river called the Messagouche
was claimed by the French as their southern boundary ; and a force under La Corne had been keeping
possession of the isthmus. On the southern bank
was a prosperous village called Beaubassin, and La
Corne had compelled its inhabitants to take the oath
of allegiance to the King of France. When Lawrence arrived, all the inhabitants of Beaubassin, about
one thousand, having been persuaded by La Loutre,
set fire to their houses, and leaving behind the fruits
of years of industry, turned their backs on their fertile fields, and crossed the river, to put themselves
under the protection of La Corne's troops. Many
Acadians from other parts of the peninsula also left
their homes, and lived in exile and poverty under
the French dominion, hoping for a speedy change
of masters in Nova Scotia.

Lawrence was obliged to abandon the work on
which he had been sent, since La Corne had a very

large force at his command ; but later in the season he went again to Chignecto with a larger body of troops.   Their landing was opposed by a band of Indians assisted by some of the Acadians, intrenched behind the dikes, and in the assault six English-men were killed and twelve wounded.   This was the first blood shed since the peace of Aix-la-Chapelle.   Lawrence's men proceeded to build a fort on the south bank of the Messagouche, which was called Fort Lawrence, and garrisoned by six hundred men.

In the same year a large French fort, Beau Séjour, was built on the northern side of the Messagouche, and a smaller one, Gaspereaux, at Baie Verte. Other stations were also planted, forming a line of fortified posts from the Gulf of St. Lawrence to the mouth of the St. John's.   An instance of the treach-ery of La Loutre about this time is recorded.   Cap-tain Edward How, an officer well known to the country and the Indians, was sent to Fort Lawrence by the Governor, that he might use his influence to keep the Indians peaceful.   He sometimes met French officers on the Messagouche with flags of truce, and messages were in that way sent between the forts.   La Loutre dressed an Indian like a French officer, and sent him down the river with a flag of truce, and Captain How came unsuspiciously to meet him, when some Indians who were concealed on the bank arose and shot him dead.

The Acadians made repeated attempts to induce Cornwallis to allow them to take the qualified oath, threatening to leave the province and to neglect sowing their fields.   Cornwallis seems to have treated them with mildness and consideration, but was firm in his refusal to take less than an oath of full allegiance. Many of those who had exiled themselves asked permission to return, but through the influences brought to bear upon them by the French, declined to fulfil the conditions required. La Loutre told them that if they returned and yielded allegiance they should be allowed neither priests nor sacraments, and as he was Vicar-General for Acadia under the Bishop of Quebec, he probably had power to make good his threat.

In the following years, the Acadians refused to bring supplies to the English forts, even at their own prices, and in 1754 three hundred of them went to work at Fort Beau Séjour. refusing the offer of employment on government works at Halifax. Their rebellious conduct was imitated by some Germans lately settled at Lunenburg, and the Governor was obliged to send soldiers to subdue them.

The commission appointed to settle the question of boundaries had broken up without accomplishing any results ; and it was resolved by the authorities in Nova Scotia and Massachusetts that an expedition should be sent against Fort Beau Séjour. The enterprise was planned by Governor Shirley and Colonel Lawrence, then in command in Nova Scotia. Great care was taken to keep the matter secret, that the garrison might be taken completely by surprise. Arms and boats had been taken from the Acadians ; and during the summer, when it was rumored that a French fleet had arrived in the Bay of Fundy, they offered memorials to the council, asking for the restoration of their arms, and exemption from the oath. This was refused ; and the deputies, on again declining to take the oath, were ordered into confinement.

The Governor then issued orders to all the French inhabitants to send in new deputies, who should express their final intentions with regard to the oath ; warning them that any who now refused would not thereafter be allowed to take it, " but that effectual measures ought to be taken to remove all such recusants out of the province." Deputies were sent in representing over five hundred of the inhabitants ; all refused to take the required oath, and were ordered into confinement. It had been determined to expel the people from the province in case they should refuse, " and," says the record of the council,

" nothing now remained to be considered but what measures should be taken to send them away, and where they should be sent to."

Meantime, Massachusetts had raised about two thousand troops for the contemplated enterprise, who were under the command of Lieutenant-Colonel John Winslow. To this force were added about three hundred regulars, and the whole was placed under the command of Lieutenant-Colonel Monckton. They reached Chignecto on the 2d of June, and the following day encamped about Fort Lawrence. De Vergor, commander at Beau Séjour, had neglected to take measures for strengthening his position, though some rumors of the intended attack had reached him. Now, however, having quite a large force at his disposal, consisting of a hundred and sixty-five soldiers, and several hundred Acadians who had obeyed the summons to come into the fort, he set to work to complete the defences.

On the 4th the English began by attacking the block-house at Pont-à-Buot, some miles east of Beau Séjour, and took it in an hour, the French running away in a panic and setting fire to the block-house and all the houses they passed on their flight to the fort. Several days were consumed by Monckton's men in making a bridge over the river and cutting a road by which to carry their cannon to an eminence north of the fort. Small parties had been sent from the fort to interrupt them, but without effecting anything. On the 13th their cannon were in place, and the attack began. The next day De Vergor received an answer from Louisbourg, whither he had sent for reënforcements, that no men could be spared, owing to a threatened assault from an English squadron.

De Vergor and his officers tried to conceal this intelligence from the Acadians at the fort, who had been led to believe that certain help was to come from Louisbourg ; but it was rumored about among them, and many of them, on De Vergor's refusal to dismiss them, escaped from the fort in the night. On the 16th the mortars were in position, and the shells made such havoc in the fort that De Vergor resolved to surrender. The terms were soon arranged, and Monckton took possession the same evening. The garrison were allowed to leave with their arms, to be sent to Louisbourg, under promise not to bear arms in America for six months. The Acadians who had been forced to take up arms were granted a general amnesty. Many of them had asked De Vergor, when they were summoned to the fort, to threaten them with death unless they complied.

La Loutre, since none of the terms of the capitulation would apply to him, fearing the vengeance of the English, escaped in disguise, and made his way through the wilderness to Quebec. Here the Bishop, who had not approved of his course in Acadia, reproached him with having neglected religion for politics. As he was without a home, friends, position, or influence in the New World, he embarked for France ; but the vessel was captured by an English ship, and the Abbé La Loutre was imprisoned on the Island of Jersey till the close of the war. He came out, to find not only Acadia, but all of Canada and the Ohio basin, irretrievably lost to France.

After Beau Séjour, the smaller forts were quickly reduced. Some vessels sent to the mouth of the St. John's found the French fort deserted and burned. The name of Beau Séjour was changed to Cumberland.

The Government had now determined to carry out the threat of expelling the Acadians from the peninsula. No doubt some justification for this act may be found in the long course of provocations given by them since they had been under English rule. They had steadily refused to take the oath of allegiance to England, and had claimed the position of neutrals. Had they maintained this position, it is quite probable that the authorities would have allowed them to keep it undisturbed ; but they had repeatedly abandoned it in favor of the French. On every occasion when the French seemed about to regain their supremacy they gave them open aid; and at other times they looked on with indifference, if not with applause, at the barbarities of the Indians against the English. And now, when the two countries were evidently on the eve of war, it was perhaps excusable in the dominant power that it should take measures to rid itself of an enemy within its own territory. Yet the exile of the Acadians remains one of the saddest incidents of history, and by almost universal consent is branded as a crime. The simple and pastoral character of the people is dwelt upon; and it is probable that the mass of them would have been innocent of hostile actions if they had been deprived of a few of the priests and leaders who were constantly inciting them against the English.

It was decided to distribute the Acadians among the various English colonies, in order that they might not go to strengthen the settlements of Canada. It was necessary to assemble them without letting them know the object for which they were called together, and then detain them until the transports were ready to take them away. They were to be allowed to carry with them their ready money and their household goods; all their other effects were to be declared forfeit to the Crown.

Arrangements were made for collecting the inhabitants at several places in different districts. At Chignecto and Annapolis the design was suspected, and most of the people escaped. Their houses were burned down, and as many of the fugitives as could be collected were put on board the transports. Winslow, who had charge of the business at Grand Pré in the district of Minas, was most successful. A proclamation was issued ordering all, "both old men and young men, as well as all the lads of ten years of age, to attend at the church of Grand Pré, on Friday, the 5th instant, at three of the clock in the afternoon, that we may impart to them what we are ordered to communicate to them." No excuse would be accepted for failure to attend ; but goods and chattels would be forfeited by disobedience, in default of real estate.

At three o'clock on Friday, the 5th of September, four hundred and eighteen men assembled in the church at Grand Pré, unsuspicious of the object for which they were summoned. The doors were closed and guarded, and the men were then addressed by Winslow, who told them :

" You are called together to hear his Majesty's final resolution in regard to you. For almost half a century you have had more indulgence granted to you than any of his subjects in any other part of his dominions, though what use you have made of the indulgence you yourselves best know. The duty which is laid on me, though necessary, is very disagreeable to my natural make and temper, as I know it must be grievous to you. His Majesty's orders and instructions are, that your lands and tenements, cattle of all kinds, and live stock of all sorts, are forfeited to the Crown, with all your other effects, saving your money and household goods ; and you yourselves are to be removed from the province. I am, through his Majesty's goodness, directed to allow you to carry away your money and household goods, so far as you can without discommoding the vessels you are to go in." He promised that families should be kept together, and that he would make the removal as easy for them as possible.

The blow was sudden and terrible ; they could not believe at first that it was anything but a threat. When they became convinced that it was really intended to tear them from their homes and scatter them among strange people, and that the guard made escape impossible, they begged to be allowed at least to go out and prepare for removal, offering to leave a number as hostages. Winslow thought it would not be safe to permit them to go out in a body ; but he allowed ten to go at a time. Afterward, seeing some movements he thought suspicious among them, he was obliged to refuse even that privilege.   It was decided to remove the men to the vessels in the harbor, and keep the women and children on shore until the transports should arrive to carry them away.   The men were so reluctant to obey the order to march to the ships that the soldiers had to drive them with their bayonets.   The women and children crowded along the way, kneeling and praying, while the men marched past them singing hymns.   Those left behind were kept near the shore, with insufficient food and clothing, for more than a month.   Twenty-four young men escaped from the ships ; but all but two of them returned, rather than stay behind and be separated from their families.

On the 10th of October the transports arrived ; and care was taken to bring families together ; but in the confusion they were separated in many cases. The number of those thus exiled has sometimes been placed at seven thousand.   This is the estimate of the number that would have to be removed which was given by Colonel Lawrence when the scheme was first proposed, and probably includes nearly the whole population of the peninsula. More than three thousand escaped to the country about the Bay of Chaleurs, some went to Quebec, and some took refuge with the Indians; so that the whole number of those removed by the English did not exceed three thousand.

The houses and barns left by the exiles were burned to the ground. The cattle and horses were seized as spoils by the officers. The dikes which the people had raised against the ocean, enclosing some of the most fertile lands in the whole region, were left to go to ruin, and the ocean broke over the deserted fields. The exiles were scattered through the British colonies, some as far south as Georgia. They became a charge upon the public, and even the support of paupers was grudgingly allotted them. A bill is on record which was sent in for the support of "three French pagans," and they were sent from town to town on one and another pretext, while their children were taken from them at the option of the town authorities. They clung with unfailing constancy to their own religion; and this, by keeping them a separate people among their captors, no doubt contributed much to the feeling against them. Yet instances are on record where their complaints were listened to and redress granted by the authorities, and where private generosity took pity on their sorrows.

Some of those who were sent to Georgia escaped

to the ocean in boats and went coasting along the shore, in hopes to reach their native country ; but they were stopped and detained on the coast of New England by orders from the authorities in Nova Scotia.   One small colony went to Guiana. Some found their way to France ; and two villages near Bordeaux are said to be inhabited by their descendants.   Some planted settlements in Louisiana in the districts of Attakapas and Opelousas, where they and their descendants went for a long time under the name of " Cajeans."

Longfellow's poem " Evangeline" is founded on the removal of the inhabitants of Grand Pré.

CHAPTER XI.

THE OHIO VALLEY.

French Posts in the West—Ogdensburg—Sir William Johnson—Conference with the Iroquois—Expedition of Bienville—The Walking Purchase—The Ohio Company—Christopher Gist—Indian Conference at Logstown—French Attack on Picqua—Expedition from Canada—Mission of George Washington—Fort Du Quesne—Fight with Jumonville—Fort Necessity—Fight at Great Meadows—Fort Cumberland—Council at Albany.

THE establishment of French forts and trading-posts at various points in the West has already been spoken of. Fort Frontenac at the head of the St. Lawrence, Fort Frederick at Crown Point on Lake Champlain, Fort Niagara at the mouth of the Niagara, and the posts at Erie, Sandusky, Detroit, Mackinaw, Chicago, and on the Maumee, the Wabash, and the Mississippi, formed a line of French stations, and supplied communication between the East and the Southwest. Missions and trading-houses were scattered through the regions of the lakes and the great rivers, at points favorable for trade and navigation ; and one French adventurer, as early as 1731, had carried a line of trading-posts one hundred leagues beyond Lake Winnipeg, and built Fort de la Reine on the Assiniboin. After the treaty of Aix-la-Chapelle the attention of both governments was drawn to the necessity of vigorous measures west of the Alleghanies.

In 1749, the mission of La Presentation was established at Oswegatchie, on the present site of Ogdensburg, by a French priest, Father Francis Picquet. He hoped by means of it to effect what the French had labored so long to accomplish by diplomacy and flattery, by the missions to the Mohawks and Onondagas, to break up the friendship of the Iroquois for the English, and win them over to the French interest. Father Picquet was with an expedition that destroyed Fort Edward during King George's War, an enterprise which he had been the first to suggest. In 1748 he proposed to the Governor of Canada to found a settlement at Oswegatchie, a point which he thought most advantageously situated for intercepting the progress of the English and for influencing the Six Nations. He was directed to incite them to the destruction of Oswego, and thus secure to the French the uninterrupted control of the great highway along the lakes and their connecting waters.

After much opposition, he established himself at Oswegatchie with soldiers and workmen, built a saw-mill, and soon had a palisaded fort and several other buildings, and some lands cleared on which to settle a colony of Indians. During the peace, the settlement grew rapidly ; in a few years there were three Indian villages gathered about the fort. At the visit of the Bishop of Quebec during the first year of the mission one hundred and thirty-two Indians were baptized. Picquet established a council from among the converts, and went with the most influential of them on a visit to Montreal, where they took the oath of allegiance to the King of France. He made a canoe voyage around Lake Ontario and up its tributaries, examined the forts, spoke to gatherings of savages, and noted the defects of the French management of the Indian trade. His success with the Iroquois was so great that the savages of that region were nearly lost to England, and perhaps would have been entirely so, had it not been for the influence of William Johnson.

This man came from Ireland and settled in the Mohawk Valley about 1738, taking charge of a large tract of land which had been granted to his uncle, Sir Peter Warren. He learned the language of the Mohawks, and became such a favorite with them that he was adopted into the tribe and chosen a sachem. They called him Warraghiyagey. He built two fortified houses, Johnson Hall and Johnson Castle. The Hall is still standing in the village of Johnstown. The Castle, farther up the river, was built of stone, with a parapet and four bastions.

The Indians were always made welcome, and were treated by Johnson with great tact, as well as confidence and liberality ; sometimes, it is said, hundreds of them would lie down about him with their blankets after a feast, and go to sleep. A story is told which illustrates his sagacity. They had great respect for dreams ; when they saw anything at Johnson's place which they particularly coveted, they were accustomed to tell him that they dreamed he gave it to them. Johnson humored them until that kind of begging grew very troublesome, and then cunningly turned their faith in dreams to his own account.

" I dreamed too," he said to a chief who had just taken possession of some coveted article.

" What did you dream ? "

Johnson told him he dreamed the tribe gave him a large tract of their hunting-ground.

The chief and his warriors were confounded. "You must have it," they said, " if you dreamed it ; but don't dream any more."

The Governor of New York made Johnson Colonel of the Six Nations, and in 1746 he was appointed Commissary of New York for Indian affairs, and in 1748 the command of all the soldiers of New

York was given to him for the defence of the frontier.

Commissioners from the several English colonies met the chiefs of the Iroquois in a conference at Albany. They agreed that they would allow no Frenchmen to settle on their lands, and that the English should negotiate with the French for the restoration of Iroquois prisoners ; and promised to use their influence to bring into the " covenant chain " the tribes dwelling west of the Alleghanies. Those about Lake Erie and the Upper Ohio had been friendly to the English during the last war.

The Governor of Canada, Count de la Galissonière, appointed in 1747, urged on the French ministry the policy of sending out competent engineers to build forts from Detroit to the Mississippi, and to colonize the country west of the Alleghanies with large bodies of French peasantry. No movement was made toward carrying out this policy ; and all that Galissonière could do was to send out men in 1749 to take formal possession of the territory west of the Alleghanies, a movement which more effectually wakened the British colonies to the danger, without securing anything to the French which they had not held before. Celoron de Bienville was put in charge of three hundred men for the purpose, and was directed to take with him representatives of the

western tribes friendly to the French, that they
might seem to give their consent to the French
claims, and also be influenced to drive English traders out of the country.

Bienville carried with him leaden plates which he
was to bury at every important point along the Ohio
and the lake shore, as far as Detroit.   These plates
were engraved with the arms of France and a Latin
inscription.   Following is a translation of the legend
on one which fell into the hands of a Mohawk chief
and was brought to Colonel Johnson's house by him
for explanation :

" In the year 1749, during the reign of Louis XV., King of France,
we, Celoron, commander of a detachment sent by Monsieur the Marquis de la Galissonière, commander-in-chief of New France, for the
restoration of tranquillity in some villages of Indians of these districts, have buried this plate at the confluence of the Ohio and Tchad-
akoin, the 29th of July, near the river Ohio, otherwise Beautiful River,
as a monument of the renewal of possession which we have taken of.
the said River Ohio, and of all those that therein fall, and of all the
land on both sides, as far as the sources of said rivers, as enjoyed, or
ought to be enjoyed, by the preceding kings of France, and as they
therein have maintained themselves by arms and by treaties, especially
by those of Ryswick, of Utrecht. and of Aix-la-Chapelle."

While the French were thus burying leaden
plates, and decorating forest trees with the lilies of
France, and sending armed men into the Ohio Valley to expel English traders from the disputed

lands, the English colonies were anxiously consider-ing the feasibility of forming settlements west of the Alleghanies. And while the colonists of the two nations were jealously watching each other, the Ind-ians were jealously watching them all. The burial of the leaden plates roused their indignation against the French, who, they were sure, were trying to steal their country away from them. And they watched with equal distrust the steady progress of the settlements of Pennsylvania and Virginia.

The western slopes of the Alleghany Mountains were occupied by the Delawares and Shawnees, both of which nations had been conquered by the Iro-quois and were subject to those fierce warriors, who exacted from them a tribute and would not allow them to bear arms. The Delawares, who had origi-nally lived on the banks of the river which bears their name, sold parts of their land to William Penn, whose treatment of them was always humane and friendly ; and they remained on the lands they still retained in amicable relations with the settlers. But as the colony grew, and more lands were needed, the Delawares were crowded back. Old title-deeds were brought forward by the proprietaries, and new interpretations put upon them, making them cover great tracts of land never intended by the savages who gave them.

One of these was called " the walking purchase."
An old deed executed in the seventeenth century
was brought forward in the eighteenth, and lands
were claimed by right of it which the bewildered
Delawares supposed they had reserved for themselves.   The land conveyed was to be a triangle
bounded on one side by the Delaware River, on
another side by one of its branches to the distance
from its mouth that a man could walk in a day and
a half, and on the third by a straight line drawn
from the point reached by the walker back to the
Delaware.   Bringing forward this deed, the proprietaries had a path cut along the margin of the creek,
that there might be no obstructions or rough places
in the way ; then they trained a man according to
the most approved methods for pedestrians, and
when he had walked his day and a half after his
training, they drew the line, not directly eastward
to the nearest point on the Delaware, but in a long
slope to the northeast, forming the broadest possible angle where it met the creek, and the narrowest
possible where it met the river.

The Delawares refused to obey the notice to quit,
as they had no knowledge of any title to the lands
but their own, acquired by ages of possession.   The
Pennsylvanians sent for the Iroquois to enforce their
demand.   The Iroquois despatched some chiefs to

settle the affair, who took the side of the English, browbeat the poor Delawares most unmercifully, and ordered them to go either to Shamokin or Wyoming. The Delawares, afraid to disobey their conquerors, moved to Shamokin and Wyoming on the Susquehanna, and as the encroachments of settlers continued, many of them with the Shawnees passed on still farther west, until now they were living about the headwaters of the Ohio. Remembering with regret their home on the Delaware, and with anger their wrongful dispossession, they were predisposed to join the French against their former friends.

In 1748, the Ohio Company was formed, for the purpose of planting settlements in the Ohio valley. It was composed of gentlemen of the provinces of Virginia and Maryland, and some in England. Among the stockholders were Lawrence and Augustine Washington, half-brothers of George. The King granted the company five hundred thousand acres of land west of the Alleghanies, south of the upper Ohio. It was designed to open a route from the settlements on the company's tract to the Atlantic coast, by connecting the headwaters of the Monongahela and the Youghiogheny with those of the Potomac, by short roads.

The Company sent out Christopher Gist to examine the country as far west as the Falls of the Ohio, to look out favorable sites for settlements and mark the passes of the mountains, the courses of the rivers, and the strength and disposition of the Indians. Gist found most of them disposed to be friendly to the English, but unwilling to commit themselves to an alliance until they could meet in a general council of all their nations. He and his men pushed on to the west, and were the first explorers of Southern Ohio. At Picqua, the chief city of the Miamis, they were invited to a council and promised the friendship of the nation. Some Ottawas came before the council broke up, with offers of amity from the French, but were sent away with the answer that the Miamis looked upon the English as their brothers and regarded as done to themselves all the hostile acts committed by the French against those brothers. Several English traders had been seized by order of the Governor of Canada and sent to the French fort at Otsanderket, or Sandusky.

Having gone as far as Louisville, Gist returned by a more southerly route, ascending the Kentucky. He had been instructed to invite the Indians to a conference at Logstown, about seventeen miles down the Ohio from the site of Pittsburg. In 1752 they came, and a treaty was made, the Indians

agreeing not to molest settlements on the lands
granted to the Ohio Company, but carefully avoiding any acknowledgment of the title of the English
to the territory.   The company built a station and
made some roads, and a few settlers, among whom
was Gist, went into the country and founded a
colony between the Monongahela and the Youghiogheny, beyond Laurel Point.

In the summer of 1752, two Frenchmen led a
party of over two hundred Indians against the Miamis, to force them to give up the six English traders
among them and renounce the English alliance.
Most of the warriors were away on a hunting-expe-
dition ; but the King refused to give up the traders.
and in the assault that followed they were bravely
defended by the few who had remained at home.
The Miamis were defeated, however, their captured
King was killed and eaten, and the French flag was
raised over the deserted fort.

Most of the Indians of the West were ready to
take up arms with the French ; and the Miamis
urged the English to carry out the plan of building
a fort on the Ohio.   But the colonies could not or
would not bear the expense ; and England did
nothing, except to declare that the valley of the
Ohio was a part of Virginia, and the encroachments
of the French were to be regarded as acts of hostil-

ity. A few guns sent over from the ordnance stores were all the substantial aid received. It was intimated that the militia of Virginia ought to be able to maintain her rights.

The government of Canada was now under the Marquis Du Quesne, who determined to drive the English back from the Ohio, and for that purpose prepared a strong party of troops to establish posts on that river. Accompanied by a large force of Indians they ascended the St. Lawrence in the spring of 1753, and crossed the lakes to Presqu' Isle, on the site of Erie. A hunting-party of Iroquois on the banks of the St. Lawrence hastened to send the news to the grand council at Onondaga. Messengers were sent out to warn the Miamis and the other friends of the Iroquois in Ohio, and runners carried the intelligence to Colonel William Johnson on the Mohawk in forty-eight hours. The Ohio tribes sent envoys to Niagara and Presqu' Isle, warning the French not to invade their country ; but the French commander threw back the wampum belts before the faces of the envoys, and told them the land was his and he meant to have it. He established and fortified posts at Waterford, south of Erie, and at Venango, now Franklin, at the junction of French Creek with the Alleghany.

When the news of these proceedings reached

Virginia, Robert Dinwiddie, the Lieutenant-Governor, determined to send a messenger to ask the French why they were invading the British dominions "while a solid peace subsisted," and for his envoy he selected George Washington, then twenty-one years of age and Adjutant-General of the State militia. As a surveyor he had grown familiar with forest life and learned something of the ways of the Indians. He started on his mission late in October, with an interpreter, Christopher Gist as guide, and four other attendants. Passing the junction of the Alleghany and Monongahela, where he noted the military importance of the place, he pushed on to Logstown, and met some Delaware and Miami chiefs in council, who agreed to ally themselves with the English, if the French should still persist in their efforts to occupy the land.

A part of the chiefs went on with Washington to Venango. The boasts of the officers there intimidated some of the Delawares, but the Half-King, chief of the Miamis, gave up the belt that symbolized his peace with the French. Washington was directed to proceed to Fort Le Bœuf, at Waterford, where he would find the commanding officer. Toiling slowly up the river through the snow and mud, crossing swollen streams by bridges which they made themselves of felled trees, the messengers arrived at the newly-built fort, surrounded by the bark-roofed log cabins that served as barracks for the soldiers, who were busily employed in making bark canoes and pine boats for the descent of the river.

Legardeur de St. Pierre, the commander, received Washington with courtesy, but told him it was his business to take possession of the country, according to the orders of his superior, and that he purposed to do it to the best of his ability, and should seize every Englishman he found in the Ohio valley. As to the question of the rights of the two nations, it was not his place to discuss that ; but he would forward the message of the Governor of Virginia to the Governor of Canada.

Having made the most of his opportunities for noting the numbers of the French and the strength and plans of their fortifications, Washington set out with his men to return. The difficulties of the way were increased by the advancing winter. When they came to the place where the horses were left, they found them so weak that they continued their way on foot. Washington was so anxious to get back that he and Gist left the circuitous route by way of the streams, and with a compass to guide them took a straight course for the fork of the rivers. Washington was twice in danger of his life. He was fired upon by a hidden Indian from

a distance of not over fifteen steps and narrowly
missed.   The Indian was taken, and Gist would
have killed him, but Washington forbade it, and released him.   Again, after they had spent a day in
making a raft, the raft was caught in the floating ice.
Washington thrust out the setting-pole to stop it,
and was thrown into the water, but saved himself
by grasping one of the logs that formed the raft.

The answer of St. Pierre led to prompt action by
the Virginia authorities.   It was determined to build
a fort at the head of the Ohio, and ten thousand
pounds were voted for the purpose by the Assembly.   Other provinces were called upon for aid, but
most of the burden fell upon Virginia.   A company
of thirty-three workmen, sent out in haste to begin
the fort and hold the place before the French should
arrive, had scarcely begun, when they were surprised
by an army of six hundred French and Indians under Contrecœur, and summoned to surrender.   Of
course there was no alternative ; they gave up the
place and were allowed to retire.   The date of the
surrender, April 17th, 1754, is usually taken as the
beginning of the " Old French War."

Meanwhile a regiment of militia was hastily col-
lected at Alexandria, and sent out under Colonel
Joshua Fry, with Washington second in command.
Washington went in advance with a part of the

force early in April, and had reached Wills' Creek, near Cumberland, when he was met by the returning party from the head of the Ohio. He sent messengers to the Governors of Maryland, Virginia, and Pennsylvania, asking for reënforcements, and then went on without waiting for Colonel Fry with the remainder of the troops, intending to intrench himself on the Monongahela at the mouth of Red Stone Creek and there await the reënforcements. He would then have been thirty-seven miles from the head of the Ohio.

The French commander, Contrecœur, set his men at work to finish the fortifications the English had begun, and named the place Fort Du Quesne, in honor of the Governor-General of Canada. More men soon arrived, and St. Pierre sent out a scouting party under Jumonville to meet the advance of the English. Hearing by messengers from the Half-King that this party was lurking in the woods, Washington stopped at a place called the Great Meadows. During the night he advanced, surprised the Jumonville party, and completely defeated them, after an action of fifteen minutes. Ten of the French, including Jumonville, were killed, and twenty-one, more than half of them, taken prisoners. This action, which took place April 23d, 1754, was the first fighting of the war in the Ohio valley.

Washington had thrown up a hasty intrenchment at Great Meadows, in a little hollow between two hills covered with trees, and after the fight with Jumonville he strengthened the fortifications, and named the place Fort Necessity.   While waiting for reënforcements, he employed his men in clearing a road toward Fort Du Quesne ; but hearing that a large body of the French were on the way to meet him, he fell back to his fort, where he was attacked on the 3d of July.   The attacking party, consisting of six hundred French soldiers and a hundred Indians, was commanded by Villiers, who was resolved to avenge the death of his brother, Jumonville.   They took possession of one of the hills, and, sheltering themselves behind the trees, fired upon the English works below.   Washington had but four hundred men, and a greatly inferior position ; but he and his men made a stubborn resistance, fighting bravely for nine hours.   Then the French sounded a parley and offered terms.   The fort was surrendered, and the next day Washington's men, with their arms. and baggage, retired to the east of the Alleghanies, according to the terms of the capitulation.   The Americans lost thirty men in the action, and the French three.   By this defeat the English flag was banished from the Ohio valley. Washington began works on Wills' Creek, which were afterward completed and named Fort Cumberland.

These hostilities led to remonstrances and protests between the French and English governments. Each declared a desire for peace and reconciliation, but war seemed inevitable, and both prepared for it. The English Government sent directions to the colonies to allow no encroachments by the French ; and the Governor of New York was directed to call a council of Iroquois chiefs and bind them to the English interests by conciliation and presents.

A congress, therefore, assembled at Albany on June 19th, 1754, commissioners coming from all the colonies as far south as Maryland. Deputies from the Six Nations were also present. Gifts were scattered among them in great profusion, and they renewed their compact with the English ; but still there was widespread disaffection among them toward their old allies. The French establishment at Oswegatchie had drawn off half the Onondagas, and the Mohawks were indignant at what they considered trespass on their lands by English surveyors. The chiefs boldly reproached the English with their inaction and the slow progress of their preparations. " Look at the French," said a Mohawk chief ; " they are men ; they are fortifying everywhere ; it is but one step from Canada hither, and they may easily come and turn you out of doors." The Iroquois claimed the lands occupied by the Delawares and Shawnoes, by right of their conquest of those nations. The Delawares and Shawnoes were still wavering, and might perhaps have been saved to the English, but the Pennsylvania agents took advantage of the assembling of Iroquois at the congress, and induced them to convey to themselves large tracts of land occupied by the conquered tribes. Those Indians heard of the transfer with great indignation, and were easily won over to the French.

The council at Albany was memorable from the fact that it projected a confederacy of the American colonies. Benjamin Franklin, a delegate from Pennsylvania, had made notes for a plan of union while on his journey to Albany, and when he arrived there he found that some of the other commissioners had also thought out plans for the same purpose. Franklin's plan was substantially adopted, after much deliberation. Philadelphia was to be the seat of government. The President, or Governor-General, was to be appointed by the King, and was to have a veto power on all measures of the Grand Council. The Council was to be elected once in three years by the legislatures of the colonies, and to meet every year. The number of delegates from each colony was to vary from two to seven. General

matters of war, trade, and taxes were to be under
the control of the Council.   The plan was favored
neither by the colonies, who thought it gave too
much power to the President appointed by the
Crown, nor by the Board of Trade in England, who
rejected it on account of the power it gave to the
people of the colonies ; but it foreshadowed the
union of the Americans, which resulted in their
independence less than thirty years later

CHAPTER XII.

BRADDOCK'S DEFEAT.

Plan of the English Ministry for Operations in America—Capture of Ships by Boscawen — Braddock's March — His Defeat — His Death — Effect of the Defeat — Washington — Alliances with the Indians.

THE English ministry now resolved upon a plan for attacking the French by four expeditions at about the same time, hoping to defeat them at every point where they had encroached on English claims, and drive them finally and forever from the disputed territory. The four expeditions were to move against the French in Acadia, at Fort Niagara, at Fort Du Quesne, and at Crown Point. The result of the operations in Acadia has already been detailed. The expedition assigned to the attack of Fort Niagara never reached its destination. That against Fort Du Quesne was most actively carried out, and most influential in its results.

While these preparations were going on, England and France were nominally at peace. Both were sending troops to America, but both professed to be taking measures for defence only. In January,

1755, negotiations passed between the two countries
on the subject of the boundaries.   France proposed
that the Ohio valley be left as it was before the last
war ; England proposed that it be left as it was at
the Treaty of Utrecht in 1713.   Then France proposed that the territory between the Ohio and the
Alleghanies be left neutral, by which she would
then have had all north of the Ohio and far on to
the west, while the neutral country would have kept
back the English settlers.   England then demanded
that twenty leagues on each side of the Bay of
Fundy should be added to the territory conceded
by the French as belonging to Nova Scotia, and the
country northward to the St. Lawrence be left
neutral ; that the French forts at Crown Point and
Niagara, and all those between the Alleghanies and
the Wabash, should be destroyed.   Of course, the
French would make no such concessions ; but some
show of negotiations was still kept up, while the
warlike movements went on.

Six thousand men had been sent out from England for service in America.   They were under
General Edward Braddock, who was made commander-in-chief of all the forces in North America,
Governor Shirley and Sir William Pepperell to be
associated with him as next in command.   Braddock
had been in service on the Continent, and his mili-

tary record was good. About three months after he sailed, a force of three thousand men was despatched from France to Canada, under Baron Dieskau.

Admiral Boscawen was sent to the Banks of Newfoundland to intercept the French squadron. Three of the French ships, the *Lys*, the *Alcide*, and the *Dauphin*, were separated from the rest and enveloped in the fogs of the Newfoundland coast, and when the fogs cleared away, on the morning of the 8th of June, they found the English fleet close upon them. " Are we at peace or war?" asked the commander of the *Alcide*. In reply Boscawen commanded his men to fire, and after a short engagement the *Lys* and the *Alcide* struck their colors. The *Dauphin* escaped to the harbor of Louisbourg. This affair naturally excited great indignation in France, and the French ambassador at the English court was withdrawn. In England it was not disapproved of, although it had been steadily asserted that only defensive measures for the protection of the English frontiers were to be taken.

Braddock arrived at Hampton Roads in February, 1755. In April he called a conference of the governors of the provinces to meet him for the purpose of raising a common fund for carrying on the war; but they were unable to pledge the support de-

manded of them.   Virginia, whose frontiers were in
the greatest danger, was most zealous in rendering
assistance, and later Franklin used his influence in
Pennsylvania to supply the pressing want of horses
and wagons.   Colonel William Johnson, at the suggestion of Braddock, was asked to treat with the
Six Nations and take charge of the expedition
against Crown Point.   The governors agreed to raise
eight hundred pounds for presents to the Iroquois,
and Johnson consented to negotiate the treaty,
though reluctantly, on account of the carelessness
the English had previously shown in regard to the
observance of their agreements with the Indians.

Braddock was full of confidence as to the result
of his enterprise.   He had great faith in himself, in
" the King's regular troops," and in the tactics of
war as he had learned them, great contempt for the
provincials who were to serve in his army, and not
the slightest suspicion that men who had spent their
lives among the Indians could tell him anything of
value about savage methods of warfare. He sent despatches to the English ministry, promising speedy
success.   To Franklin he said, " I shall hardly
need to stop more than three or four days at Fort
Du Quesne ; then I shall march on to Niagara, and
from there to Frontenac."

" To be sure, sir," answered Franklin, " if you

arrive well before Du Quesne with those fine troops, so well provided with artillery, that place, not completely fortified, and, as we hear, with no very strong garrison, can probably make but a short resistance.   The only danger I apprehend of obstruction to your march is from ambuscades of Indians, who, by constant practice, are dexterous in laying and executing them ; and the slender line, near four miles long, which your army must make, may expose it to be attacked by surprise in its flanks, and to be cut like a thread into several pieces, which, from their distance, cannot come up in time to support each other."

Franklin says Braddock smiled at his ignorance, and answered, " These savages may, indeed, be a formidable enemy to your raw American militia ; but upon the King's regular and disciplined troops, sir, it is impossible they should make any impression."   He paid no attention to Washington's advice that he should secure the aid of one hundred Indians under the interpreter Croghan, and treated them so scornfully that they withdrew in anger.

The troops were all gathered at Fort Cumberland, on Wills' Creek.   Braddock spent some weeks there in preparations, disciplining the provincial troops to make them as much like regulars as possible, and disgusted with his slender success.   " The American troops," he wrote in one of his letters, " have little courage or goodwill.   I expect almost no military service from them, though I have employed the best officers to drill them."

The wagons and horses procured by Franklin at last arrived, and on the 7th of June the army was ready to march.   There were one thousand of Braddock's regular soldiers, twelve hundred of the provincial militia, a few sailors, and a few Indians. Washington was made an aide-de-camp.   Two companies from New York were under the command of Horatio Gates, afterward famous as the American commander at Saratoga ; one of the wagons was owned and driven by Daniel Morgan, destined to render important service in South Carolina during the Revolutionary War ; and there was Hugh Mercer, who was to fall at Princeton.   Side by side with these future leaders of the American rebels was Lieutenant-Colonel Thomas Gage, the future commander of the King's forces in their struggle with his rebellious subjects.

Many of the French troops had been sent away from Fort Du Quesne ; but on the news of the English expedition reënforcements were summoned, and the slowness of Braddock's march gave them ample time to reach the fort.   The route through Pennsylvania would have been much shorter than

that through Virginia. But the former expedition
of Washington had taken the route by way of Wills'
Creek, and the shorter route seems scarcely to have
been considered. Five hundred men had been sent
forward the last day of May to open the road, and
carry stores to Little Meadows. The rest of the
army moved slowly, making only five miles in three
days.

Washington looked on with impatience, while
Braddock insisted on moving exactly in accordance
with the methods practised in European warfare.
" We halted," he says, " to level every mole-hill
and bridge every brook, by which means we were
four days in getting twelve miles." Even after the
road had been widened by the advancing axe-men,
it was almost impossible for the horses to drag the
heavy wagons loaded with useless baggage through
the miry ravines and over the rocks and stumps of
trees, and they grew weak with the fatigue and the
insufficient food afforded by the wild grass. After
crossing the Great Savage Mountain, and toiling
painfully through the thick gloom of the Shades of
Death, the army reached Little Meadows, where
some attempt at fortification had been made by the
five hundred axe-men.

Here a council of war was held, and Washington's
suggestion was adopted, that twelve hundred men

should be selected to push on in advance with the
artillery and the lighter baggage.   Braddock went
on with the twelve hundred, leaving the remainder,
with the heavy wagons, in charge of Colonel Dunbar.
Even then the progress of the advance party was
very slow, and it was not until the 8th of July that
they arrived at the fork of the Monongahela and
Youghiogeny rivers, twelve miles from Fort Du
Quesne, where they encamped on a stream known
as Crooked Run.   Braddock had at first refused to
send forward any Indians as scouts ; now it was with
great difficulty that he could induce any of the few
remaining with him to undertake the perilous task.
Their march was haunted by the skulking allies of
the French, who picked off stragglers and faithfully reported every movement of the British army
at Fort Du Quesne.

Braddock's men were now on the same side of the
Monongahela as the fort—that is, on the eastern
side ; but a high rocky ridge very near the river on
that side left such a narrow defile beside the stream,
that the General thought best to cross at a ford
near his camp, and, reaching a point above the narrow defile, to recross at a second ford at the mouth
of Turtle Creek, eight miles below the fort.   Early
on the morning of the 9th of July, the army crossed
the upper ford, and marched splendidly down the

river in their scarlet uniform, with drums beating and colors flying, the finest spectacle, Washington said long years afterward, that he had ever witnessed.

At noon they recrossed the river, and entered a woody and hilly country cut through by three deep ravines, with seven miles yet to march. Gage led on a detachment through the narrow path, attended by the engineers with the workmen.

Indian scouts had carried swift intelligence of the English advance to Fort Du Quesne, and Contrecœur, thinking it would be impossible to hold out against such an army, talked of retreat. But one of his captains, Beaujeu, advised sending out a party of soldiers and Indians to form an ambuscade. Contrecœur consented, and the Indians were called together from their bark huts around the fort.

Not one was willing to follow Beaujeu in the dangerous undertaking, and he gave it up for the time. Another invitation met with an answer no more favorable ; but the third time, when he said, " I am determined to go ; and will you let your father go alone?" a sudden enthusiasm seized them, and they were ready to follow.

On the morning of the 9th, Beaujeu, Dumas, and Lignery led out more than eight hundred men, of whom six hundred were Indians. Among the Indians was the chief Pontiac, afterward well known in American history. The English army was moving on without a single scout to give warning of the danger, when it was suddenly confronted by the fantastic figure of Beaujeu in a fringed hunting-dress and wearing on his neck a silver gorget, closely followed down the hill by a multitude of white men and savages. Beaujeu gave the word of command, and the Indians dropped into the ravines and joined the French on the hill in a murderous fire on the British regulars, who, though bewildered by the hideous yells and shrieks that arose from the ravines, returned the fire, and Beaujeu was one of the first to fall dead. His loss dismayed the Indians, and they began to fly, but were rallied by Dumas, who sent them to attack the flanks of the English army, while the French soldiers kept up the fire in front. Hiding behind the trees, the Indians picked off the Englishmen with unerring aim. A reënforcement was sent on by Braddock ; but the advance party was driven back, leaving two of their pieces to the enemy, and meeting the reënforcements which were attempting to form, they became mingled and confused with them, and the entire force was thrown into disorder and unable to effect anything.

Braddock pushed bravely forward, and rode hither

and thither, issuing commands, and trying to inspire his troops with his own courage. Four horses
were shot under him, but again he mounted and
again renewed his efforts. His officers were not
outdone in bravery. Washington had two horses
shot under him and his clothing torn by bullets ;
Gates was shot through the body ; and only twenty three of the eighty-six officers escaped unhurt.
Twenty-six were killed and thirty-seven wounded.
But the English troops were panic-stricken ; they
would not follow their officers ; they loaded their
muskets and fired upon their own comrades, or into
the empty air. The provincials, understanding better the methods of the Indians, maintained their
self-control, and, stationing themselves behind trees,
returned the fire in the Indian method from the
cover. Washington urged Braddock to order all
the men to fight in that way; but still the General
could not see that there was any occasion for setting
aside the rules of regular warfare. He drove the
men out from their hiding-places, and insisted that
they should form in platoons. At length he fell,
mortally wounded, but continued to give orders as
he lay bleeding on the ground.

After three hours of such fighting, during which
half the men were killed or wounded, the soldiers, in
an uncontrollable panic, rushed back from the field

and fled in confusion across the river, throwing away their arms. Braddock was carried from the field by some provincials. The enemy did not follow across the river, but returned to the field to secure the plunder. Braddock's orders brought his men to a stand, but they were too frightened to maintain it, and broke once more into a straggling retreat, and on the 11th reached the reserves at the camp. The panic spread to Dunbar's men; all the stores at the camp were destroyed, and the whole army fled helpless through the woods, and past the settlements toward Philadelphia.

Braddock lay in a lethargy, rousing himself at times to give commands, and once murmuring, " Who would have thought it? Who would have thought it?" Shortly before he died, on the night of the 13th, he turned to his lieutenant and said, " We shall better know how to deal with them another time." The soldiers made his grave at Great Meadows, near Fort Necessity, where it still may be seen. The lower ford, where his army crossed to the fatal field, is known as Braddock's Ford.

The news of this defeat carried dismay through the provinces. It left the frontier settlements of Pennsylvania and Virginia open and unprotected from the Indians; and every unusual noise, even the

maudlin howl of a drunken man in the streets, was
thought by the terrified inhabitants to be the deadly
yell that heralded the tomahawk and the scalping-
knife. In August, Washington was appointed Commander-in-Chief of all the forces of the colony.
His conduct during Braddock's expedition had
brought him to the favorable notice of the country,
and attracted attention in England. He had, it is
said, been marked by an Indian chief, who persist-
ently aimed at him, and told some of his warriors
to do the same. Failing to bring him down, they
concluded that some powerful manitou was watching
over his life.

"I point out that heroic youth, Colonel Washington," said a clergyman, Rev. Samuel Davis, in
a sermon, "whom I cannot but hope Providence
has preserved in so signal a manner for some important service to his country." And Lord Halifax said, "Who is Mr. Washington? I know nothing of him but that they say he behaved in Braddock's action as if he really loved the whistling of
bullets."

One of the most disastrous results of the defeat
was its effect upon the Indians. It inspired them
with contempt for the English soldiers and respect
for the military ability of the French. It decided
the defection of the Delawares and Shawnoes, and

incited them to petty ravages on the border. Scarooyadi, successor to the Half-King, refused to listen to French persuasions, and remained true to the English. He said the defeat was due to the " pride and ignorance of that great general that came from England. He is now dead ; but he was a bad man when he was alive. He looked upon us as dogs, and would never hear anything that was said to him. We often endeavored to advise him, and tell him of the danger he was in with his soldiers ; but he never appeared pleased with us, and that was the reason that a great many of our warriors left him."

Washington was anxious to secure the aid of the Indians ; and Scarooyadi was willing to go out at once. " Let us unite our strength," said he. " You are numerous, and the governors along the seashore can raise men enough ; but don't let those from over the seas be concerned any more. They are unfit to fight in the woods. Let us go out ourselves, we that came out of this ground."

The Cherokees were also faithful to their friendship with the English colonies. Their chief proposed a conference with the Governor of South Carolina, notifying him of the attempts of the French and their allies to win over his nation. The Governor met the principal Cherokee warriors in their own country, two hundred miles from Charleston ; the alliance was renewed, and a large tract of land was ceded by the Cherokees to the colony. Fort Prince George, three hundred miles from Charleston, was built on the ceded lands.

CHAPTER XIII.

BATTLE OF LAKE GEORGE.

Expeditions under Shirley and Johnson—Shirley at Oswego—Movements of Dieskau—Building of Fort Edward—Advance of Dieskau—First Engagement—Fight at the Camp—Fight with Macginnis—Reward of Johnson—Erection of Fort William Henry—Fortification of Ticonderoga—Hostilities on the Ocean—Plans for the Ensuing Year.

THE third expedition designed to establish the supremacy of England in the American territory which she claimed as her own, was to advance under Governor Shirley to attack Fort Niagara ; and the fourth under Johnson to Fort Frederick at Crown Point. These two expeditions were to be composed of troops supplied by the northern colonies, and warriors of the Six Nations. In June nearly six thousand men were gathered at Albany. Among them were Israel Putnam, of Connecticut, who was to have so large a share in the deeds of the Revolutionary War ; John Stark, of New Hampshire, destined to make himself famous at Bennington and Saratoga ; and Ephraim Williams, of Massachusetts, who had just made a will at Albany by which he left a bequest to found the free school that is now Williams College.

After capturing Fort Du Quesne, Braddock was to march northward and meet Shirley at Niagara. The fort there was in poor condition ; and Vaudreuil, Governor of Canada, was anxious for its safety, having heard from Indians of the preparations that were being made by the English. " The preservation of Niagara," he wrote to the French minister, " is what interests us the most ; if our enemies should become masters of it and keep Chouaguen (Oswego), the Upper Countries would be lost to us, and besides we should have no more communication with the River Ohio."

But there was no immediate danger of the English becoming masters of Niagara ; the news of Braddock's defeat was received before the last of Shirley's men had started up the Mohawk. They were to ascend the river in bateaux, and the bateaux were to be managed by forest-rangers who had been gathered for the expedition. The news of the defeat so frightened them that many deserted ; and when the army arrived at the carrying-place, at the head of the Mohawk, the men who were to transport the military stores by sledges also failed them. The soldiers were disheartened, Shirley was slow and irresolute, and they did not reach Oswego till

the 21st of August.   A month was passed in building boats to take them across Lake Ontario ; and
just as they were ready to embark, on the 18th of
September, heavy rains and winds set in, and continued with little intermission for three weeks.
Most of the Indians and some of the soldiers deserted, and sickness disabled many more.   It was
therefore decided that the attempt should be abandoned until the following year, that Colonel Mercer
should be left at Oswego with seven hundred men.
and Governor Shirley should return to Albany with
the rest.

The French had designed to send their army under
Baron Dieskau to take Oswego, expecting thereby to gain uninterrupted communication between
their own forts, Frontenac and Niagara, at either
end of Lake Ontario, and weaken the English influence over the Iroquois ; and General Braddock's
papers, which were captured, revealed the English
plan of the campaign.   Dieskau was about to start
for Oswego with his army when information reached
Montreal that Johnson's army was on its way toward
Crown Point.   Vaudreuil decided that it was of more
importance to send the aid there than to attack
Oswego ; and Dieskau reluctantly consented to the
change of plan.   The French force assembled at
Crown Point consisted of seven hundred regular

troops, sixteen hundred Canadians, and seven hundred Indians, about half of the Indians being converted Iroquois from the mission villages of Canada.

The troops at Albany designed for Johnson's force were sent on early in July, under General Phinehas Lyman, and were occupied in building a fort on the eastern bank of the Hudson at the beginning of the portage to Lake George, which was named Fort Edward. On the 8th of August, Johnson set out from Albany with the artillery, bateaux, and provisions. He passed Fort Edward and encamped on the southern shore of Lake St. Sacrament, which he soon afterward named Lake George, in honor of George II. The camp was surrounded by woods and swamps on all sides except that which faced the lake.

It was Johnson's intention to build a fort at this point, and when his bateaux should arrive, to go up Lake Champlain to Ticonderoga, fortify that place, and then march against Fort Frederick. Ticonderoga is a point projecting into the lake, fifteen miles above Crown Point. But no fort was built, nor defences of any kind. The Indians came in slowly. The old Mohawk chief, Hendrick, told Johnson that Shirley had discouraged the warriors from enlisting under Johnson, between whom and himself there was a feeling of jealousy, and had

tried to induce them to go with him to Oswego.
But in time a large number of them regained their
confidence in Johnson, and joined him in his camp.
While the thirty-four hundred men were wasting
their time in Johnson's camp, Dieskau's men were
making active preparations at Crown Point for the
expected attack.

After waiting some time, Dieskau resolved to advance toward the English army, hoping to conquer
it and leave the way open to Albany and Schenectady ; he could then march on those places and cut
off communication with Oswego, after which the
capture of that place would be easy.   Taking with
him fifteen hundred men, six hundred of whom
were Indians, and two hundred regulars, he went up
the lake in boats, and landed at South Bay, on the
present site of Whitehall.   The army marched for
three days, intending to attack Fort Edward.
Halting on the road to Lake George, which had been
taken by mistake instead of the one leading directly
to Fort Edward, Dieskau sent a party of Indians to
reconnoitre, who returned with the intelligence that
their approach was known both at the fort and at
the camp.   The Indians, with their usual fear of
cannon, were averse to attacking the fort, but were
willing to advance against the camp.   Dieskau assented, and marched toward Lake George.

When it was known in Johnson's camp that the
French were approaching, warning was sent to Fort
Edward. One of the messengers, a wagoner named
Adams, was taken by the Indians and killed; the
other returned with the intelligence that the enemy
were about four miles north of the fort. A council of war was held the next morning, the 7th of
September, and it was decided to send out a
thousand troops and two hundred Indians to meet
the enemy. Hendrick was the only one who saw
the folly of the movement. "If they are to be
killed," he said, "they are too many; if they are to
fight, they are too few." But Hendrick was overruled, and putting himself at the head of his
Mohawks, he rode out to the fray at sunrise the
next morning, the only mounted man of the party,
unable, from his age and weight, to go on foot.
The detachment was headed by Colonel Ephraim
Williams.

As soon as Dieskau learned of their approach
he prepared an ambuscade, arranging his men in a
line which crossed the road and curved toward the
advancing English on both sides of it. The French
troops were therefore disposed in the form of a
horse-shoe, those at one end being hidden by a ridge
covered with trees and bushes, and those at the
other crouching in a swampy spot also concealed

from the road by a thick undergrowth. When the English should have marched forward to where the French line crossed the road, Dieskau's men could close in on both sides and surround them.

As they entered the trap, Hendrick was riding in advance. He had gone some distance within the enclosing lines, but a part of the division was still without, when an Indian suddenly appeared close to him and said, " Whence came you ? " " From the Mohawks," answered Hendrick. " Whence came you ? " " From Montreal," was the reply, and immediately a shot was fired, contrary to the orders of Dieskau, who had directed his men to be quiet until the English were completely within the French line. The shot was the signal for a general assault, and the firing began on both sides and in front of the astonished troops. One moment they had been riding through a silent wilderness ; the next they were surrounded by blazing muskets and whooping savages. Hendrick was one of the first who fell, Williams and many other officers shared his fate, and the command devolved upon Lieutenant Nathan Whiting.

The English gave way and retreated, fighting as they went, many of them spreading themselves out so as to oppose a wide front to the enemy, and darting from tree to tree where they could find shelter

and fire upon their pursuers ; the Canadians and
Indians picking them off in the same way, and the
French regulars advancing in a body and firing upon
those who remained in a mass retreating along the
road.

When the noise of the battle was heard at the
camp, the soldiers there, who had at last begun the
building of some hasty defences after Williams had
gone out with his men in the morning, hurriedly
dragged the cannon up from the lake shore and
heaped up a breastwork of felled trees. A reënforcement of three hundred men, under Lieutenant-
Colonel Cole, was sent out to the help of the retreating division, and a stand was made at a little
sheet of water, which received the name of Bloody
Pond, and is pointed out as the grave of the unfortunate Frenchmen who fell upon its banks. Among
them was the Chevalier Legardeur de St. Pierre, who
was in command of the Indians. He was the officer
to whom Washington delivered his letters from Governor Dinwiddie at Fort Le Bœuf.

When the fugitives reached the camp they climbed
over the breastwork of felled trees and wagons,
and waited for the attack. Dieskau had intended
to rush forward with the retreating division of the
English and enter the camp at the same time. But
the Indians halted as soon as they came in sight of

the guns, and the Canadians followed their example. Dieskau advanced toward the centre of the camp with his regulars, and when the Indians and Canadians scattered themselves about the swamp and took shelter behind the trees instead of sustaining the regulars, he asked in disappointment, "Are these the boasted troops?" The regulars, however, behaved well ; they halted a hundred and fifty yards from the camp, and opened fire by platoons. It was about half-past eleven when the battle began. The three guns in the centre returned the fire of the French, and Johnson's men, sheltered behind the trees, picked off Dieskau's regulars with deadly precision. Johnson was slightly wounded in the beginning of the fight, and the command devolved upon Lyman, who conducted the defence with the greatest spirit and bravery. Unable to stand the fire, the French regulars went to each side of the camp in succession, and fired into it, but without much effect.

Excited and emboldened by their success, and reënforced by the Mohawks, who had fled when the French appeared in sight of the camp, the Americans leaped over their defences and fought hand-to-hand. They had no bayonets, but they struck with their muskets, and clubbed and beat so furiously that nearly all the regulars who had survived their fire were knocked down and killed. Dieskau, wounded three times during the action, would not be carried away, but seated himself on the stump of a tree exposed to the fire, and tried to direct the movements of his men.   When they were driven into a disorderly retreat, he was left on the field.   As they were flying he put his hand into his pocket, intending to take out his watch and give it to one of the pursuers who was about to capture him ; but the man supposed he was drawing his pistol, and hastily fired, inflicting an incurable wound.

Lyman would have followed up the retreat, and a close pursuit might have resulted in the capture of almost the entire army ; for two hundred troops were on the way from Fort Edward under the command of Captain Macginnis, and the French soldiers would have been caught between the two parties. But Johnson gave orders to call back the men ; and when the French found themselves secure from pursuit they halted beside Rocky Brook.   Here the half-starved men were preparing supper when the detachment from the fort fell upon them and put them to flight, after a sharp engagement, in which Macginnis was mortally wounded.   The French baggage and ammunition were captured.

The battle of Lake George, resulting in a **victory**

so complete, revived the spirit of the English colonists from the depressing effects of Braddock's defeat. Although the victory was not followed up by the occupation of Ticonderoga and the capture of Crown Point, the original object of the expedition, the country looked upon it as a great success. Johnson received a baronetcy and five thousand pounds from England, to reward him for the victory, which was largely due to Lyman. Dieskau was sent to England a prisoner, but returned to France at the peace of 1763, and not long afterward died from the effect of his wound.

During the autumn Johnson kept his men at work strengthening their position, and built a stockade fort at the south end of Lake George, which was called Fort William Henry. At the approach of winter he garrisoned that and Fort Edward, and allowed the rest of the provincial soldiers to return to their homes. The French took possession of the important post of Ticonderoga, and busied themselves in fortifying it ; two thousand soldiers were said to be assembled there in the autumn, with a large body of Indians.

But war had not even yet been declared between the two countries whose colonists were thus meeting on battle-fields in the new world, aided by regular troops from over the seas. These hostilities were carried on under the name of measures of defence, by which each side professed to resist the aggressions of the other on territory of which it claimed the rightful ownership.   The French, however, deeply resented the capture of their two ships by Admiral Boscawen, an act which could not be defended on any such ground ; and they soon had still more cause for resentment.   Sir Edward Hawke was sent out with a fleet under orders to take all French ships he met with, whether men-of-war or merchantmen ; and letters of marque were issued to cruisers.   Great numbers of French vessels were on the return from Martinique with the products of the Jesuit plantations, and the fishing-boats were on their way from Newfoundland and the Labrador coast, laden with the results of the summer's work. Before the end of the year three hundred French vessels and seven or eight thousand French sailors had been carried into English ports.   The king's share of the spoils amounted to seven hundred thousand pounds.

This alone was enough to bring on a war.   But the French were not ready ; and they returned an English man-of-war which had been taken by some French ships, protesting against the acts of England on the seas and stigmatizing them as piracy.   Preparations for the inevitable war went on, both nations seeking alliances among the other powers of Europe, appealing to the resentments, the prejudices, and the cupidity of their sovereigns. Prussia joined with England ; Austria, Russia, and Saxony were on the side of France. In the general European struggle which followed, known as the Seven Years' War, the events of the colonial war in America were but lightly considered, though they determined the fortunes of a continent.

Governor Shirley was still continued at the head of affairs, though it began to be evident that his military capacity was by no means brilliant. He called a council of governors in the city of New York in December, 1755, and laid out a plan for the campaign of the ensuing year, substantially the same as that which had been arranged for that year, nothing having been effected but the conquest of Acadia. Forts Du Quesne, Frederick, and Niagara still remained to be taken ; and expeditions for their capture were determined on for the coming summer, while a force was to move up the Kennebec to the settlements on the Chaudière.

CHAPTER XIV.

FRENCH SUCCESSES.

Declaration of War—Lord Loudoun Commander-in-chief—Inaction of Abercrombie—Adventure of Bradstreet—Capture of Fort Bull —Montcalm—Capture of Oswego—Movements of Webb—Loudoun s Troops Quartered on the Cities—Devastation of the Shenandoah Valley—Dinwiddie's Plan of Defence—Washington's Suggestions—Destruction of Kittanning—The Iroquois.

WAR was at length declared by England, May 17th, 1756. Governor Shirley was removed from the command of the forces in America, and a still more incapable officer was appointed to the place, the Earl of Loudoun. Lord Loudoun's chief recommendation for the post was his zeal for the assertion of the rights of the mother-country over her colonies. He was also appointed Governor of the Dominion of Virginia, and his power as military chief was supreme over all the colonial governments. The provincial soldiers were to be put under officers of the regular army whom Loudoun might appoint ; and he was given authority to quarter his soldiers on the inhabitants of the colonies at will. General James Abercrombie was to be second in command. One hundred and fifteen thousand pounds was voted to the northern provinces to re-imburse them for the campaign of 1755 ; at the same time they were forbidden to negotiate with the Indians, all dealings with whom were to be left to Sir William Johnson, who was responsible alone to Lord Loudoun.

Loudoun's slowness and indecision, combined with a great affectation of business habits, are exhibited by a story of Franklin, who went to New York in the beginning of April to sail for Europe in a packet which was to set out immediately, but was kept waiting till the end of June for his lordship's letters, which were always to be ready to-morrow ; " and yet," says Franklin, " whoever waited on him found him always at his desk, pen in hand, and concluded he must needs write abundantly." One morning while he was waiting for the ship's depart-ure Franklin met in the earl's antechamber a mes-senger from Philadelphia named Innis, with a packet of letters from the Governor to the earl. Franklin wished to send back some letters by him to Phila-delphia ; and Innis told him he was to call the next morning at nine for Lord Loudoun's answer to the Governor, and should then set out at once. Frank-lin prepared his letters and gave them to Innis the same day. "A fortnight after," continues Frank-lin, " I met him again in the same place. ' So you are soon returned, Innis ' ' ' Returned ! no, I am not gone yet.' ' How so ?' ' I have called here this and every morning these two weeks past for his lordship's letters, and they are not yet ready.' ' Is it possible, when he is so great a writer ? for I see him constantly at his escritoire.' ' Yes,' said Innis, ' but he is like St. George on the signs—always on horseback, but never rides on.' "

The same characteristic was manifested in all of the earl's proceedings. Abercrombie was to go in advance with two battalions, but it was the middle of June before he reached New York. On the 25th he was in Albany. Oswego was threatened by the French, and he was urged to relieve it at once. Men, stores, and boats were ready, but Abercrombie was not. He was busy with preparations to quarter his soldiers on the town, and when that was done he began to talk of fortifying Albany with a ditch and stockade, and ordered a survey for that purpose.

Colonel Bradstreet, who had been sent to Oswego with provisions and military stores, was surprised on his way back by a body of Canadians and Indians about ten miles from that place. A fight ensued, in which Bradstreet put the enemy to flight, but he had not men enough to venture on a pursuit. One of the prisoners revealed the designs of the French and their movements preparatory to an attack on Oswego, which Bradstreet reported to Abercrombie, who had ten thousand regulars and seven thousand provincials at his command. The roads were opened, and the two forts at Oswego were ready for occupation and well provided with stores of all kinds. Abercrombie ordered a regiment of regulars to prepare to go to Oswego, but before they were ready Lord Loudoun arrived, on the 29th of July. More time was spent in debating the question of the status of the provincial officers and troops, and the regiment did not move until the 12th of August. The French under De Lery and De Villiers had been active during the spring in getting possession of the approaches to Oswego from Albany, and in the conciliation of the Indians of New York. De Lery came from Montreal with two hundred and sixty-five men, and on the 27th of March surprised the garrison of Fort Bull, at the Oneida portage, capturing them after a short resistance; and all but five were massacred, the fort was blown up, and the military stores destroyed. A party of Indians descended upon some ship-carpenters who were working at Oswego, and returned to Niagara in triumph with three prisoners and twelve scalps. These small successes and the martial activity of the French inclined the wavering warriors of the Iroquois toward their alliance;

and the Indians of the upper country about the lakes began to flock to Fort Niagara to form war-parties.

During the summer the French forces were placed under the command of one of the ablest soldiers of his time, Louis Joseph, Marquis de Montcalm de Saint Veron. Small, quick, and active, Montcalm saw at a glance what ought to be done, and wasted no time in talking about it. Remaining only a few days at Quebec, he sent a force of men to Fort Carillon at Ticonderoga, and another, under De Villiers, to the Bay of Niaouré, to a spot now known as Six Town Point, in Jefferson county, to observe the movements of the enemy and keep him in check. Another regiment was sent by Montcalm to Niagara, accompanied by a skilful engineer, Pouchot, to strengthen the fortifications there.

On the 5th of August, Montcalm, taking two regiments of regular troops with him, left Fort Frontenac, and, encamping at the Bay of Niaouré, sent De Villiers and Rigaud de Vaudreuil to take a position not far from Oswego. Montcalm followed, and by the 12th of August the forces were gathered before the forts at Oswego and ready for operations.

Fort Oswego, or Pepperell, called Chouaguen by the French, stood near the site of the " stone house of strength,'' built by Governor Burnet in 1726, and was a large stone fort with four bastions. On an eminence across the river which commanded it Governor Shirley had placed Fort Ontario. The garrison consisted of sixteen hundred men under the command of Colonel Mercer, many of them raw recruits.

On the night of the 12th of August, the day when the regiments started from Albany to relieve the fort, the French opened trenches before Fort Ontario and felled trees for an abatis, finishing the work by daybreak. The batteries opened fire that day, and the garrison returned it with spirit as long as their ammunition lasted ; for, in addition to the other blunders, Fort Ontario had been left with a very slender store. At three o'clock in the afternoon, they spiked their guns and crossed to Fort Oswego in boats sent over by Colonel Mercer.

The French took immediate possession of the deserted works, and the guns of Fort Oswego were turned upon them. Mercer had sent a party under Colonel Schuyler to a hill four and a half miles up the river, where they were intrenched, and designed to harass the French. But Montcalm despatched Vaudreuil with a party of Canadians and Indians to cut off communication between the fort and the hill, while his men kept up a continuous fire on Fort

Oswego with their batteries and such guns of Fort Ontario as they could use. Mercer was killed by a cannon-ball on the 13th, and on the 14th the garrison resolved to surrender, Montcalm promising that they should receive " all the regard which the most courteous of nations could show."

The English lost forty-five men killed, and all the rest prisoners, one hundred and twenty-one cannon, six vessels of war, two hundred boats, and three chests of money, together with stores of ammunition and provisions. After removing the stores, Montcalm destroyed the forts in the presence of the warriors of the Six Nations who had accompanied him. Those Indians had always looked upon the erection of the forts as an infraction of their rights, and this act on the part of Montcalm was an acknowledgment of the justice of their claim and a profession of the intention of the French to uphold them in it, and not continue the trespass by keeping the forts for themselves.

In Montcalm's account of the surrender he says : " Their stores were provided with everything to maintain our army during the next campaign. The least superstitious attribute our success to Providence. We have lost, notwithstanding, eighty men, and our little army had been swamped if that valor so justly attributed to the troops of Old England

had extended to her colonies.   Ours is now more
flourishing than ever ; trade entirely re-established ;
Lake Ontario ours without any opposition.   We can
hardly recover from our astonishment.   The bul-
wark of New England was originally but the house
of an individual whom the Iroquois had permitted
to build ; of this the king took possession some
years afterward for purposes of trade.   He increased it with all the works which we demolish-
ed.   Their loss is incredible.   The Canadians and
Indians have had a very considerable slice of the
cake ; the latter perpetrated there a multitude of
horrors and assassinated more than one hundred
persons included in the capitulation, without our
being able to prevent them or having the right to
remonstrate with them.   This species of animal I
look upon as mad dogs ; when they are intoxicated
they are uncontrollable. "

It is said that Montcalm, notwithstanding his
pledge of honorable treatment to the prisoners, delivered up about twenty men of the garrison to the
Indians to recompense them for the same number of
their men who had fallen during the siege.   It is
possible that this and the slaughter of sick and
wounded prisoners mentioned above, was, as he
says, beyond his power to prevent.   The rest of the
prisoners were taken to Montreal, and exchanged

not long afterward.   The British flags were sent to Montreal, Quebec, and Three Rivers, where they were hung in the churches as trophies of the victory. The Abbé Picquet, founder of the mission of La Presentation, on the site of Ogdensburg, was with this expedition, and raised a cross on the scene of the French victory, to which was affixed the motto, *In hoc signo vincunt*, "In this sign they conquer." By its side he raised a column with the King's arms and the inscription, *Manibus date lilia plenis*, "Bring lilies, with full hands."

Webb, who had set out from Albany the day the French began their operations at Oswego, was slowly advancing when he received the news of Montcalm's victory.   Waiting only to fell trees to obstruct the passage of Wood Creek, a stream whose head-waters were near those of the Mohawk, and formed a part of the water communication between Albany and Oswego, he fled back to Albany in haste and terror.

Montcalm, supposing the English forces at Albany would now be turned against the French forts on Lake Champlain, hurried to Ticonderoga.   But Loudoun had no idea of advancing.   The expedition against Forts Carillon and Frederick was given up ; and the general turned his attention to quartering his troops for the winter, after strengthening the works at Forts Edward and William Henry.

The cities of New York and Philadelphia protested against being forced to give free quarters to the soldiers in the houses of the citizens ; but Loudoun threatened to bring all the troops in North America and billet them upon those cities if they resisted.

While these things were going on, or failing to go on, at the north, and soldiers were lying inactive in the safety of the large northern cities, the frontiers of Pennsylvania and Virginia were suffering from the constant inroads of hostile savages, and it was impossible to raise men in numbers sufficient to impose the least check upon them. Washington had command of all the forces raised, or to be raised, in the province ; but it was almost impossible to get men to respond to the calls for gatherings of the provincial soldiers.

The valley of the Shenandoah was especially exposed to these attacks. No farm-house was safe, and no man sure of his life for a moment, on the road or the farm, in his own house, or even in the little stockaded forts. Winchester was in a state of continual alarm. Washington was sent for, and decided that a force of militia must be raised, and, aided by some of the soldiers from Fort Cumberland, must scour the woods in search of the marauding parties, which in many instances were led by Frenchmen.

A messenger was therefore despatched to Fort Cumberland ; and all captains of militia were ordered to gather their men and read to them an exhortation, setting forth the danger, and appealing to their patriotism and their interest, to assemble on the 15th of April to join the expedition. The officers at Fort Cumberland sent back word that no men could be spared ; that detachments had been sent out in various directions, and the garrison was no more than sufficient for the defence of the fort. The messenger reported that the woods were filled with lurking savages ; his own clothes were pierced with bullets, his horse shot under him, and he had barely escaped with his life. The plan for assembling the militia turned out no better ; on the appointed day only fifteen men presented themselves.

The Indians grew bolder ; houses were burned and families murdered all about Winchester, and the inhabitants, growing frantic, gathered about Washington, imploring him to do something to avert the calamity ; but he was paralyzed by the impossibility of raising men. In a letter to Governor Dinwiddie he wrote :

"I am too little acquainted with pathetic language to attempt a description of these people's distresses. But what can I do? I know their danger, and participate in their sufferings, without hav-

ing it in my power to give them further relief than
uncertain promises.   The supplicating tears of the
women and moving petitions of the men melt me
into such deadly sorrow, that I solemnly declare,
if I know my own mind, that I could offer myself a
willing sacrifice to the butchering enemy, provided
that would contribute to the people's ease.''

This letter called forth an order from the Governor for a force of militia from the upper counties
to go to the relief of the frontier ; and the Assembly
voted an appropriation of twenty thousand pounds
and an increase of the provincial forces to fifteen
thousand men.   Governor Dinwiddie proposed to
expend the money in building a chain of forts along
the Alleghanies from the Potomac to the border of
North Carolina, and to garrison the forts with the
new militia to be raised.   In vain Washington laid
before the Governor the difficulties of carrying out
such a plan.   To place the forts near enough
together for the scouts to keep watch of the whole
line, and to prevent the marauders from breaking
through at any point, without assistance from distant forts, would have called for a much greater
outlay of money and vastly more men than the
province could possibly raise.

Washington's own plan was, to build not more
than four or five strong forts, with large garrisons,

the largest and strongest to be at Winchester, a point where many roads met, where news could be quickly received from all parts of the valley, and where the defenceless inhabitants could take refuge in case of alarm. But Dinwiddie persisted in his design of building twenty-three forts along the frontier, and of maintaining Fort Cumberland at great expense, though it was so far away from the routes taken by the Indians that everything was over before the garrison could be notified. The erection of a central fort at Winchester was, however, agreed upon.

But the preparations for these great defensive works went on very slowly, and meantime the savages kept up their incursions. The people of the Shenandoah valley, despairing of protection, left their homes in large numbers, and moved to the eastern settlements. It seemed that the province of Virginia would soon be practically bounded on the west by the Blue Ridge.

A bold and successful attempt at retribution was made this year in Pennsylvania. An Indian town called Kittanning, about forty miles from Fort Du Quesne, was the rendezvous for parties of marauding Indians; and about one thousand people on the frontier had fallen victims in their raids. They were led by the chief Shingis, and another known as Cap-

tain Jacobs, a bold and brave Indian, who boasted
that he could " take any fort that would catch fire."

To put a stop to these raids, a party of two hundred and eighty Pennsylvanians placed themselves
under the command of Colonel John Armstrong.
One of the officers under him was Captain Hugh
Mercer, afterward of Revolutionary fame, who had
served as a surgeon in the army of the Young
Pretender, and after his defeat at Culloden escaped
to America. The men marched rapidly from Fort
Shirley on the Juniata, and reached the Alleghany
without a suspicion on the part of the savages that
vengeance was on their track.

On the night of the 7th of October, Armstrong's
men drew near enough to hear the rejoicings of
the Indians over their victories—the whoops, and
screams, and sound of drums. When the carouse
was over, the Indians made fires in the fields and
went to sleep beside them without sentinels.
Armstrong's men hid themselves until the moon
had set and all the warriors were asleep ; then, dividing into two parties, they attacked the village
and the sleeping warriors in the fields at the same
time. The Indians fought with desperate bravery ;
Captain Jacobs defended himself to the last, fighting
through the loop-holes of his log house. The village had been set on fire, and as the flames drew

near his dwelling, he was offered quarter, which he refused, saying he would kill a few before he died. He and the warriors with him were at length driven out by the fire, and some escaped to the woods. Captain Jacobs attempted to get away, but was shot ; as was also his son, who was said to be a giant seven feet high. The whole town was destroyed by the fire ; the repeated explosions of loaded guns and bags and kegs of powder showing how well the Indians were prepared for future raids.

Both Armstrong and Mercer were wounded. On the return march, which was made as rapidly as possible for fear the alarm might reach Fort Du Quesne and a party be sent out in pursuit, Mercer was separated from his companions, and only reached the fort after fourteen days of lonely wandering through the woods, finding his way by the water-courses, and living on two dried clams and a rattlesnake, with a few berries.

The Six Nations were now fast passing over from their neutral position to the side of the French ; the younger braves would have taken up the hatchet at once to fight under Montcalm for the prospering cause. The English, losing these fickle allies by their failures, were still to meet more reverses, and bring their military pretensions into still greater contempt.

CHAPTER XV.

LOUISBOURG AND FORT WILLIAM HENRY.

An Indian Raid—Encounter between Stark's Men and the French—
Vaudreuil's Attempt at Fort William Henry—Loudoun's Council—
Affairs in the South—Plan to Take Louisbourg—Admiral Hol-
bourne—Withdrawal from Louisbourg—Opinion in England—In
America—Siege of Fort William Henry—Webb's Cowardice—
Monroe's Surrender—Massacre by Montcalm's Indians—Descent
on the German Flats—Situation at the Close of the Year—The
Duke of Newcastle—William Pitt.

DURING the ensuing year, 1757, the British cause
in America reached its lowest ebb. The French,
under the brilliant leadership of Montcalm, achieved
so many successes that it seemed as if the Bourbon
lilies would soon float over every stronghold of the continent. Loudoun continued to give away advantages
by his slowness and cowardice; and the few brave
dashes made by parties of provincials were of little
effect, because not followed by any movement of the
main forces. During the winter, which was very long
and cold, the frozen waters of Lake Champlain formed
a highway for war-parties on their deadly errands.
An Indian chief, Aouschik, who had killed one of
Montcalm's engineers the summer before, mistaking
him for an Englishman, demonstrated the sincerity of

his regret by bringing in thirty-three English scalps
during the year. In the course of a discussion of a
treaty between his nation, the Nipissings, and the
French, he exclaimed, "What need of councils, de-
liberations, and proposals, when action is needed?
I hate the Englishman. I thirst for his blood. I
am going to bathe in it;" and he broke into a
hideous war-song, and led out his braves.

In January, John Stark led seventy-four men from
Fort William Henry, on snow-shoes and skates, to
Lake Champlain. They attacked a party of Frenchmen who were travelling in sledges from Fort
Carillon to Fort Frederick, and took three of the
sledges, with their horses, and seven prisoners. But
just as they reached the land, in retreating, they
were attacked in turn by two hundred and fifty
French and Indians. Stark's men took shelter behind hills and trees, and fought till evening, when
they retreated, leaving fourteen killed and six
missing.

In February, Montcalm formed a plan for capturing Fort William Henry. Fifteen hundred men,
under the command of Rigaud de Vaudreuil, start-
ing on the 23d, crossed Lakes Champlain and
George, marching sixty leagues on snow-shoes.
Their provisions were drawn on sledges, by dogs;
and at night they spread bear-skins on the snow, or

raised tents in stormy weather.   On the 18th of
March they were in front of the fort, but found
themselves disappointed in their hope of a surprise ;
they had been discovered, and the garrison was on
the alert.   Rigaud thought it useless to attempt to
carry the fort by assault, but set his men at work to
destroy everything outside the works.   For four
nights they worked under fire, burning up the boats,
the mills, magazines, and palisaded houses, and the
cabins of the rangers.   Three hundred and fifty
bateaux and four brigantines were consumed.   The
fire of the garrison inflicted some damage, but they
made no attempts by sorties to drive off the French
or stop their depredations.

A council of governors held at Boston in January
had agreed to raise four thousand men in the
northern colonies, and New York and New Jersey
were to be called on for proportionate numbers to
increase Lord Loudoun's army for the summer
campaign.   In March, another council was held at
Philadelphia, and Washington obtained permission
from Governor Dinwiddie to be present, wishing to
represent to Lord Loudoun the interests of Virginia.
He was anxious that another attack should be made
on Fort Du Quesne, at the same time with the
operations in the noith, since a large part of the
garrison would be drawn away to the Canadian

frontier. Loudoun did not approve of the plan, as he desired the southern colonies simply to stand on the defensive. He gave orders, however, in accordance with Washington's advice, to withdraw the garrison from Fort Cumberland, leaving Maryland to supply that point, and make Fort Loudoun, at Winchester, the head-quarters of the Virginia militia. Stanwix was stationed on the frontier of Pennsylvania, Colonel Henry Bouquet had charge of the Carolina border, and Webb was furnished with nearly six thousand men to defend the important posts about Lake George.

Loudoun's own work for the summer was to be the reduction of Louisbourg. Abandoning for the time the idea of capturing the forts on the English borders, he resolved to take the greater part of his forces to Halifax, where he was to be joined by an English squadron, and proceed to Louisbourg. The New England provinces had been greatly disappointed at the surrender of that fortress by treaty after they had taken it in 1745 by their almost unaided prowess, an achievement which they justly regarded with pride; and, in addition to this, the fact that Louisbourg, when held by the French, was a harbor of refuge for the cruisers that preyed upon the colonial vessels, made the project for re-taking it very popular in New England.

Admiral Holbourne arrived at Halifax early in July with a squadron and a reënforcement of five thousand troops under Lord George Howe. On the 6th of the same month, Loudoun sailed from New York with six thousand men, having first laid an embargo on all the ships in the ports of British North America — an assumption of power which aroused the indignation of the colonies, and was not approved by the English Government.

Arrived at Halifax, Loudoun set his men at work, levelling ground for a parade and planting a vegetable garden to furnish protection against the scurvy. Then he kept them exercising in drills, and sham fights, and mock sieges, until the impatience of some of the subordinate officers broke out into open criticism. At the beginning of August, the troops were embarked for Gabarus Bay; but on the 4th information was received from a captured sloop that the French had nineteen ships of war and three thousand regular troops, besides many Canadians and Indians. The English had but seventeen ships of war, and Admiral Holbourne dared not attack the French nineteen. Loudoun also prudently resolved to put off the capture of Louisbourg until another summer, and some of the soldiers were left at Halifax, while he returned with the greater part of them to New York.

Horace Walpole had written in February of this year, "I do not augur very well of the ensuing summer ; a detachment is going to America under a commander whom a child might outwit or terrify with a pop-gun." After news of the fiasco at Louisbourg reached England, he wrote, "Shortly after came letters from the Earl of Loudoun, stating that he found the French twenty-one thousand strong, and that, not having so many, he could not attack Louisbourg, but should return to Halifax. Admiral Holbourne, one of the sternest condemners of Byng, wrote at the same time that he, having but seventeen ships and the French nineteen, dared not attack them. Here was another summer lost ! Pitt expressed himself with great vehemence against the earl ; and we naturally have too lofty ideas of our naval strength to suppose that seventeen of our ships are not a match for any nineteen others." *

---

* The clerk of a church in Halifax, on the news of the abandonment of the enterprise against Cape Breton, gave out, for the expression of his own feelings and those of the people generally, some stanzas of the forty-fourth psalm :

> O God, we with our ears have heard,
>   Our fathers have us told,
> What works thou in their days hadst done
>   Even in the days of old.
>
> Thy hand did drive the heathen out,
>   And plant them in their place :

Loudoun was only two days out on his way to
New York, when he was met by tidings of more
misfortune to the British arms.   As soon as it was
known by the French that he had sailed for Louisbourg, Montcalm resolved to strike another blow in
New York, for which he had been making preparations during the entire spring and summer.   Nothing had been left undone to incite the Indians and
unite them for a blow at the English fortifications at
Lake George.   A grand council was held at Niagara
on the 1st of July, at which the Iroquois gave belts

Thou didst afflict the nations,
But them thou didst increase.

But now we are cast off by thee,
And us thou putt'st to shame ;
And when our armies do go forth,
Thou goest not with the same.

Thou mak'st us from the enemy,
Faint-hearted, to turn back ;
And they who hate us, for themselves
Our spoils away do take.

Like sheep for meat thou gavest us ;
'Mongst heathen cast we be.
Thou didst for nought thy people sell ;
Their price enriched not thee.

Thou mak'st us a reproach to be
Unto our neighbors near,
Derision and a scorn to them
That round about us are.
Rise for our help and us redeem
Even for thy mercies' sake.

to the Hurons, Ottawas, and other allies of the
French, as a token of their intention to join the
enemies of the English ; and a belt was given in reply, which was covered with vermilion, signifying
an invitation to war.　They desired the Iroquois to
bring to their father—that is, the French Governor—
some of the bad meat they loved so well.　By the
" bad meat " they meant the English.

Another congress was held at Montreal, at which
thirty-three nations were represented, including
chiefs from Acadia to Lake Superior.　" We will try
our father's hatchet on the English, to see if it cuts
well," said a chief of the Senecas.　Montcalm sang
the war-song with them every day of the council,
and they loved him as a leader whom they never
had seen beaten, who could open the way for them
to an unlimited quantity of plunder and scalps.　The
tribes were assembled at Fort St. John, on the River
Sorel.　Their missionaries came with them, and
masses and hymns of the church alternated with the
fantastic dance and the unearthly yells that heralded
the strife.　When all was ready, they ascended the
river and Lake Champlain in a fleet of two hundred canoes, and landed at Ticonderoga.

Several minor engagements took place while
Montcalm was preparing for the main attack.　A
party went out under Marin to the vicinity of Fort

Edward, and returned in triumph. "They did not amuse themselves with making prisoners," said Montcalm, as the one captive and the forty-two scalps were taken from the boat, and exhibited before the admiring eyes of the Indians. A slight skirmish took place at Harbor Island near Sabbath-Day Point. A party of three hundred was sent out from Fort William Henry under an officer named Palmer, to make observations, when a band of Ottawas who had been hiding for twenty-four hours suddenly rushed upon the twenty-two boats of the English, and made such havoc that only twelve escaped. One hundred and sixty were taken prisoners; the rest were drowned, or fell under the fury of the savages. After this victory, the Ottawas wanted to go home. They felt that they had glory enough, and ought not to tempt the fortunes of war any farther. But Montcalm held another council, and bound all the Indians, by the presentation of the great belt of six thousand shells, to stay until the end of the expedition.

Fort William Henry was close to the shore of the lake, on ground so low that it seemed from a little distance to be resting on the water. The walls were low, and bastions rose at the four corners. The land immediately about the fort had been cleared and planted as a garden by the garrison.

On the east was a morass, and the other sides were protected by a ditch. On the southeast was an eminence, the summit of which commanded the fort, and would have been a better site for the works. On the top of this hill a camp was formed with intrenchments, which contained about seventeen hundred men, and the fort four or five hundred.

Montcalm's whole army, fifty-five hundred regulars and Canadians and sixteen hundred Indians, crossed from Ticonderoga to the foot of Lake George. Here, as there was a scarcity of boats, a division was made. The Chevalier De Levis, with twenty-two hundred soldiers and six hundred Indians, marched by land along the rugged trail on the western side of the lake, while the rest of the Indians set out in their bark canoes, and the following day Montcalm embarked with the remainder of the army and all the baggage in two hundred and fifty boats. After rowing that day and most of the night, they came in sight of three fires arranged in a triangle which marked the camp of De Levis.

Here they halted, held a council of war, and selected a place for landing which was hidden from the fort by a point of land extending into the lake. During the night, two of the canoes had attacked two English boats which were out on the lake, and after a struggle, in which the Nipissings lost a great chief, one of the English boats was captured, and all the men in it were slaughtered, save two who were held as prisoners.

The next morning, August 2d, the Indians threw out a line of canoes across the lake, and raised the war-cry. The English, taken by surprise, withdrew in haste from their tents and outlying barracks, while the detachment of De Levis scoured the woods, burned the barracks, chased the cattle and horses, and slew a small foraging party whom they surprised in the woods. Montcalm landed about a mile and a half from the fort, at the north-west, and advanced in three columns. One detachment of Indians and Canadians, under La Corne, took a position on the road leading to Fort Edward ; another, under De Levis, formed an encampment south of the fort ; while Montcalm, with the main body of the army, was on the west shore of the lake, at the edge of the forest. The 3d of August was employed in preparing for a siege.

On the 4th, Montcalm sent a summons to Colonel Monroe, commanding at the fort, to surrender, and intimated that in case the garrison should resist, and the fort be finally taken by siege, he could not answer for the behavior of his Indians. Monroe had not more than twenty-two hundred men ; but relying on assistance from General Webb, who was at Fort Edward, fifteen miles away, with four thousand men, he answered that he would not surrender. "I will defend my trust," he said, "to the last extremity." The French then pushed on their preparations with vigor; they dug trenches, brought fascines for the batteries, and gabions for shelter, and drew the artillery from the landing-place. The first battery was at length prepared, and opened on the fort in the morning of the 6th, to the great delight of the Indians, who had seen but little artillery practice, and were nearly beside themselves at the noise of the big guns. The fire was returned, but with much less power, while the trenches were carried so close to the fort that the Indians could stand near enough to fire upon the works without danger from the guns. Another battery was erected, and the sharp-shooters drew closer around the fort, hiding not only in the zigzags, but behind every forest tree or cover of any kind.

The walls of the fort were fast giving way under the fire of the batteries, and the garrison were falling under the deadly bullets; but Monroe still held out, hoping for relief; for General Webb was well aware, from the first, of the approach of the French army, and of Monroe's brave defence. When Montcalm was coming over the lake, Webb was in the neighborhood of Fort William Henry; and Israel

Putnam, who was on the lake with a party of rangers, discovered the movement of the French and hastened to Webb with the news, urging him to oppose the landing ; but Webb—enjoining secrecy on Putnam, it is said—fell back to Fort Edward.

On the second day of the siege, Sir William Johnson arrived at Fort Edward with some Indians and militia, whom he had hastily gathered after hearing of the departure of Montcalm's army from Ticonderoga. Finding that Webb was determined to do nothing, he asked to be allowed to make up a body of reënforcements from those who would volunteer to go. Webb consented at first, but afterward withdrew his consent ; and the whole four thousand at Fort Edward remained inactive. A letter was despatched by Webb to the fort, probably on the day of Johnson's arrival, advising Monroe to surrender, as it would be impossible for him to send any help unless he himself should be reënforced from Albany, and giving an exaggerated account of the strength of the French. The messenger was taken by a party of French on the road between the two forts, who read the letter, and then sent it on to Monroe.

On the sixth day of the siege, August 9th, when half of the guns of the fort had burst, and the ammunition was nearly gone, Monroe, knowing that he had nothing to hope for from Webb, hung out a flag of truce. In arranging the terms of capitulation, Montcalm invited the Indian chiefs to the council, in order to make it binding on them. The garrison were to march out with the honors of war, carrying their private effects, and delivering up the fort, with the intrenched camp and all its dependencies, and all the artillery, provisions, and warlike stores, to his Most Christian Majesty the King of France. The garrison and other troops were not to serve against his Most Christian Majesty or his allies for the space of eighteen months.

All French prisoners taken by land since the beginning of the war were to be delivered at Fort Carillon within three months; and, according to receipts given by the French officers to whom they should be surrendered, an equal number of the troops at Fort William Henry should be released from their engagement not to serve in the English armies. An officer was to be left as a hostage until the return of the escort to be provided for the English troops. The sick and wounded were to remain with Montcalm, who promised to take proper care of them and return them as soon as they were recovered. As a mark of esteem to Colonel Monroe and the garrison, for their honorable defence, Montcalm gave them "one piece of cannon, a six-pounder."

The English retired to the intrenched camp, and the French took possession of the fort, while the Indians spent the night in a wild carouse in honor of the victory.   When the English marched out in the morning, carrying their arms and baggage, and accompanied by an escort from the French army, the rage and cupidity of the Indians were at once excited ; they were never able to understand the consideration shown to prisoners by civilized nations, and they had been drawn to the fight by the hope of plunder, as well as the thirst for blood. At a favorable spot a short distance from the camp, they fell upon the luckless soldiers, stripped them of everything they carried, and even of the clothes they wore, and hewed them down without mercy. Attacked in this unexpected way, the troops who had just shown so much bravery in the defence of the fort were thrown into a panic of uncontrollable terror, and fled in all directions, some to the woods, some to the French soldiers for protection.   Twelve to fifteen hundred were taken captive by the Indians, and many were killed.

In regard to the conduct of the French officers and soldiers during this horrible scene, the accounts are conflicting.   According to one English statement, the French officers neglected and even refused during the massacre to take any of the measures stipulated in the surrender, and neither officers nor troops gave any protection ; according to French accounts, Montcalm besought them to kill him, but spare the English, who were under his protection, while De Levis rushed into the midst of them again and again, at the peril of his life, to arrest the slaughter, many of the French officers received wounds in attempting to protect those whom they had rescued from the fury of the savages, and Montcalm bade the English defend themselves.

The great number of the captives seems to make it improbable that any very determined effort was made to protect them ; but there is no doubt that the French officers, with whom rested the responsibility of carrying out the terms of the capitulation, did all that could be done by commands and entreaties to stay the fury of the savages, yet would not give any order to their soldiers which would imperil the friendship of the Indians. But they had industriously excited the fury of the savages by appealing to their lowest passions, and could not control it when their own purposes were accomplished.

About six hundred of the troops reached Fort Edward after escaping to the woods. Montcalm released the prisoners still kept by the Indians near the French camp, sending them to the fort with a powerful escort, and Rigaud de Vaudreuil was sent to ransom those who had been carried away. Fort William Henry was then razed to the ground, the English vessels were destroyed, and nine hundred men were set at work to load the stores for transportation. Among them were provisions for six months for an army of five thousand men.

The news of the capture of the fort and the slaughter by the Indians aroused the colonies, and Webb called loudly for help, fearing an attack on Fort Edward. Militia were sent from Massachusetts and Connecticut, but the French had departed without attempting anything further, and the shores of Lake George were a solitude.

Late in November of this year, a force of three hundred French and Indians, under an officer named Bellêtre, made a descent upon a settlement on the Mohawk called German Flats, near Fort Herkimer. Sixty houses, with the mill and other buildings, were burned, forty of the settlers were killed, and a hundred and fifty were carried away prisoners. A large amount of plunder was taken, one Indian, it is said, having thirty thousand livres (about six thousand dollars) in money. The mayor of the village lost four hundred thousand livres' worth of property.

Bellêtre was entrusted with messages by some of the Iroquois to their "father," the Governor of

Canada, professing faithfulness, and asking for aid to resist the English. Sir William Johnson sent an interpreter to some Oneida and Tuscarora Indians at the German Flats, to demand why they, having knowledge of the intended attack, had not warned the people of the settlement. An Oneida chief replied that they did give warning to the Germans at the settlement, telling them to prepare for an attack, and send word to Warraghiyagey (Sir William Johnson); that the warning was disregarded and the message not sent, the Germans declaring they did not fear the enemy; and that they sent a warning, accompanied by a belt of wampum, on the day preceding the attack, of which no more notice was taken. The Germans present acknowledged the truth of the Indian statements before the interpreter.

Lord Loudoun was in New York when Fort William Henry was taken. One of his plans was, to form an encampment on Long Island, which he imagined would in some way protect the country. As the winter approached, the troubles about quartering soldiers were repeated. Boston refused, and Loudoun yielded, after having written, "I have ordered the messenger to wait but forty-eight hours in Boston; and if, on his return, I find things not settled, I will instantly order into Boston the three regiments from New York, Long Island, and Connecticut ; and if more are wanted, I have two in the Jerseys at hand, besides three in Pennsylvania.''

Thus closed a year of disasters to the British cause in America. The French were in actual possession of very nearly all they had claimed previous to the war. They had the valley of the Mississippi, except a fort on the Upper Tennessee ; they had the basin of the St. Lawrence and its tributary waters in northeastern New York ; and they had made an open passage to the west by the capture of Oswego. They had won over many of the Iroquois tribes ; and the Cherokees, who still remained faithful to the English, showed signs of alienation. Acadia was in constant danger from the strong force of men and ships at Louisbourg. If they were not checked, they would have nothing to do but carry war into the heart of the English colonies. At the same time, the British had not been more successful in Europe. Imbecility seemed to control all the acts of the administration and the military authorities. The Duke of Newcastle was again the nominal head of the ministry—Newcastle, the ignorant and incompetent nobleman, who is reported, if not with truth, yet with a happy hit at his characteristics, to have said, "Oh, yes, yes, to be sure, Annapolis must be defended ; troops must be sent to Annapolis—pray, where is Annapolis? Cape Breton an island? Wonderful! Show it to me on the map. So it is, sure enough. My dear sir, you always bring us good news. I must go and tell the King that Cape Breton is an island.''

But William Pitt was made Secretary of State, and Newcastle was obliged to leave to him the entire management of the war.

The disgraceful defeats in America had roused a storm of indignation in England. Loudoun was severely censured. "Nothing has been done," said Pitt, "nothing attempted. Every door is open to France." Loudoun was recalled ; the quarrels with the colonies about raising a common fund for war purposes and taxation by Parliament were abandoned ; all provincial officers, from colonels downward, were made equal in rank to corresponding officers in the regular army ; and the colonies were asked to raise as many men as possible, and to clothe and pay them, Pitt promising that the King would recommend Parliament to reimburse them, while all munitions of war were to be provided by England.

While vigorous measures were thus taken by the English Government, and the outlook for the coming year was more encouraging, the victorious French in Canada began to feel that they were on the eve of reverses. The men had left their fields untilled, to follow Montcalm ; rain had destroyed the crops, so that in some parishes there was not enough left to furnish seed ; and France sent no supplies. Not only the army, but the entire body of inhabitants, were put on a reduced allowance. Montcalm predicted that New France must fall sooner or later, such were the numbers of the English, and such the difficulty of obtaining supplies in Canada.

CHAPTER XVI.

LOUISBOURG AND TICONDEROGA.

Plan of the Campaign—Siege of Louisbourg—The Surrender—Effect of the Victory—Destruction of French Settlements—Expedition against Ticonderoga—Skirmish in the Woods—Death of Lord Howe—The Attack—The Flight—Terror of the General—Conduct of Bradstreet.

FOR the prosecution of the war in 1758, Abercrombie succeeded Lord Loudoun, with command of the forces that were to attack Ticonderoga and Crown Point. Lord Howe, a young nobleman of military ability and great personal popularity, was made second in command. Admiral Boscawen was given charge of the fleet destined for Louisbourg. Colonel Jeffrey Amherst, who had served with distinction in Germany, was made a major-general and sent to America to command the land forces to coöperate with Boscawen ; and under him were Brigadier-Generals Whitmore, Lawrence, and James Wolfe. The reduction of Fort Du Quesne was intrusted to Brigadier-General Joseph Forbes, who was called, from his obstinacy, "the Head of Iron." A large number of men was raised in the colonies, and twelve thousand were sent from England with Amherst, so that the entire British force in America was not far from fifty thousand.

Amherst, delayed by storms, did not reach Halifax till the end of May, when he met Boscawen's fleet just coming out of the harbor. The Admiral had given him up, and, leaving a strong force to guard the town, was about to sail without him. On the 2d of June, the entire force arrived at Gabarus Bay. There were twenty-two ships of the line, and .fifteen frigates, with one hundred and twenty smaller vessels ; and the army amounted to over eleven thousand men. In the brigade under Wolfe were Isaac Barré, the eloquent advocate of the cause of America in the British Parliament a few years later, and Richard Montgomery, a young Irishman, twenty-one years of age, destined to die under the walls of Quebec in a later struggle.

Amherst, hoping to surprise the garrison at Louisbourg, ordered great care and silence to be observed in making the landing. But in the morning the shore was enveloped in a dense fog, and as it cleared away, a high wind drove the surf on the beach so heavily as to make landing impossible, and give the French time for preparation. Lawrence and Wolfe, however, went out in the evening and reconnoitred the shore, notwithstanding the dangerous roll of the surf. They found that the French had thrown a

chain of posts across the country, and placed batteries in a position to command the shore where a
landing would be most likely to be attempted.

For six days they waited for the waves to subside ;
on the 8th of June, though the sea was still rolling
heavily, a landing was found to be possible, and under cover of a fire from seven of the frigates, the boats
were rowed toward the shore at Cormoran Creek,
while three sloops were sent past the harbor to draw
off the attention of the enemy.   Many of the boats
were upset, and some of them broken, by the
violence of the waves.   The French reserved their
fire till the boats were close to the shore, and then
poured on them a sudden volley which struck down
many of the men, and disabled some of the boats.
Wolfe's flag-staff was shivered ; but, forbidding his
men to return the fire, he urged on the rowers, and
leaping into the sea, led his men through the surf.
In a few minutes the whole division was on shore.
The French retreated in disorder from their intrenchments, and the British pursued, taking seventy
prisoners, and only retreating when they came within
range of the guns of Louisbourg.

It was not till the 11th that the artillery and other
supplies could be landed.   On the 12th the French
abandoned their outposts and concentrated their
whole force on the defence of the town.   Wolfe

pushed on his men around the northern and eastern shores of the bay to Lighthouse Point, a promontory on the northeast side of the entrance to the harbor. Between this and the town, which occupied another promontory on the western side of the harbor, was Goat Island, standing in the middle of the entrance to the bay. Here the French had a battery. Wolfe placed a battery on Lighthouse Point, from which he could command Goat Island and fire upon the ships; and by the 25th the Goat Island battery was silenced. Leaving a detachment in charge of the battery at the Point, Wolfe took possession of another position, near the town, where he erected a battery to play upon the fort and the ships.

The siege went on for weeks; but its progress, though slow, was steady and sure. The heavy surf and the continuous rains interfered with the landing of munitions from the fleet and the work of the engineers. On the 9th of July, six hundred Frenchmen made a sally from the fort, and surprised a detachment of the English, killing their commander, the Earl of Dundonald, and putting his men to flight; but another English detachment coming up, the French were driven back with the loss of twenty dead and eighty prisoners.

The commander of the fort, the Chevalier de Drucour, held out bravely; he had under him be-

'tween five and six thousand men—soldiers, sailors, and Indians—with five ships of the line, and four frigates, three of which he had ordered to be sunk at the entrance of the harbor. On the 21st of July, his three largest ships of war took fire from a shell. On the 22d the citadel was burned, and the town of Louisbourg was soon a pile of ruins ; forty of the fifty-two cannon were disabled, and on the night of the 25th two young English captains took boats of the fleet and, boarding the two remaining vessels, set fire to one and carried off the other. The celebrated Captain James Cook participated in this enterprise.

With the town in ruins, the cannon silenced, the ships gone, and the English ready to sail into the harbor, Drucour proposed to capitulate ; but thinking the terms offered too severe, he would have refused and submitted to a general assault. The clamor of the inhabitants, however, decided him to yield. The garrison, with the sailors and marines —five thousand six hundred and thirty-seven in all— were made prisoners of war and sent to England ; and Cape Breton and Prince Edward's Island were taken possession of by the English troops.

The capture of Louisbourg, after so many reverses, aroused great enthusiasm throughout America. Captain Amherst, brother of the general, carried the news to England. Eleven stand of colors, the trophies of victory, were borne through the streets of London by a procession, to the sound of martial music, laid at the feet of the sovereign, and then hung up in St. Paul's Cathedral. Boscawen and Amherst were honored with official acknowledgment of their services ; but the daring and dash of Wolfe made him the popular hero of the enterprise.

In August, seven ships of the line and three frigates under Sir Charles Hardy were sent to carry a body of soldiers under Wolfe to destroy the French settlements along the coast, beginning with the villages of the unfortunate Acadians in the northeast, and passing along the shores of the Gulf of St. Lawrence to Gaspé, and thence as far up the river as the season would permit, while Monckton was sent to the settlements on the Bay of Fundy and the River St. John. The villages were laid in ruins, and the inhabitants were scattered or carried away. The intendant in charge of Mont Louis, on the St. Lawrence, offered a hundred and fifty thousand livres to save the stores which were gathered at that flourishing fishing-station ; but there was no authority for anything but destruction, and the place was left in ruins.

Amherst had hoped to follow up the capture of Louisbourg with that of Quebec. But the length of the siege and the lateness of the season made it unadvisable to attempt it, and the news from Lake George decided him to move his troops in that direction.

At the beginning of July, 1758, the largest army that had ever been gathered on American soil by any European nation was encamped on the shore of Lake George, preparing for an attack on the French fortresses at Ticonderoga and Crown Point. There were six thousand three hundred and sixty-seven regulars, and nine thousand and twenty-four provincials. Abercrombie was commander-in-chief, and under him was the young and gallant Lord Howe, whose brother was afterward commander of the British army in America, in the time of the Revolution. Among the provincials were Stark, Putnam, Bradstreet, and Robert Rogers with his famous company of rangers.

Rogers and his men had made a reconnoissance and brought back a plan of the works of Fort Carillon and the surrounding country. The fort was on a point of land extending into Lake Champlain where it is joined by the outlet of Lake George. In front of the fort and south of it was the little bay formed by the junction of the waters; on the east was Lake Champlain. Between the fort and the waters of the lake where they widen slightly at the north of the little peninsula, the ground was low and marshy; the only approach by land was on the northwest, and there Montcalm, who was in command with about three thousand men, had made an intrenchment, with an abatis of felled trees, whose parapet was covered with interwoven branches.

On the 5th of July, Abercrombie's army embarked on Lake George in one hundred and thirty-five whale-boats and nine hundred small boats. The artillery was placed on rafts, and the fleet moved down the lake with banners and music. The first night they landed at Sabbath-Day Point; but before midnight they reëmbarked, and by nine in the morning had reached the little river which forms the outlet of the lake, where they landed and formed in columns.

This river, which is very winding, and interrupted by rapids and falls, is nearly four miles long. The direct road from Lake George to Ticonderoga crossed it by two bridges, and at the bridge nearest the fort the French had built saw-mills. Montcalm, when he learned of the presence of the English on the lake, sent out two regiments to oppose the landing, but afterward recalled them, only placing three pickets at the portage, and sending out three hundred men under De Trépézée for observation.

Instead of landing on the east side and taking the road, the English, seeing that the French had burned the bridges, landed on the west side and marched through the woods, following the windings of the river. Trépézée's men, thus left behind, and cut off from the fort, struck into the woods to march around the English, and get to their own army before the landing should be finished, but they lost their way; and having groped about in the woods for twelve hours, they unexpectedly came face to face with an advance party of the English under Lord Howe, near Trout Brook, or Bernes River. In the skirmish that ensued, the Frenchmen fought bravely, hand-to-hand, or sheltering themselves behind the forest trees. Lord Howe was one of the first to fall, struck by a musket-ball in the breast, and died immediately. Maddened by the loss of their favorite leader, his men fought still more fiercely, and the French were soon overpowered. Not more than twenty escaped; Trépézée was mortally wounded; a hundred and fourteen were made prisoners; the rest fell on the battle-field or were drowned in the stream.

The death of Lord Howe was an irreparable loss to Abercrombie's army. All spirit and decision in the ordering of its movements seemed to die with him. Abercrombie had no generalship, no courage, and no confidence in the advice of provincial officers. With the soldiers, Howe had gained a wonderful popularity. A French writer who was at Ticonderoga says of him, calling him, with a Frenchman's difficulty in getting hold of English names, "Lord Ho, or Hau":

"Abercrombie had with him a young nobleman of great ambition, who was a decided favorite with the army, and had succeeded in imparting to it his own brave spirit. He had come in April to reconnoitre the position of Fort Carillon, and seemed to be intrusted with the direction of every plan of attack in the campaign. He had induced all the officers to dress like the common soldiers, warned by Braddock's defeat, where the officers were picked out as marks for the bullets. He persuaded the men to cut their hair short, and all were supplied with a kind of gaiters like those worn by Indians and Canadians, and called *mituzzes*. Their haversacks were rolled in a blanket. They had each thirty pounds of meal, a pound of powder, and four pounds of balls, besides their cartridge-boxes full; an army thus equipped would need no magazine for a month. Their canteens were filled with rum. Both officers and men mixed their own meal with a little water, and baked it in cakes by putting it on a flat stone under the ashes, an arrangement which

answered ·very well for a light expedition. The
soldier thus found everything necessary for his use,
and was no more loaded than ordinarily. The
officers and men had only one shirt apiece, which
was doubtless of cotton and well made. Lord Ho
set the example by himself washing his own soiled
shirt and drying it in the sun.''

It was probably this hearty way of mingling with
the soldiers, and making the details of camp life and
equipment interesting, which, united to his brilliant
courage and his recognition of every man's value,
inspired the affection of the army. After his death,
Stark remembered how closely Lord Howe had
questioned him about the situation of Ticonderoga
and the approaches to it, as he lay on a bear-skin in
his tent, that night at Sabbath-Day Point. Massachusetts erected a monument to his memory in
Westminster Abbey.

The next morning, the 7th, Abercrombie took
his army back to the landing-place. Bradstreet went
forward with a detachment, rebuilt the bridges, and
took possession of the saw-mills near the second
bridge, about two miles from the fort, which were
in an advantageous military position. The army
then followed, and encamped there for the night.

In the morning, Abercrombie sent out his chief
engineer and other officers of the regulars, to recon-

noitre. They saw the abatis of felled trees in front
of the lines ; but, owing to the thick woods and the
morass, were unable to make very clear observations.
The engineer and many of the officers judged the
breastwork to be a very slight defence. Stark
warned the general that it was stronger than it
looked. But, with his usual contempt for provincials, he disregarded the warning, though a minority
of the British observers agreed with Stark, and determined to march on the work at once, without
waiting for the artillery. He was farther persuaded to move quickly by the report that Montcalm
already had six thousand men, and was daily expecting De.Levis with three thousand more from
the Mohawk. As a matter of fact, De Levis had
already come in with his eight hundred men, and
the whole force did not exceed three thousand.
Montcalm was undecided all the morning whether
to remain or retreat to Crown Point, but at length
determined to wait for the attack, and his men were
marched into the intrenchments during the forenoon.

Abercrombie's forces were arranged in three lines.
In the first were Bradstreet's boatmen, with the
rangers on one side and some companies of light
infantry on the other. The second was composed
of Massachusetts militia. Behind these were the

regulars, openings being left in the two forward lines for their advance. The rear guard was composed of Connecticut and New Jersey militia. Abercrombie, who remained far in the rear, gave orders that not a shot should be fired until the breastwork should be surmounted.

At one o'clock on the 8th, the advance began. The regulars marched through the spaces between the companies of provincials, and led on the attack, the grenadier companies first, followed closely by Murray's Highlanders. Marching on through the underbrush and over the swampy ground, they made a dash at the abatis, and then they realized the fatal strength of the intrenchments. The abatis consisted of felled trees, with sharp branches pointing outward; and the top was made still more formidable by interwoven branches piled closely upon it. Stumps of trees and rubbish of all kinds added to the obstruction, which extended for a hundred yards in front of a breastwork of logs, and sloped gradually downward from it toward the assailants.

The French held back their fire till the hapless regulars were hopelessly entangled among the sharp branches and stumps, climbing over the bogs, and stumbling among the rubbish. Then came a sudden blaze from muskets and cannon, and hundreds of them were mowed down. But still they struggled on; many of the Highlanders, active and lightly equipped, forced their way to the breastwork, but only to die by the bayonet. Half of the regiment fell, and nearly all of the officers were either killed or wounded. Fresh troops rushed on, only to meet the same fate; their musket-balls fell harmless against the defences, while the merciless fire from behind the breastwork had full play upon them. The whole afternoon passed; Montcalm saw every movement, and promptly sent reënforcements to such points as needed them. When the English attempted to turn the left, aid was sent to the left; when they concentrated between the centre and the right, Montcalm was speedily there with a reserve. De Levis and Bourlamaque were equally vigilant and active.

During this terrible slaughter, Abercrombie was at the saw-mills, and there was apparently no one to give general orders or withdraw the men from the useless sacrifice; but it was at length ended by an accident. Some of the English, advancing through the woods, saw firing directly in front of them, supposed it to come from the French lines, and returned it promptly; but when the smoke cleared away, they saw that they had fired upon an advance party of their own men. Confused and panic-stricken, they turned and fled ; the panic spread, and the whole army was soon in bewildered flight.

Abercrombie had lost, in killed and wounded, nineteen hundred and forty-four, but his army still largely outnumbered Montcalm's, which had lost in all three hundred and ninety. It was in reality four times as large. According to the number he supposed Montcalm had, Abercrombie's was twice as great ; and even had De Levis arrived with the three thousand men he was wildly reported to have, the English force would still have outnumbered the French by three thousand. Yet this discrepancy was largely offset by the carefully prepared intrenchments.

The English held Mount Defiance, which commanded the fort, and a battery there might have done good execution ; but Abercrombie seems not to have had any idea of renewing the attack, but rather to have thought only of putting as many miles as possible between himself and the foe. Hardly had the soldiers reached the saw-mills, and begun to rally, after finding they were not pursued, when he gave orders for a retreat to the landing-place. Supposing he had intelligence of a pursuit by the enemy, the troops broke into another flight, while apparently the general did not try to arrest them, or restore order. A French writer who was at Carillon says Montcalm's men found more than five hundred pairs of shoes with buckles in the mud on the road to the falls the next day.   Arrived at the landing-place, they would have thrown themselves into the boats in the same confusion ; but Bradstreet was there with a small force that had not yet lost their heads, and forming a guard in front of the landing-place, would not allow a man to embark. ' Order was restored to some extent, and the troops remained at the landing for the night. The next morning they crossed the lake, to the site of Fort William Henry.   Here the general employed them in preparing defences, while he sent his artillery and ammunition to Albany for safety, and even ordered them to be sent on to New York.

Thus disgracefully ended the expedition for which such elaborate preparations had been made, and from which so much had been expected.   The troops had fought with unflinching valor for four hours, and nothing but the blunders of the general was responsible for the failure.   The regulars bore the brunt of the battle, and more than four fifths of the loss fell upon them.   The Highlanders lost half their number.   These men belonged to clans which had always been faithful to the cause of the Stuarts, and disaffected toward a government which they still regarded as an usurpation ; but they had been formed into regiments by the keen-sighted policy of Pitt, and soon showed themselves to be among the most daring and effective soldiers that England could bring into the field. The Indians brought by Johnson took no part in the battle, remaining simply as spectators.

A letter from the Earl of Bute to Pitt, in regard to the battle, illustrates the value of the judgment passed at home upon the conduct of the generals: "I think this check, my dear Pitt," he wrote, "affects you too strongly. The general and the troops have done their duty, and appear, by the numbers lost, to have fought with the greatest intrepidity, to have tried all that men could do to force their way. The commander seems broken-hearted at being forced to a retreat."

CHAPTER XVII.

FRONTENAC AND DU QUESNE.

Skirmishes near Lake Champlain—Rogers and Putnam—Bradstreet's Expedition—Capture of Fort Frontenac—General Forbes in Pennsylvania—Grant's Defeat—Capture of Fort Du Quesne.

STRENGTHENING their intrenchments, and receiving reënforcements of three thousand Canadians under Rigaud de Vaudreuil, and six hundred Indians, the French employed the time after the battle in organizing and sending out detachments to surprise parties of the English, attack outlying settlements, and bring in prisoners, plunder, and scalps. The thousands of men lying at Lake George under Abercrombie seemed powerless to protect the country about them to the distance of twenty miles. On the 17th of July, a party of twenty men was cut off near Half-Way Brook. On the 27th, a detachment of five hundred Canadians and Indians made an attack near the same place on a convoy of fifty-four wagons. Sixteen prisoners, a hundred and ten scalps, and a large amount of plunder were the result.

Rogers was sent out with seven hundred men to intercept this party on the way back to the camp, but failed to find it, and was then directed to scour the country south and east of Lake Champlain. On the 8th of August, he was surprised by a force under a Canadian officer named Marin, and a sharp contest ensued. The French at first gained the advantage ; but the bravery of Rogers and his rangers soon turned the fight in their favor. Major Israel Putnam and twelve or fourteen others, being separated from the rest, were taken prisoners, and all but Putnam were murdered. He was tied to a tree after an Indian had struck him in the cheek with his tomahawk, and wood was piled about him and kindled ; but just then he was seen by Marin, who hurried to his rescue, took him from the hands of the savages, and carried him away a prisoner. A few months afterward he was exchanged.

About this time Fort Stanwix, afterward a post of considerable importance, was built by Brigadier-General Stanwix, on the site of the present village of Rome. It stood on the portage between the Mohawk River and Wood Creek, the only spot where the water communication between Schenectady and Oswego was interrupted ; being therefore on the highway between the Hudson and Lake Ontario, it was a post of military importance.

The only thing of consequence accomplished by any of the forces under Abercrombie was due to the bravery and sagacity of Bradstreet, who applied for permission to lead a detachment against Fort Frontenac. He had cherished for three years an ambition to take this fort, but had not succeeded in persuading his superiors that it was possible. A council of war now unwillingly gave him permission, and twenty-seven hundred provincials were placed under his command. They were met at Fort Stanwix by one hundred and fifty Iroquois, of whom forty-two, under the Onondaga chief, Red Head, joined the expedition. In attempting to pass down Wood Creek, Bradstreet was seriously hindered by the obstructions that General Webb had placed in it when he turned back from his tardy march to Oswego, after its surrender. The removal of the logs from the river involved a great deal of labor. Having embarked the artillery and stores, the army marched to Oneida Lake, and thence went by water to Oswego, where the large wooden cross was almost the only memorial they found of the struggle of two years before.

Embarking in open boats at Oswego, they crossed the lake and landed within a mile of Frontenac. This fort was a quadrangle, about one hundred yards square ; it had sixty guns and sixteen small mortars, thirty of the guns being mounted, and contained a large quantity of stores, some of which were to be sent to Fort Du Quesne and other western posts, and merchandise intended for the Indian trade. It was garrisoned by one hundred and ten men under an officer named De Noyan.

The commandant was warned of the threatened attack, and sent to the Governor of Canada for re-enforcements ; but none came before Bradstreet arrived. A French writer intimates that the Governor neglected to send them on account of personal dislike to the commandant of the fort. " He [the commandant] was a philosopher and a poet, and sometimes meddled with physic. His aim was to be a little spicy, which had gained him some enemies. Vaudreuil, who was not learned, detested him, although under some obligations to him. He was sixty-eight years old, and infirm, but at this advanced age retained all his spirit, and would have done honor to the post that had been given him, if he had had a large enough force."

Bradstreet planted a battery behind an epaulement of some old intrenchments, and opened fire. A breach was soon made, and the next morning the garrison surrendered. Besides the stores in the fort, the shipping on the lake, consisting of nine vessels of from eight to eighteen guns each, fell into

the hands of the victors.   Some of the vessels were
heavily laden with furs of great value.

Abercrombie had given strict orders that the fort
and stores should be destroyed, although there was
no apparent reason why it could not have been
held, and accordingly Bradstreet destroyed all the
artillery and stores, and all of the vessels but two,
which he sent to Oswego with the most valuable
part of the cargoes, and left the fort in ruins.   It
was afterward restored by the French.

After his success at Louisbourg, Amherst, hearing of Abercrombie's disaster, decided to go to New
York with a portion of his army, and do something
if possible to retrieve the defeat.   Landing at Boston in September, with five battalions, he went to
Lake George, held a conference with Abercrombie,
and, leaving the reënforcements, returned to Halifax to await orders from England.

The third expedition planned for the year—that
against Fort Du Quesne — was in command of
General Forbes, whose force consisted of twelve
hundred Highlanders, three hundred and fifty
Royal Americans, and nearly five thousand provincials of Pennsylvania and Virginia, with some
from South Carolina.   The Virginia regiments were
under the command of Washington, who was ordered
to Fort Cumberland, arrived with his troops on

the 2d of July, and at once began cutting a road to Raystown (now Bedford) in Pennsylvania, where Colonel Bouquet was stationed, awaiting the arrival of General Forbes.

It was decided not to take the army to Fort Du Quesne over the road already made, which had been followed by Braddock's army, but to open a new one through Pennsylvania from Raystown. Washington strongly opposed the waste of time ; but the Pennsylvanians were determined to have a route to the west through their own territory. Braddock's despatches had given the officers of the English army an idea that the road passed over by his men was extremely rugged and difficult, abounding in mountains, ravines, and torrents, so that the Pennsylvania traders had little difficulty in persuading them that it would be far better to take the proposed new route, which was fifty miles shorter, and, as they represented, less obstructed.

General Forbes arrived at Raystown with his army in September, having been two months on the way from Philadelphia. He was very ill, and was carried in a litter. Colonel Bouquet was sent forward to Loyal Hanna (now Ligonier), about forty-five miles from Raystown, with a detachment of two thousand men, where he formed a military post.

In August, intelligence had been received that the French had only eight hundred men at Du Quesne, including Indians.   But now four hundred more, under an officer named D'Aubry, had arrived from the west.   This was unknown to the English, and Colonel Bouquet resolved to attempt a brilliant achievement—the capture of the fort with his own men before the arrival of the main force.   Without the knowledge of General Forbes, he sent forward eight hundred men under Major Grant, some of whom were Highlanders, and some Virginia men from Washington's force, under Major Lewis. Washington had equipped them in light Indian hunting-dress, for greater expedition on the march.

Fort Du Quesne was fifty miles distant from Loyal Hanna.   Grant was instructed to reconnoitre the country around the fort, and gain all the information he could about the force of the enemy; but he was anxious, like his superior, to seize the glory of victory before Bouquet's men should be sent out ; and, moreover, he was ignorant, like most of the British officers, of Indian modes of warfare, and was confident of victory if he could bring the French to an open battle.

He placed his men on a hill that still bears his name, and sent out a party at night to reconnoitre the fort.   They set fire to a log house near the wall, and in the morning, the 14th of September, had the drums beaten in several places. The French, through their scouts, had long before learned of his approach, but kept perfectly quiet, even after this display of bravado. Grant then arranged his regulars in battle order, leaving Major Lewis behind with the provincials to protect the baggage, and sent an engineer with a guard to take a plan of the works in sight of the fort. Still there was no sign from the French ; but just as Grant began to think the garrison was overcome with fear, and would give up without striking a blow, there was a sudden sally of men under D'Aubry, who attacked his army in front, while countless Indians rose from ambush on both sides.

Grant and his Highlanders fought with great bravery ; but, as had happened with Braddock's men, they were thrown into confusion by the fire of the concealed Indians. Lewis came up with the greater part of the Virginians, who fought cour- ageously, but could not save the day. The Indians came out from their concealment when the English ranks were in hopeless confusion, and fought hand- to-hand with their tomahawks. Grant and Lewis were both taken prisoners, and the whole force was put to flight.

When Lewis went forward to the battle with the

main body of Virginians, he left Captain Bullitt
with fifty men to guard the baggage. Now, as the
panic-stricken fugitives fell back, pursued by the
triumphant savages, Bullitt, having sent the valuable
baggage still farther back, hastily threw up a barricade with the rest of the wagons, and rallied a few
of the flying soldiers behind it. When the Indians
drew near, a destructive fire was opened from the
barricade; many fell, and the rest were checked,
but more arrived, and they advanced to storm the
barricade, when Bullitt made a sign of surrender,
and advanced with his men until they were within
thirty feet of the enemy; then they suddenly
lowered their guns and fired a volley, and rushed
on with their bayonets. The Indians, in their turn,
were panic-stricken, and retreated, giving Bullitt a
chance to collect the scattered fugitives and retreat
to Loyal Hanna.

This rash movement cost Bouquet nearly three
hundred men, of whom twenty-one were officers.
The conduct of the Highlanders, and especially of
the Virginians, was highly applauded and publicly
acknowledged by General Forbes, and Bullitt was
rewarded with a major's commission.

Forbes reached Loyal Hanna with his army on the
5th of November, when a council of war was held,
and it was resolved not to proceed that year, since

the season was far advanced, the road yet lacked fifty miles of completion, and the Indians had deserted. But some prisoners who were taken and brought into camp gave information that led to a change of plan ; the garrison was weak and the provisions low, and the capture of Fort Frontenac by Bradstreet had cut off all hope of supplies.

The heavy baggage was left behind, and the army pushed forward, Washington leading the advance. The route was strewn with the dead bodies of Grant's men, and it is said that a row of stakes was found fixed in the ground, on each of which was displayed the head of a Highlander, and beneath it his kilts. When the Scotch regiment saw this, they broke into a low murmur of rage and fury, constantly increasing in volume and violence, as they rushed forward, breaking their ranks and brandishing their claymores, to take swift and terrible vengeance.

But vengeance was beyond their reach. As the army marched cautiously on, passing the bleaching bones of the unburied dead who had fallen three years before on Braddock's disastrous field, and on the 24th of November were within a day's march of Fort Du Quesne, they heard a heavy explosion from the direction of the fort, and saw smoke and flames rising into the air. The commandant, having no hope of a successful resistance, with only five hundred men and no provisions, had abandoned the fort, blown up the magazine, set fire to the buildings, and had his men on the way down the Ohio in boats. The next day, Washington's troops marched in and took possession of the ruined fort. The defences were put into the best possible condition, and Fort Du Quesne was re-named Fort Pitt, in honor of the English minister who had planned the campaign for the year, and to whose vigorous measures its successes had been largely due. The name survives in that of the city, Pittsburg, which has grown up around the spot where stood the old fort. The Indians submitted quietly to the new domination, and the English had at last gained a foothold west of the Alleghanies.

A curious story is told of the device of a Highlander, Allan Macpherson, to escape torture by his Indian captors. He and several companions had been captured near Fort Du Quesne, and he had witnessed the horrible tortures undergone by some of his comrades before the merciless savages would put them to death. He told an interpreter to tell them that he knew how to make a medicine from herbs which would render the skin proof against all kinds of weapons, and he offered to prove it at the risk of his own neck. The Indians eagerly consented, and, gathering a quantity of herbs, he made a decoction which he applied to his neck ; then laying his head on a block, he challenged them to strike. One of the strongest warriors came forward and dealt a mighty blow. Not until they saw his head flying from his shoulders did the savages suspect Macpherson's design ; and it is said they were so pleased at the Highlander's cunning that they remitted the tortures intended for the rest of his companions.

CHAPTER XVIII.

NIAGARA AND LAKE CHAMPLAIN.

Plan of Operations for the Year—Weakness of the French—Siege and Capture of Fort Niagara—Death of Prideaux—Western Forts Occupied by the English—Attack at Oswego—Inaction of General Gage—Amherst at Ticonderoga and Crown Point—Operations on the Lake—Punishment of the St. Francis Indians—Adventures of Rogers.

FOR the campaign of 1759, the British Parliament voted liberal supplies of men and money, and the American colonies, encouraged by the successes of the preceding year, raised large numbers of troops. Amherst superseded Abercrombie as commander-in-chief. The plan for the year embraced three expeditions: Fort Niagara was to be attacked by Prideaux, assisted by Sir William Johnson; Amherst was to march his force against Ticonderoga and Crown Point; and Quebec was to be assailed by an army under Wolfe and a fleet under Saunders. Prideaux and Amherst, after the capture of the forts, were to descend the St. Lawrence, take Montreal, and join the army before Quebec.

At this time Canada was much weakened; its resources were nearly exhausted, and the French

Government, absorbed with the war in Europe, sent but scanty assistance. The occupation of Louisbourg by the English rendered it difficult for ships to ascend the St. Lawrence; a large amount of stores had been destroyed at Fort Frontenac, the French reverses had cooled the ardor of the Indians, and Canada had not a strong reserve force in its colonists, as had the British provinces. There were not over fifteen thousand Canadians able to bear arms, and the French soldiers in the country numbered but little more than three thousand. To add to the distresses of the Canadians, they had been plundered by traders and contractors. It is said that the worst swindling was in the interest of a company which operated under the name of one of its agents, Cadet. Having the contract to furnish the army with provisions, they collected all the worn-out horses in the country, and served them up to the starving soldiers; and from this, whenever the men saw a jaded skeleton of a horse, they called him "a cadet."

Vaudreuil, the Governor, having received warning from France of the intentions of the English, sent a small force to Niagara under the engineer Pouchot, not expecting to be able to hold the post, and not wishing to sacrifice many men, or to spare the troops from the more important points. Pouchot repaired the defences, and when the alarm was given that the

English were near, sent for men from Presqu' Isle, Venango, and Detroit.

Prideaux, in command of two British regiments, a battalion of Royal Americans, two battalions from New York, and a train of artillery, was joined by Johnson with a detachment of Indians. They began their march from Schenectady on the 20th of May, and, after a difficult journey, reached Oswego, where a detachment under Colonel Haldimand was left to take possession and form a post, and the remainder of the force embarked on Lake Ontario, and on the 1st of July landed without opposition about six miles east of the mouth of the Niagara.

The fort was on a narrow promontory between the lake and the river. Prideaux made preparations to invest it by planting batteries on the land side, while his boats cut off the approach by water. To a summons on the 8th to surrender, Pouchot answered that the King had entrusted him with the place ; that he was in condition to defend it ; and that if General Prideaux were ever to enter it, he should at least gain his esteem by a courageous defence, before making any terms with him.

Prideaux began his trenches on the 10th, and on the 11th a sally was made from the fort ; but the English placed themselves in line of battle, and the French were obliged to retire. Prideaux was steadily advancing the work, opening trenches and placing batteries, when, on the 19th, he was killed by the bursting of a shell from a Coehorn mortar in one of the trenches, where he had gone to issue orders. Amherst appointed General Gage to succeed him, but before the arrival of Gage the command devolved upon General Johnson, who carried on the siege according to the plans of Prideaux.

On the 23d, Pouchot, receiving intelligence that about sixteen hundred French and Indians were on the way to his relief under D'Aubry and De Lignery, sent word that if they did not feel strong enough to attack the enemy, who were four or five thousand strong, they should approach on the other side of the river, where the English were only two hundred strong, and could not easily be reënforced. After driving them back, they could reach the fort by bateaux which would be sent over to them.

The besieged then awaited anxiously the approach of the reënforcement, on which all their hopes depended. The defences were steadily giving way under the heavy fire from the batteries, and the garrison were picked off by the marksmen in the trenches. Johnson had placed his main army above the fort to intercept the approach from the south. On the 24th, being informed by scouts that the force of French and Indians under D'Aubry and De

Lignery was approaching, he detached a force of grenadiers and light infantry and some Mohawks under Colonel Massey, to meet them. A regiment under Colonel Farquhar was placed midway between them and the fort, ready to assist the advance, or go to the aid of the besieged in the event of a sally.

The Mohawks advanced and gave the signal for a parley with De Lignery's Indians; but as it was not answered, they fell back and took their station on the flanks of the British regiments. D'Aubry formed his men, and gave the order for attack. His Indians attempted to break up the English ranks by the tactics which had succeeded at Braddock's defeat; but the grenadiers scattered them with a few volleys, ar 1 they disappeared so suddenly that the French believed they had previously agreed to desert.

D'Aubry led on his men to attack the English front, but the Mohawks threw themselves on the flanks of the French army, and plunged them into disorder, while the English made an impetuous charge. The French fought desperately for about half an hour, when they were broken and completely routed. They fled through the woods, and were pursued by the victorious army. Many were slain, and a few escaped; the remainder were captured, D'Aubry and sixteen other officers being among the prisoners.

The firing had been heard at the fort in the morning, and the besieged had anxiously awaited the event of the battle which was to decide the fate of the fort. At first the rattle of musketry seemed to be drawing near, and the beleaguered garrison believed the English were driven before the relieving force. Then the noise of the firing fluctuated, sometimes nearer the fort and again farther away and fainter. At length it receded rapidly, grew fainter, and ceased. Then the garrison knew that their reënforcements had been driven back; but how disastrously they were defeated, they did not know till an Onondaga Indian, who had asked leave to go out from the fort to fight with them, returned with great difficulty through the lines of the besiegers at two o'clock, and reported that the survivors had all been put to flight, and every officer was either killed or captured.

At four o'clock Sir William Johnson sent Major Harvey to inform Pouchot of the result of the battle, and ask him to surrender without more bloodshed. Pouchot professed to doubt the report, and sent one of his officers with Major Harvey to see if D'Aubry and his subordinates were really in the hands of the enemy. On their report, the garrison became disorderly, and ready to abandon everything in confusion, and it was with difficulty that Pouchot restrained them until the terms of capitulation were arranged. They marched out with the honors of war, on the 25th, and laid down their arms on the shore of the lake. They were in great fear of the Indians, remembering the scene at Fort William Henry ; but Johnson kept his word that they should not be molested, and restrained the savages from any assault on the conquered garrison.

As the stations beyond Niagara were now completely cut off from communication with the east, and had given up a large part of their men to join D'Aubry, they were no longer capable of resistance. Presqu' Isle, Venango, and Le Bœuf were easily taken by Colonel Bouquet, who had been sent to summon them to surrender.

Colonel Haldimand had been left at Oswego with five or six hundred men. They had not had time to intrench themselves fully, but had formed a sort of wall about their camp with the barrels of pork and flour that had been provided and stored there in great profusion, when De la Corne came down from La Presentation (Ogdensburg) with five or six hundred Canadians and a large body of Indians, accompanied by the zealous Abbé Picquet, founder of the mission at that point.

Haldimand's men, having no apprehension of

danger, were scattered through the woods, cutting trees for their intrenchments, when they were fired upon by De la Corne's scouts, who then pressed on to the camp.   What followed is related by a French writer who was present :

" If De la Corne had followed his advance-guard, the English would have lost everything.   But the Abbé Picquet, who heard the beginning of the firing, thought it was his duty, before his troops should attack, to make a short exhortation and give them absolution.   This led to the loss of their opportunity ; and the English ran to arms and placed themselves behind the barrels.

" De la Corne arrived after his detachment, who were scattered around the English, but did not approach nearer, on account of their superiority.   He wished to have them renew the attack, but some Canadians, who would rather retreat than fight, cried out that the blow had failed, and, in spite of their officers, regained their boats as soon as possible.   The Abbé Picquet, who tried to rally them, was thrown down, when he caught hold of one and called out, ' Save at least your chaplain ! '   We sustained but a small loss, as the English did not pursue.   Had this body been defeated, Niagara might have been saved, for their army could not have received the troops and supplies."

The English lost only two killed and eleven wounded. The French commandant at Toronto set fire to his buildings and took his small garrison to Montreal, as soon as he heard of the fall of Niagara.

Fearing the army from Niagara would next be marched on Montreal, Vaudreuil sent De Levis up the river to guard the approach to that city from the lake. He took possession of Oswegatchie, or Ogdensburg, to defend the passes of the St. Lawrence, but had only few men. Amherst ordered General Gage to go and get possession of that important post. But Gage found difficulties and made excuses until the season was so far advanced that it was impossible. He had been appointed to succeed Prideaux, but did not reach Niagara until after Johnson had taken the fort. He was afterward, in 1763, appointed commander-in-chief of the British forces in America, and was royal Governor of Massachusetts when the Revolutionary War broke out.

For the reduction of the forts at Ticonderoga and Crown Point, Amherst had somewhat more than eleven thousand men. He began preparations early in May at Albany, preparing boats, gathering stores, and disciplining the new recruits. He sent Major West with a detachment to build a small

stockade fort between Fort Edward and Lake
George, and in June his army was slowly moved on
to encampments near Fort Edward.

On the 21st of June, the general marched six
thousand troops to the border of the lake, and
traced the plan of a fort on the spot where Fort
William Henry had stood. The remainder of the
troops and the boats were now brought up ; but the
embarkation did not take place until the 21st of
July ; but in the interval, the sloop *Halifax* and a
floating battery of eight guns which had been sunk
the previous year, were raised from the lake and
prepared for service.

The army moved down the lake in four columns,
in a fleet of whale-boats, bateaux, and artillery-
rafts, very much as Abercrombie's men had gone to
their defeat the year before, and left the boats
nearly opposite the former landing-place. The
vanguard, pushing on rapidly over the road to the
falls, met a detachment of French and Indians,
whom they overpowered and scattered after a slight
skirmish, and the main body pressed on and took a
position at the saw-mills. From prisoners it was
learned that Bourlamaque commanded at Ticonderoga with thirty-four hundred men. Montcalm
was at Quebec.

The next morning, Amherst prepared to attack

where the British army had suffered defeat in 1758. But the French, conscious of their inability to defend the lines against so overwhelming a force, abandoned them, and withdrew into the fort, while the lines were taken possession of by the grenadiers, and the remainder of the army encamped in the rear.

In the centre they found a lofty cross surmounting a grave, and on the cross a plate of brass with the inscription :

Pone principes eorum sicut Oreb et Zebec et Zalmanna.

"Make their nobles like Oreb and Zebah and Zalmunna ;"— a quotation from the eighty-third psalm.

The French kept up a fire through the 23d, which fell harmless on the well-protected lines. Bourlamaque, then, seeing the uselessness of a defence, silently withdrew most of his men in the night, leaving four hundred to keep up the firing and conceal the retreat of their comrades. During the two following days, they maintained a vigorous fire, doing some damage to the British, who were advancing their lines toward the fort ; then they too abandoned the place, having first loaded and aimed the guns, charged some mines, and placed a lighted fuse to the powder magazine.

An explosion and the light of the burning works assured the English of the retreat of the French, of which they had already heard from a deserter, and Colonel Haviland pursued them down the lake with a few troops, and took sixteen prisoners and some boats laden with powder. At daybreak, a sergeant volunteered to enter the burning fort, and raise the English flag in place of the white banner of France.

After the flames were extinguished, Amherst, who had lost about seventy-five men, went to work to repair the fortifications and complete the road from the lake. Some sunken French boats were raised, and a brig was built. Amherst was slowly preparing to attack Crown Point, and sent Rogers with his rangers to reconnoitre. But on the 1st of August they learned that the French had abandoned that fort also; and on the 16th that Bourlamaque's men were encamped on the Isle aux Noix, at the northern extremity of Lake Champlain, commanding the entrance to the Richelieu. They had been joined by some small detachments, and numbered about thirty-five hundred men.

Amherst spent his time fortifying Crown Point, and building boats and rafts, and on the 11th of October he had the brig from Ticonderoga, a raft for artillery, and a new sloop ready to sail, and em-

barked his troops.   One boat with twenty-one men
was captured ; and with this prize the French vessels disappeared, and carefully avoided an action.
Three of them, chased by Amherst's vessels under
Captain Loring, were so hard pressed that the crews
ran one aground and sank the others.   But a storm
with contrary winds kept back the English vessels.
It was too late to descend to Montreal and go to the
help of Wolfe ; the time for that had been passed
in elaborate and useless preparations.

The repair of the forts, if not unnecessary, was
not at all pressing.   It was not probable that the
French with their exhausted army would very soon
attempt to recover the forts on Lake Champlain ; if
the English were to conquer and keep Canada, they
would be of no use ; if another campaign had still
to be fought, there would be time enough to
fortify.   The immediate and pressing need was, to
sustain Wolfe.

Amherst was very fortunate in his enterprises ; he
had overwhelming numbers and an exhausted foe,
so that his generalship was not put to any severe
test.   He was cautious to excess, slow and sure in
what he attempted ; the trouble was, that he did
not attempt enough.   With the help of the great
army lying useless at Lake Champlain, Wolfe's
victory might possibly have been more speedy,

and would almost certainly have closed the struggle.

In September, General Amherst sent Captain
Kennedy with a flag of truce to offer peace and
friendship to the St. Francis Indians, living at the
lake of that name.   These Indians were steadfast
friends of the French, and had long harassed the
frontier settlements of New England.   Rogers says
that, to his own knowledge, they had killed or carried
off four hundred persons within six years.   They
kept Captain Kennedy and his whole escort as
prisoners, and sent no answer to the message.

Amherst then sent Robert Rogers with two hundred men to attack their settlements. with orders
to take complete vengeance on the warriors for
their cowardly attacks on defenceless settlements,
but by no means to injure any women or children.

St. Francis is within three miles of the St.
Lawrence, and about midway between Montreal
and Quebec.   The route lay through an almost unbroken forest.   " We marched," says Rogers in his
journal, " nine days through wet, sunken ground,
the water most of the way near a foot deep ; it
being a spruce bog.   When we encamped at night,
we had no way to secure ourselves from the water
but by cutting the boughs of trees, and with them
erecting a kind of hammocks."   It was twenty-two

days before they came in sight of the Indian town, and the party was by that time reduced one fourth through the hardships and accidents of the march.

In the evening, Rogers reconnoitred the town. The warriors were holding a feast, dancing, singing, and carousing. Waiting till they had lain down to sleep, at three o'clock in the morning, Rogers marched his men within five hundred yards of the village, where they laid aside their baggage and made ready for the attack.

Just before sunrise he gave the order, and his men burst into the sleeping town. The Indians, who had gone to sleep without placing sentinels, were completely surprised. Bewildered with their excesses and the sudden awakening, they could make no resistance. Many were slain in their sleep, others struck down as they were attempting to fly. Some reached the river and embarked in canoes; but they were pursued, and the boats were sunk. Some concealed themselves in the cellars and lofts of their houses, and were consumed in the flames when the town was fired. By seven o'clock in the morning the ruin was complete. All the houses were burned but three, which were saved because they were stored with corn, that Rogers needed for his men. Two hundred Indians had been killed, and twenty women and children were made prisoners, of whom all but five were released. Rogers had lost but one friendly Indian killed, and a captain and six privates wounded.

He was now, however, in a very dangerous position, for he learned that there was a party of three hundred Frenchmen with some Indians below him on the river, that his boats had been taken, and that a smaller force was lying in wait for him farther up the stream. There seemed to be no way to extricate his men from this peril except by following the upper branches of the Connecticut, and descending that river to Fort Number Four. The route was rugged and difficult, and they were poorly supplied with provisions.

They had marched eight days, and their food was nearly exhausted, when Rogers divided them into small companies to take different routes and sustain themselves on the way as best they could. All were to meet at the mouth of the Ammonoosuc, where provisions were expected ; but when Rogers's own party reached the place, they were not there. Rogers, with three others, embarked on a pine raft and dropped down to Fort Number Four, whence he speedily sent food to the starving men above. One party lost the way, and was four days without food ; some died, and some lost their reason ; the remnant, after devouring their leather straps and

the covers of their cartridge-boxes, found a few
roots that kept them alive until they reached the
Connecticut and met one of the supply-boats sent
by Rogers.

CHAPTER XIX.

THE SIEGE OF QUEBEC.

Situation of the City—Sailing of the English Fleet—Officers and
Forces of the English—Advance of Durell—Mistake of the French
—First Blow—Passage up the River—Skirmish with Peasants—
Attempts to Fire the Fleet—Incidents of the Siege—Occupation
of the East Bank of the Montmorenci by the English — The
Scholars' Battle—Firing of the City—Passage of Ships by the
Town—Battle of Montmorenci.

To watch for and signal the approach of the
British fleet which was hourly expected at Quebec,
three stations were chosen by the French : the first
at Isle du Portage, the second on a height near Ka-
mouraska, and the third on the Isle of Orleans.

On the east, and partially on the south of the
promontory on which the city is built, sweeps the
deep and rapid current of the St. Lawrence, at the
north is the embouchure of the St. Charles, and
slightly to the west a sudden curve of the same
stream. The promontory is very steep along the
St. Lawrence, and may be described as a bluff vary-
ing in height from one hundred and sixty to three
hundred feet. In that direction nature seemed to
have anticipated the work of the military engineer.
The Lower Town, at the foot of the cliff, was defend-

ed by batteries on the quays; and the avenues leading from the river were barricaded. The communication between the Lower Town and the Upper Town
was secured by a strong picketing, and commanded
by a battery.

To prevent the approach of the enemy from the
valley of the St. Charles, it was determined to close
the entry to that stream. At a point opposite the
gate of the bishop's palace, a boom was run across,
consisting of logs chained together and kept in place
by anchors. Above this boom three merchant vessels were sunk; and on a platform built upon them
was placed a battery of heavy guns, commanding
the entire bay. In front of the boom five barges
were set, each armed with a cannon. On the left
bank was placed a battery of four guns to protect
the whole. Farther up, near the Charlesbourg road,
a bridge of boats was thrown across the St. Charles,
and defended at each end by a horn-work.

On the city side, a line of intrenchments, with
artillery, ran from the bridge to the palace gate.
From the opposite bank of the St. Charles, the
northern shore of the St. Lawrence, to the mouth of
the Montmorenci, eight miles below, was intrenched
and at all accessible points fortified, the line being
continued for a short distance along the right bank
of the Montmorenci.

On the landward side, the defence of the city was not formidable, consisting only of a rampart of moderate height, with neither parapet nor embrasures, and unprotected by fosse or glacis. For nine miles above the city, every apparently accessible point was intrenched and guarded ; among others the spot then called the Anse du Foulon (the fuller's bay), but now known as Wolfe's Cove.

There were gathered for the defence of Quebec about thirteen thousand men, of whom only six worn battalions were French regulars, the rest being raw Canadian militia ; so that the generous Wolfe afterward hesitated to call such a force an army. A council of war was held toward the close of May, when the order of battle was issued and general regulations given for the conduct of the campaign.

Vauquelin was made commander of the bay, with authority over craft of all kinds. The army occupied its intrenched camp from the redoubt on the left bank of the St. Charles to a point on the Montmorenci above the great falls. The right, consisting of the brigades of Quebec and Three Rivers under St. Ours and De Borne, forty-four hundred and twenty men in all, was placed along the plain to the river Beauport. The centre consisted of the regulars, two thousand strong, under Senezergues, and the Montreal militia, eleven hundred and fifty strong.

under Prudhomme, and was placed on the heights of Beauport. The brigade of the Island of Montreal, under Herbin, twenty-three hundred strong, formed the left, and was placed along the high ridge down the St. Lawrence. A reserve force of three hundred and fifty cavalry, fourteen hundred volunteers of Canada and Acadia, and four hundred and fifty Indians, under Boishebert, stretched down to the Montmorenci and along its right bank. The artillery was under the command of Mercier, and the militia of the city was left as a garrison under the king's lieutenant, De Ramsay.

It was the opinion of the French commander that no attack would be made directly on the town from the river front, but that an attempt would be made to pierce his extended lines somewhere between the Montmorenci and Beauport River, and possibly between the latter and the left bank of the St. Charles. For the event of a successful assault in either neighborhood — and Montcalm was by no means overconfident — lines of retreat were carefully marked out, all arranged with the general design of swinging the army back behind the St. Charles as a new line of defence, with the right on the city fortifications, and the left extended as far as possible.

That the authorities were not sanguine, is clear from the final sentence of their instructions : " It · is incumbent on us to exert our most strenuous efforts to defend and preserve Quebec, or at least to retard the reduction of it as long as possible, because it is evident that the fate of the colony will depend entirely on that of its capital."

These precautions were taken in good time. In the middle of February, a powerful squadron set sail from England, under command of Admiral Saunders, described by Walpole as "a pattern of most sturdy bravery united with the most unaffected modesty." With him sailed General James Wolfe, chosen to command the expedition to Quebec. The fleet arrived off Louisbourg on the 21st of April, but the port was blocked with ice, and the squadron rendezvoused at Halifax, and proceeded to Louisbourg a few days later. The naval force consisted of twenty-two ships of the line, five frigates, and nineteen smaller war-vessels, together with a crowd of transports, on which the land forces were embarked on the 1st of June. These were divided into three brigades, under command of Generals Monckton, Townshend, and Murray, all in the prime of manhood, eager for personal glory and zealous in the service of their country.

Colonel Guy Carleton, afterward Lord Dorchester, was quartermaster-general, Major Isaac Barré was adjutant-general, and Richard Montgomery was

among the captains.   The whole military force is
commonly estimated at something more than eight
thousand men, though some French writers put its
strength at eleven thousand.   It might be described
as a corps of picked men ; braver or better disciplined troops have seldom embarked in a more
hazardous enterprise, or been more ably commanded.

Admiral Durell was sent forward with the van, in
the hope that he would intercept a squadron of
supply-ships from France, but was too late.   The
whole fleet got under way by June 4th and joined
Durell on the 23d, at Isle aux Coudres.   It is said
that as the vessels of the latter hove in sight at this
point on their way up the river, they were flying the
French flag ; and the watchers at the signal-stations,
seeing the welcome ensign, despatched hasty ex-
presses to Quebec to announce that succor was at
hand.   But after pilots had put off to the ships in
canoes, the white colors were struck, and the Union
Jack run up in their place, to the dismay of the
Canadians along the shore.   A priest who saw the
change through a glass dropped dead at the sight,
from the sudden revulsion of feeling.   On the 26th
the squadron anchored off the Isle of Orleans.

The passage up the river had been unusually
fortunate, and surprised the French greatly, since

they had taken pains to remove the buoys from the channel, and expected that the heavy ships of the line would run aground at various difficult points. The rapidity of the passage was long explained by the fact that charts of the St. Lawrence had been found in one of two French vessels captured by Admiral Durell near the mouth of the river; but French authorities assert that a certain Denis de Vitré, captain of a French frigate taken during the war, consented to pilot the fleet to Quebec for a commission in the British navy.

During the night of the 26th forty rangers landed on the island, and, pushing cautiously into the interior, came upon a party of armed peasants, engaged in burying their valuables. There was a hasty skirmish, in which both parties were badly frightened; a fight in the woods at midnight between a band of marauders and a party of men concealing their treasures being by no means a cheerful kind of encounter.

The next day troops were landed, debarking at a cove under the Church of St. Lawrence, on the walls of which was a placard asking "the worthy officers of the British army" that the place might be spared. Wolfe probably pushed on at once to the point of the island nearest Quebec.

Above the island, and nearly opposite the city,

lay Point Levi, the only unprotected spot within easy reach of the invaders.   Montcalm had urged in the council of war that it should be fortified and garrisoned with four thousand troops, but his opinion was overruled by the Governor-General. Wolfe instantly chose it as an available point from which to attack Quebec, though it was said to be held by a strong detachment, and he also selected the spot on which he stood as the site of fortifications to cover the hospitals and army-stores, which might find perfect security in that beautiful island with the fleet at anchor in front.

The day had been stormy, but the evening came on clear though dark ; and the French chose it for their first attempt to burn the English fleet.   They put fire-ships afloat with the ebbing tide, each laden with grenades, shells, useless muskets loaded to the muzzle, and tar-barrels.   As they were swept in the direction of the transports, the flames broke out among them and spread rapidly and fiercely, to the accompaniment of a random fusillade.   A panic arose among the soldiers on the beach, for the unaccustomed character of the danger terrified them ; but the sailors were cool, and ready with a remedy.   Well-manned boats set out, and, after waiting for the subsidence of the irregular firing, pushed on and grappled the fire-ships, turning them ashore, where they burned harmlessly away, and served as a cheerful illumination to the warlike scene.

On the morning of the 28th, Wolfe issued a proclamation to the inhabitants of Canada. He set forth the determination of the English king to deprive France of her American settlements; enumerated the advantages of Great Britain in the struggle; alluded to the cruelties practised by the French on the English colonies, as justifying severe reprisals, but promised the most considerate treatment if the Canadians would accept the protection of England, and abandon France, which had practically abandoned them. Speaking in the name of his master, he said : "It is not against the industrious peasants, their wives and children, nor against the ministers of religion, that he designs making war. He laments the misfortunes to which this quarrel exposes them, and promises them his protection, offers to maintain them in their possessions and permit them to follow the worship of their religion, provided that they do not take any part in the differences between the two crowns, directly or indirectly."

Of course all these fair promises were worthless, for the conditions on which they were made were not such as the Canadians were very likely to comply with. As a natural consequence, the struggle was destined to degenerate into a cruel and bloody one at all points save the regular field of battle, where it was bloody without being unnecessarily cruel.

On the night of the 29th of June, Monckton, to whom the movement against Point Levi was entrusted, sent over a detachment which took possession of Beaumont Church and barricaded it. Early in the morning more men passed over, and before evening the British troops had possession of the pretty village of Point Levi. The opposition amounted to nothing more than skirmishing, as the force in possession of the position was neither strong enough nor skilful enough to make · an obstinate defence, though the nature of the ground was favorable to it.

During the morning occurred one of those tragedies that exhibit the brutality of war. A party of rangers had pushed forward from Beaumont Church to reconnoitre, and had taken possession of a large and fine, but apparently deserted, farm-house. The soldiers heard the sound of voices, and, after a hasty search, set fire to the buildings and fell back, but were recalled by the shrieks of women and children who had hidden in the cellar and were perishing in the flames. We are told that they worked gallantly though ineffectively to rescue their victims, and it would be pleasant to believe the best ; but so many strange things happened during the campaign that the historian grows weary of trying to explain away atrocities.

On the morning of July 1st, the French pushed over their floating batteries to attack the post at Point Levi, but the frigate *Trent* interposed, and easily drove them off. Monckton's and Townshend's men were set at work on the heights opposite Quebec and on the western end of the island, raising fortifications and planting batteries ; and by the 9th everything was ready for action at those places.

In the mean while, scouting and skirmishing went on constantly. Major Scott pushed up along the right bank of the St. Lawrence as far as the Chaudière, but to no purpose. On one occasion, about twenty of the command, under a lieutenant, coming across a man and his three sons in a log hut, dragged them off out of pure wantonness, though two of the boys were mere children. The man and the oldest boy, a lad of fifteen, went quietly enough, but the frightened children screamed convulsively ; and the scouting-party grew alarmed lest the screams should attract pursuit. It is said that they actually saw a band of Indians on their trail and heard the war-whoop ringing through the woods. They endeavored to calm the children, but the poor things screamed the louder ; then they tried to cast them off in the woods, but they clung to their captors all the tighter ; and, as a last resource, to silence their hysterical sobs, the soldiers murdered them.

With his supplies in safety and a point secured from which an active bombardment could be maintained against the city, Wolfe began his first effort to break the enemy's lines. Under cover of the fleet, which swung into place on the 9th of July, and commanded the French position along the river below the city, Wolfe moved the bulk of his army, under Townshend and Murray, to the north bank of the St. Lawrence, just below the mouth of the Montmorenci. The east or left bank of this stream is higher than the opposite one ; and along these heights the British troops encamped, facing the left of the French line, with nothing but the river intervening. Artillery was placed in position, and the men were ordered to intrench.

On the morning of the 10th, Captain Dank's company of rangers, which had been sent into the woods to protect men engaged in making fascines, was suddenly attacked by Indians, and nearly destroyed. The action took place so close to the lines that the men who rushed to the rescue could actually see the savages scalping their dead comrades and murdering the wounded.

Wolfe reconnoitred the Montmorenci upward in the hope of finding a crossing that he might force, and so turn the left of the French position, but without success. There were two Indian attacks on the reconnoitring party, but they were easily repulsed, though not without the loss of forty officers and men.

It was found that the only pathway to the French lines on the Montmorenci side lay through the ford below the falls, which was practicable at low tide, and might be covered by the fire of the batteries on the heights above, and of such light-draught vessels as could get close to the shore. The prospect for an attack at this point was so unpromising, that Wolfe waited until he should have studied other points before he determined to strike there. It is said that Montcalm, when urged by De Levis to attempt to dislodge his enemy, remarked : " While there, he cannot hurt us. Let him amuse himself."

Meanwhile, on the night of the 12th of July, a body of sixteen hundred French, under Dumas, crossed the St. Lawrence above the city and set out for Point Levi, doubtless with the expectation of finding it held by a weak force. The French marched in two columns. and, in the excitement of the night movement, the rear body mistook that in front for the enemy, and poured a volley into it, which was promptly returned. There was an instant panic, and both parties set cff in the wildest disorder for the boats, reaching the beach in time to recross the river early in the morning of the 13th, with a loss of seventy killed and wounded. Wolfe regretted that they got away without making an attack and giving him an opportunity to defeat them. This affair is known among Canadians as "The Scholars' Battle," because the firing was begun by some of the boys from the city schools, who were in the ranks.

A lively bombardment of the city followed, which was especially effective from the Point Levi batteries, and on the 16th the town was set on fire. The firing was renewed at intervals, and four times the city was in flames. To sum up at once the results of weeks of cannonading, it may be said, in the words of Wolfe himself, that the Upper Town was considerably damaged, and the Lower Town entirely destroyed. The destruction fell heaviest upon the church and private individuals ; the cathedral and most of the finest residences were in ruins within a month. Of course all this was useless, except in so far as it kept up the appearance of activity on the part of the besiegers. It did not at all affect the military strength of the place.

On the night of the 18th of July occurred one of the most significant events of the expedition. Two men-of-war, two armed sloops, and two transports filled with troops, the whole under the command of Captain Rous, ran up the river past the town, escaping without injury, as the French failed to notice them in time to bring their guns to bear ; and the next day two hapless sentinels who were held responsible were hanged in sight of both armies. A battery in position at Sillery dropped a few shots among the English vessels and made them move on up the river, and the gunners of the city, grown unusually vigilant, struck the mast out of Wolfe's barge, which was skirting the southern shore to join the ships that had run the gauntlet.

The passage of the forts opened up the whole river, and rendered the English masters of the stream above and below. But the first fruits of the achievement were not promising. '' This enabled me,'' said Wolfe in his report to Pitt, '' to reconnoitre the country above, where I found the same attention on the enemy's side, and great difficulties on ours, arising from the nature of the ground, and the obstacles to our communication with the fleet. But what I feared most was, that if he should land between the town and the River Cape Rouge, the body first landed could not be reënforced before they were attacked by the enemy's whole army.''

He thought of landing three miles above the

town, but the enemy brought cannon and a mortar to
play on the shipping. '' And,'' to use his own words,
'' as it must have been many hours before we could
attack them—even supposing a favorable night for
the boats to pass by the town unhurt—it seemed so
hazardous that I thought best to desist.''

Merely to divert the attention of the enemy,
Wolfe sent Colonel Carleton up the river with the
troops that had already passed the town. On the
22d he landed at Point aux Trembles, dispersed a
party of Indians, captured a few civilians, and procured correspondence, which plainly showed that
the people in Quebec were hungry and disheartened,
and almost as disgusted with the defence as the
English were with the attack.

Wolfe returned to the position on the Montmorenci after his trip above the town, convinced
that he would have to make an attempt to break
into Montcalm's intrenched camp somewhere between the St. Charles and the Montmorenci. '' I
now resolved,'' he says, '' to take the first opportunity which presented itself of attacking the enemy,
though posted to great advantage and everywhere
prepared to receive us.'' If he was somewhat
daunted at the prospect, it is probable that there
was much discontent and discouragement throughout the expedition. Indeed, there are extant let-

ters written to the Governor of Nova Scotia by a
minister who accompanied the expedition, express-
ing the greatest contempt for the capacity of the
commander-in-chief, and repeating the criticisms on
his conduct which were current on shipboard.

But the young general was not the man to give
up an enterprise merely because it looked desperate.
On the shore of the St. Lawrence, near the mouth
of the Montmorenci, was a detached redoubt, apparently out of reach of musketry from the hill
and Wolfe determined to make this the key of al
attack. His design was to seize it ; then, if the
French disputed its possession, a general engagement would be brought on, which was what he
aimed at. If they gave it up without a struggle, it
might afford a point from which to reconnoitre their
lines in security.

As the water shoaled along the northern shore so
that the men-of-war could not get into position to
bring their guns to bear, the admiral armed two
light-draught transports which might be run aground
to cover a descent on the redoubt, and the frigate
Centurion was brought close to the mouth of the
Montmorenci to cover the ford below the falls.
The artillery on the height along the left bank of
that stream was placed in position to enfilade the
left of the enemy's intrenchments.

The plan of action was, to put a part of Monckton's brigade from Point Levi, and the grenadiers of the army, on the boats, and make a dash for the redoubt ; while the brigades of Townshend and Murray were to be ready to march from their camp on the left bank of the Montmorenci, and cross the ford in support of their comrades.

At ten o'clock in the forenoon of July 31st, the 15th and 78th regiments of Monckton's brigade, thirteen companies of grenadiers, and two hundred Royal Americans, embarked in small boats, and the flotilla moved into the northern channel of the St. Lawrence. The two armed transports, Wolfe being on one of them, were run aground at about eleven o'clock ; and the cannon from those vessels, from the *Centurion*, and from all the fleet, from the heights of Montmorenci and from Point Levi, opened fire, every available gun in the circle of the British position about Quebec joining in the chorus.

Close inspection showed Wolfe that the detached redoubt was really covered by fire from the French lines, and that musketry from the grounded vessels would be of no avail in helping the attack. This was a disappointment ; but he was not to be diverted from his purpose. Some delay was occasioned by a feint on the left of the French line, which looked like a movement to cross the Montmorenci above the falls, and make a counter attack ; but this was checked by a display of the 48th regiment in motion beyond Point Levi, which caused Montcalm to send two battalions to guard against a crossing above the town.

It was four o'clock in the afternoon when Wolfe signalled for a renewal of the cannonade, and at five he ran up a red flag at the mizzen peak of one of the stranded transports, as the sign to advance. The flotilla dashed forward with a will, and the troops of Townshend and Murray set out for the ford. The French met the advance of the boats with a lively shower of shot and shell, which, however, did little damage ; but the advance was checked by a reef running out from the shore, on which many of the small craft ran aground ; and, as a consequence, the whole flotilla of fifteen hundred boats was thrown into confusion.

Order was soon restored, and the general and several naval officers took a flat-bottomed boat, and examined the shore for a landing-place, signalling in the mean time for Townshend to halt. An opening in the reef was found in the course of half an hour, and the flotilla was put in motion once more. The grenadiers and Royal Americans were first on shore. The orders were for the grenadiers to form in four divisions, wait for the landing of Monckton's troops and the approach of Townshend to within supporting distance, and then attack.

But they attacked without waiting or forming— "ran on," to use Wolfe's words, "toward the enemy's intrenchments in the utmost disorder and confusion." This excess of valor and lack of steadiness was fatal. The French had abandoned the detached redoubt, and the mass of grenadiers pushed boldly up the slope at the intrenchments. It was an assault which would have been useless, even if successful, as Monckton had not landed, and Townshend and Murray were not within reach ; but it was not destined to succeed. The Canadians received the grenadiers with a close and effective fire, which not only checked their advance, but drove them back in dismay, leaving some scores of scarlet-clad bodies along the green hill-side.

The grenadiers sought shelter behind the abandoned redoubt, while their officers exposed themselves to no purpose, in the endeavor to re-form them under fire. "I saw," says Wolfe, "the absolute necessity of calling them off, that they might form themselves behind Brigadier Monckton's corps, which was now landed and drawn up on the beach in extreme good order."

Not only were the grenadiers withdrawn, but it was resolved to abandon the attack. It was growing late in the evening, the state of the tide was such that the line of retreat by the ford would be cut off in case of disaster, and a storm which had been threatening for some time broke in fury. But these were, perhaps, the mere pretexts for a retreat. The main reason was, the rapid repulse of the picked troops of the army, who were beaten without getting an opportunity to fight.

The French made no attempt to interrupt the movement, as Monckton's men reëmbarked, and Townshend withdrew, but "some of their savages," says Wolfe, "came down to murder such wounded as could not be brought off, and to scalp the dead, as their custom is."

Wolfe lost in this affair thirty-three officers and four hundred and ten men, killed or wounded. In his honest and straightforward account, he argues that the place chosen for the attack was well covered by British artillery, and afforded opportunity for the employment of all the troops at once, and the line of retreat, in case of repulse, was secure. The disadvantages were no less marked. "The beach upon which the troops were drawn up was," he said, "of deep mud with holes, and cut by several gullies, the hill to be ascended very steep and not everywhere practicable, the enemy remaining in their intrenchments, and their fire hot. If the attack had succeeded, our loss must certainly have been great and theirs inconsiderable, from the shelter which the neighboring woods afforded them. The River St. Charles still remained to be passed before the town was invested. All these circumstances I considered ; but the desire to act in conformity with the King's instructions induced me to make this trial, persuaded that a victorious army finds no difficulties." In a general order, the commander rebuked the grenadiers sharply for their undisciplined enthusiasm.

CHAPTER XX.

THE CAPTURE OF QUEBEC.

Attacks of the French on Scouting Parties—Reprisals by the English —Attempt by Murray—Illness of Wolfe—Townshend's Plan— Wolfe's Opinion of it—Montcalm's Prediction—Transfer of the Army—The Anse du Foulon, or Wolfe's Cove—Landing and Ascent of the Troops—Diversion at Beauport—Position on the Plains of Abraham—Arrival of Montcalm—Arrangement and Numbers of the Troops—The Battle of the Plains of Abraham— Rout of the French—Death of Wolfe—Death of Montcalm.

NOTWITHSTANDING Wolfe's proclamation enjoining neutrality upon the Canadians, they withstood the depredations of the soldiery, and in some instances joined with the Indians in murdering and scalping scouting-parties. A protest from Wolfe to Montcalm brought the usual answer that the French officers could not control their wild auxiliaries—the same answer that in after-years the British themselves used to make when American commanders complained of Indian atrocities. As a curious measure of retaliation, the English troops were allowed to scalp all Indians, and Canadians fighting disguised as Indians, which was practically only an exemption of the regular troops. The foraging parties had been ordered to burn and lay waste the country,

sparing nothing but churches, but molesting women
and children " on no account whatsoever."

On the 28th of July, when the French renewed
their attempt to burn the English fleet by casting
loose a huge fire-raft of light vessels bound together, Wolfe sent a flag of truce to the garrison with
this message : " If the enemy presume to send down
any more fire-rafts, they are to be made fast to two
particular transports, in which are all the Canadian
and other prisoners, in order that they may perish
by their own base inventions."

The defeat at Montmorenci tended to increase
the existing irritation. The whole of August was
spent in mere raiding. It was estimated, by one
who took part in the devastation, that fourteen hundred farm-houses were burned and their orchards
ruined. An expedition against St. Paul's Bay encountered some resistance, but succeeded in burning
several pretty villages. The Louisbourg grenadiers,
coming across a priest who had thrown himself into
a house with a party of his parishioners, drew them
out by a stratagem, and then killed and scalped
thirty-one of them.

The only serious bit of campaigning that relieved
this petty marauding was the expedition of General
Murray up the river. He set out with twelve hundred men for the purpose of aiding Admiral Holmes

in an attempt to destroy the French ships above the town, and to open communication with Amherst ; but they escaped him by lightening and running into shallows, out of the way.

Murray found the north shore carefully watched at all points, and was beaten off twice in attempting to land. The third time he got a foothold at Dechambault, burned a magazine, captured a few prisoners, and discovered, by letters which fell into his hands, that Johnson had captured Niagara, and that Amherst was in possession of Crown Point. He then returned without having accomplished anything of importance.

During August, Wolfe, never in robust health, was stricken with a fever. As soon as he began to recover, he called together his brigadiers, and directed them to take into consideration the problem of the siege. He gave it as his opinion that the town would surrender if the French army were defeated ; that the army, and not the town, should be attacked ; and submitted three plans, all looking toward an attempt to carry the intrenched camp at some point between the St. Charles and the Montmorenci.

But General Townshend proposed an alternative which met the approval of his associates, was finally adopted by the commander-in-chief, and resulted in the capture of Quebec.   In support of the idea of getting a position on the heights of Abraham, he said : " If we can maintain a new position on that side, we shall force Montcalm to fight where we choose ; we shall then be not only situated between him and his magazines, but also between his camp and the forces opposed to Amherst.   If he offer us battle and he should lose the day, then Quebec, probably all Canada, would fall into our hands, a result far greater than could occur from a victory at Beauport ; and, again, if he cross the River St. Charles with forces enough to confront us in the position we have supposed, the Beauport camp, thereby weakened, might be all the more easily attacked."

However, there was nothing sanguine in the tone of Wolfe's mind at this juncture.   He had been two months before the city, the summer was rapidly passing away, and little was accomplished.   The whole case is summed up frankly in his own letter to Pitt, in which he gave Townshend's plan, and said he had acquiesced in it ; but he detailed the difficulties in the way of carrying it out and recapitulated the elements that had hitherto retarded success—the vigilance of the Indian scouts preventing surprise, the batteries on the heights commanding the fleet in case of a direct assault on the town from the river, and the difficulty of receiving any help from the fleet in the position it must necessarily take, if the Upper Town were chosen for the attack. "In this situation," said he, "there is such a choice of difficulties that I own myself at a loss how to determine."

Curiously enough, we have what is supposed to be a record of Montcalm's opinions at about the same time, in a letter sent to Paris. After describing the ill success of the besiegers, he says their only hope is in "effecting a descent on the bank where the city is situated, without fortifications and without defence. They would then be in a position to offer me battle, which I could not refuse, and which I should not gain. . . . My Canadians, without discipline, deaf to the voice of the drum and martial instruments, disordered by this movement, could not form their ranks again. Moreover, they are without bayonets to oppose to those of the enemy; they could only fly, and there I should be, beaten without remedy."

This remarkable military prophecy was followed by a still more remarkable political prophecy which is quoted elsewhere. It is to be regretted that the authenticity of so wonderful a document as this letter should be questioned; but Carlyle, who quotes it in his "Frederick the Great," declares in a note to the last edition of the work that it is a forgery. His reasons are not given ; but the fact that the letter was first published in London in 1777 is suspicious, as its fabrication might then have had a political end in view.   Moreover, it is hard to understand why Mont-calm should have written a long letter of this sort at a time when there was very little prospect of getting it to France.   But something stronger than mere con-jecture is needed to overturn the authority of the doc-ument.   On the 29th of August, five vessels ran past the town, and the next day four more.   On the 1st of September the sick and wounded were brought to the Isle of Orleans ; on the 2d, a large body of the troops in position there withdrew ; on the 3d, the main body set all the houses and fortifications on fire, embarked in flat-bottomed boats, and moved to Point Levi ; and on the 4th, the troops on the Island of Orleans were shifted to the same place.   The whole available force of the army was then on the south side of the river.

On the 7th, 8th, and 9th, Admiral Holmes, com-manding the squadron above the city, stretching from Sillery to Point aux Trembles, manœuvred to divert the attention of the French.   Montcalm was on the alert, and sent Bougainville up the river with about three thousand men to watch the enemy's movements.   The bank was regularly patrolled, and guards were stationed at the Anse des Mères,

Anse du Foulon, and the Cove of Samos, all of which the French general persisted in regarding as impracticable, probably because he was urged to take additional precautions by Vaudreuil. A month earlier, he had said in a letter to the Governor touching these points : '' Vigilant patrolling is all that is needed in addition ; for we need not suppose that our enemies have wings to enable them in one night to cross the flood, debark, ascend broken-up, steep ways, and resort to escalade—an operation all the more unlikely to take place, as the assailants would have to bring ladders.''

On another occasion he wrote to Vaudreuil, who was concerned about the Anse des Mères : '' I swear to you that one hundred men posted will stop an army, give us time to wait till daylight, and then come up from the right. At the slightest nocturnal alarm, I shall march to your relief with the regiments of Guyenne and Bearn, which encamp in line to-morrow. Show light to-night in canoes ; and if darkness be great, light up fires.'' It seems singular that he who had left nothing to chance below the city, should have trusted so much to chance above it.

After a careful exmination of the northern bank, Wolfe and his officers had chosen for the contemplated descent a spot about three miles above the

city, called the Anse du Foulon, now known as
Wolfe's Cove.   There a narrow path ran up the bank,
and was defended at the top by an escarpment.   The
position was guarded by about one hundred men ;
but, unfortunately for the French, the place was in
command of Vercors, who, three years before, had
surrendered Beau Sejour, and was more notable
for his skill in peculation than for his soldiership.

Some of the English troops marched on the south
bank to a point eight miles up the river, and there
embarked, but were set ashore again.   On September 11th, Wolfe issued an order warning the army
to be in readiness to land and attack the enemy, and
hinting at a night's service in the boats.   On the
12th, a deserter from Montcalm's camp reported the
bulk of the French army below the town, and the
general incredulous as to any serious design at any
point above.   On the evening of that day, Wolfe
issued his last general order, declaring that the
Canadians were disheartened, that Amherst was advancing, and that a vigorous blow would determine
the fate of Canada.   Those first ashore were enjoined
to form with expedition, march straight on the
enemy, and charge whatever appeared.   Much was
to be expected from them in dealing with " five
weak French battalions mingled with a disorderly
peasantry."

The same evening, the heavier vessels below the city stood in toward Beauport shore and lowered away their boats filled with seamen and marines, as if for an attack. The rest of them set all sail and moved rapidly up to join Holmes's squadron at Cape Rouge, eight miles above the city, to which point Murray and Monckton marched from Point Levi, and the whole army embarked.

It was nine o'clock when the first division of sixteen hundred men, composed of the light infantry commanded by Colonel Howe, the regiments of Bragg, Kennedy, Lascelles, and Anstruther, a detachment of the Highlanders, and the American Grenadiers, took their places in the flat-bottomed boats, and the flotilla dropped down the river with the tide, Holmes's squadron following with the rest of the troops at an interval of forty-five minutes. Wolfe, though scarcely recovered from his illness, was as usual in the lead ; and there is a tradition that, as he sat in the boat, floating along between the clear water and the starlit sky, the sense of the nothingness of that glory for which he had so thirsted came over him, and he repeated these lines from Gray's Elegy :

> " The boast of heraldry, the pomp of power,
>   And all that beauty, all that wealth e'er gave,
>   Await alike the inexorable hour :
>   The paths of glory lead but to the grave."

"Now, gentlemen," he said, "I would rather be the author of that poem than take Quebec." And doubtless the capture of the Canadian citadel was an easier task than the composition of that almost faultless threnody.

It was a circumstance in favor of the English expedition, that the French were expecting a convoy of provisions from Bougainville, and, warned of the fact, the boats gave the proper answer when the French sentinels challenged along the shore. One of the English vessels, however, unaware of the attempt to land, and on the watch for the convoy, came near ruining the enterprise by firing on the flotilla. The rapidity of the ebbing tide carried part of the boats a little below the appointed landing.

An hour before daylight, the light company of the 78th Highlanders, which was the first to land, began to scramble up the wooded precipice. The captain, Donald Macdonald, answered the challenge of the sentinel in French, and gained a few moments. But the noise of the advance startled the guard, which turned, fired an irregular volley down the precipice, and fled. According to an English account, Vercors, the captain, alone stood his ground and resisted stoutly ; according to a French account, he was captured in his bed.

With very little loss, the troops reached the heights

and formed on the Plains of Abraham, the table-
land stretching away for nine miles above the city.
As fast as a boat was emptied, it was despatched to
the fleet, and reloaded with the men of Townshend's division. The battalions formed on the narrow beach, marched up the winding path, and re-
formed on the open ground above. At dawn, the
whole army was in line, but only one gun had been
brought up the hill.

Montcalm had been deceived by the movements
of the boats below the town during the night, as
they seemed to be threatening different points
between Beauport and Montmorenci ; and, though
he heard the sound of a cannon and the rattle of
musketry from the westward after daylight, he had
no notion of what had happened, until couriers gal-
loped into the camp at six o'clock with the intelligence.

" It can be but a small party come to burn a few
houses and retire," he said. But when the news
was confirmed, he exclaimed : " Then they have at
last reached the weak side of this miserable garrison ! We must give them battle and crush them
before mid-day."

Gathering all his available force, he moved rapidly
across the St. Charles by the bridge of boats, and
past the ramparts of the town, Vaudreuil being left

to guard the lines.   As early as eight o'clock, the
head of the column was in sight, and by nine Montcalm was forming his line of battle.   It has been
said that he should not have fought at all : Bougainville was within an easy march ; the English army
was weak, and could not attempt to attack a superior, or even an equal force, resting on the works
of the city ; the season was far advanced, and the
raising of the siege merely a question of days.   To
deliver a hasty battle seemed mere madness.   Montcalm may have been fluttered by the appearance of
the British in so dangerous a position, and so have
made an unwise decision ; or it may be that he was
convinced he had a fair chance of victory, and saw
that victory won under such circumstances meant
the complete destruction of his enemy.   Perhaps he
simply saw the end approaching which he had so
long anticipated ; and, believing there was nothing
effective to be done, determined to do something
gallant.

Wolfe's line of battle was formed with the right
on the precipice, scarcely a mile from the ramparts
of the town.   The 35th regiment was on the extreme right, the Louisbourg grenadiers joined them,
and the 28th prolonged the line to the 43d, which
constituted the centre.   Toward the left, the 47th,
the 78th Highlanders, and the 58th followed in suc-

cession, the last regiment holding the brow of the ridge overlooking the valley of the St. Charles and completing the first line. In the second line, the 15th regiment rested its right upon the river-bank ; the two battalions of the 60th, or Royal Americans, occupied the plain to the left, Colonel Burton with the 48th regiment was held in reserve, and Colonel Howe with the light infantry, grouped in some houses and neighboring coppices, protected the left flank. Wolfe with Monckton took his station on the right of the first line, Murray commanded on the left, and Townshend had charge of the second line.

Montcalm's right was formed of the regiment of La Sarre and Languedoc, with a battalion of the Colonial troops ; the regiments of Bearne and Guyenne were in the centre, supported by a strong body of militia ; the Royal Roussillon and a battalion of the marine held the left. The commander took his place in the centre.

The ordinary English historian is accustomed to give the strength of Wolfe's army at forty-eight hundred and twenty-eight men, and that of Montcalm's at seventy-five hundred and twenty, basing the latter figure on the authority of an '' intelligent Frenchman,'' casually mentioned in Knox's Journal, but not named. The ordinary French historian allows Wolfe eight thousand and Montcalm four thousand five hundred troops.   But the best author- ities estimate the strength of each army at less than five thousand men, and as nearly numerically equal.   The English troops, however, were a solid mass of tried veterans, confident in themselves and confident in their leader ; the French troops were an incongruous mixture, part of whom mistrusted themselves, and part of whom mistrusted their com- rades, while the commander mistrusted his army as a whole.   Artillery played but little part in the bat- tle.   To offset the single cannon that Wolfe had dragged up the precipice, Montcalm brought up only two guns.

If it was inconsiderate folly on the part of the French general to risk a battle, it must be acknowl- edged that he fought it like a bold and skilful sol- dier.   About ten o'clock, after an hour's cannonad- ing, the fighting opened on the right, where the French skirmishers, mainly Canadians and Indians, pushed up the slope from the valley of the St Charles, turned the left flank of Murray's brigade, and attacked Howe's light infantry. The object of the movement, which was gallantly executed, seemed to be to roll back the English line and crowd it over the precipice.   Townshend, who exhibited singular ability throughout this campaign, pushed forward the 15th regiment and the Royal Americans to the help of Howe, and restored the fight.

Meanwhile the French centre and left advanced rapidly, driving in Wolfe's skirmishers, whose retreat for a moment disordered the main line. But the disturbance passed away, and the British waited quietly for the approach of the enemy. The French line came on, firing quickly at a distance of a hundred yards. Wolfe, who was moving along his line exhorting the men to reserve their fire till they could deliver a volley at a distance of forty yards, was struck in the wrist with a bullet ; but he wrapped his handkerchief about his hand, and paid no further attention to the wound. When at last the English troops received the order to fire, they delivered one of those close and deadly volleys for which they are celebrated, and under the crash of that battle-bolt the French column staggered. St. Ours was killed, Senezergues fell mortally wounded, and many minor officers and men were stretched upon the field. The pressure of the fire. was so fierce that the Canadian militia broke, notwithstanding the efforts of Montcalm to keep them steady ; and while the French left and centre hesitated and wavered, the right, checked by Townshend's dispositions, began to recoil before a counter-attack of the 58th and 78th regiments.

Wolfe, seeing that the crisis of the fight was at
hand, ordered an advance along the whole line.
The movement, which began as a slow but steady
advance, with deadly volleys clearing the way, soon
took the form of a triumphant charge, the French
breaking away in all directions.   At this juncture
Wolfe was struck a second time, somewhat more
seriously, and as he pressed on in the pursuit at the
head of the Louisbourg grenadiers, he was struck in
the breast by a shot from a redoubt.   He staggered,
but catching hold of Lieutenant Brown, of the 22d,
murmured : "Support me, that my brave fellows
may not see me fall."   The lieutenant, a volunteer
named Henderson, and a private soldier of the 22d,
carried him a little way to the rear, with the help of
Captain Williamson of the Royal Artillery.   There
he asked to be laid down.   They wanted to know
if he would have a surgeon, but he said : " It is
needless ; it is all over with me."

One of the group about him cried out : " They
run, see how they run !"

Like a man roused from sleep, Wolfe, who had
been sinking rapidly, asked : " Who runs ?"

" The enemy, sir," was the answer.   " Egad !
they give way everywhere."

" Go one of you, my lads," said Wolfe, " to Colonel Burton.   Tell him to march Webb's regiment

with all speed down to the St. Charles, to cut off the retreat of the fugitives from the bridge." Then, turning on his side, he died with the ex- clamation : " Now, God be praised ! I will die in peace."

About the same time that Wolfe was struck down, Carleton fell severely wounded, and Barré re- ceived a ball in the head, from the effect of which he afterward lost the sight of one eye. Monckton also fell, disabled but not dangerously hurt, as he was advancing between the 43d and 47th regiments, and the command devolved upon Townshend, who, after disposing of the last organized resistance in a coppice toward the left of the victorious forces, took measures to withdraw from the pursuit and re-form the troops to meet the expected advance of Bou- gainville from up the river. The 47th and 58th regi- ments had pushed the fugitives up to the very gates of St. Louis and St. John, while the 78th Highland- ers, drawing their broadswords, followed the strag- glers, slaughtering as they went ; many of the Frenchmen joining to the cry for quarter the protest that they had not been at Fort William Henry The remnants of the left and centre of Montcalm's army found refuge within the fortifications of the city, while all that was left of the right wing fell back in confusion beyond the St. Charles.

Montcalm had been mortally wounded while making a gallant effort to rally his men. Death came to him more slowly than to Wolfe; but he met it with a Christian resignation not less admirable than the fiery heroism of the British commander. When he had been carried to the general hospital, a convent of the Augustine nuns on the St. Charles, about a mile from the town, and put to bed, with his wound dressed, he asked the surgeon if his hurt was mortal. When told that it was, he said: "I am glad of it." He then inquired: "How long can I survive?" "About a dozen hours; perhaps more, peradventure less," was the answer. "So much the better," said Montcalm; "I shall not live to see the surrender of Quebec."

Shortly afterward Monsieur de Ramsay, the King's lieutenant, in command of the fortifications of the city, called upon the general and asked his advice on various points touching the defence. The dying man made answer: "I'll neither give orders nor interfere any further. I have business that must be attended to of much greater moment than your ruined garrison and this wretched country. My time is very short; therefore, pray leave me. I wish you all comfort, and to be happily extricated from your present perplexities." He then called for

his chaplain and prepared for death, which came to
his relief on the evening of September 14th.

The battle was scarcely over when Bougainville
appeared upon the field ; but the resolute front and
superior numbers of Townshend dismayed him, and
he fell back unpursued to Cape Rouge. There he
was joined the same evening by Vaudreuil, who
had abandoned the intrenched camp below the St.
Charles with the remnants of the French army.
Word was sent to M. de Levis, then at Montreal, to
come and assume command in Montcalm's place,
and it is not improbable that an energetic leader
such as he was might have done something to retrieve the evil effects of the first battle of the Plains
of Abraham ; but by the time he was ready to move,
Quebec had surrendered.

On the day succeeding the action, Townshend
began the construction of works against the city and
cut it off from communication with the surrounding
country ; and on the 17th the fleet moved up for
an attack on the Lower Town. Provisions were
scarce, the inhabitants of the city were disheartened, and the prospects of a protracted defence were
gloomy. Consequently, M. de Ramsay completed
negotiations for the surrender of the place at once.
The capitulation was proclaimed on the morning of
the 18th, and in the afternoon the representatives of

the army took possession of the Upper Town, the representatives of the navy assuming the honor of occupying the Lower Town. The terms granted were honorable, as Townshend and Admiral Saunders were only too glad to secure their easy conquest by liberal concessions. The garrison marched out with the honors of war, the people were secured in all their rights and privileges, and the Catholic church was guaranteed the enjoyment of freedom and the possession of its property. On the part of the French commander, the surrender must, on the whole, be regarded as somewhat pusillanimous, since a messenger from De Levis arrived on the 18th with a promise of help, which that officer would certainly have tried desperately to make good.

So ended the memorable siege of Quebec. The battle which decided the result was a mere skirmish, if we consider only the numbers engaged and the losses ; for the English acknowledge a loss on their own part of but fifty-five killed and six hundred and seven wounded of all ranks, and only claim a loss on the part of the French of fifteen hundred killed, wounded, or missing. But the romantic circumstances attending the action—the night movement on the great river, the ascent of a precipice to find a field of battle, the fall of the two commanders, one so heroic in his victory, and the other so manly in his defeat, the decisive results of the brief struggle—all these things make the story of the capture of Quebec a favorite with the historian and the artist.

To be sure, the decisive character of the engagement on the Plains of Abraham was mainly due to the fact that it was England that won the victory ; for the result gave her one of those strong natural positions on a great commercial channel which her mastery at sea has enabled her to hold in different parts of the world.   Though the war was still to linger on, the event was no longer doubtful, as the possession of Quebec afforded the means of bringing the naval power of Great Britain to bear effectively ; and the support of that power rendered Quebec invulnerable.   The French might win another battle on the spot where Wolfe had defeated them, but it was destined to be a barren victory.

The news of the fall of the capital of Canada reached England two days after the news of the defeat at Montmorenci, and caused the wildest rejoicings—save in one small Kentish village, where sympathy with the widowed mother of the dead victor restrained the expression of public gratification. The remains of Wolfe were taken to England for interment, and his memory was honored by his countrymen with lavish gratitude.   Montcalm was buried in a church in Quebec, in a tomb scooped out by a hostile shell.   To-day a monument erected to the honor of both heroes looks down on the scene of their struggle –a memorial of one of those few conquests in the history of the world in which the vanquished have preserved possessions, language, religion, and the fair fame of the men who died for the lost cause.

CHAPTER XXI.

THE SURRENDER OF CANADA.

Siege of Quebec by De Levis—Battle at Sillery Wood—Amherst on the St. Lawrence—Surrender of Isle Royale—Surrender of Montreal and the Whole of Canada—The Treaty of Paris—Predictions of the Revolt of the Colonies.

NOTWITHSTANDING the successes of 1759, Canada was not yet completely conquered. If Amherst had moved on faster and taken Montreal, the work would have been finished ; but his failure to do so gave the French forces an opportunity to rally, and the indefatigable De Levis, who had succeeded Montcalm, gathered what remained of the army at Montreal, and made preparations for attempting the recovery of Quebec. The people of Canada were still more pressed with want than the year before ; wheat sold at from thirty to forty livres a bushel (six or eight dollars), a cow was worth nine hundred livres, and a sheep from two to three hundred.

After several fruitless attacks had been made on the British outposts during the winter, De Levis refitted all the vessels yet remaining early in the

spring and gathered the stores still left at the forts
on the Richelieu.   On the 17th of April, he left
Montreal with all his force, and descended the river,
gathering up the detached troops on the way ;
the whole amounting to more than ten thousand
men.

Quebec had been left in charge of Murray, with
seven thousand men, a supply of heavy artillery, and
stores of ammunition and provisions ; but the number of men had been much reduced by sickness and
by hardship encountered in bringing fuel to the
city from forests, some as far as ten miles away.
Their position, however, had been very much
strengthened ; Murray had erected redoubts, with
artillery, outside the fortifications, and repaired five
hundred of the injured houses for the accommoda-
tion of his troops.

De Levis encamped at St. Foy, and on the 27th
advanced to within three miles of the city.   Murray
took the unaccountable resolution of sallying out
with his reduced and dispirited army to meet the
enemy in the open field—a measure which he afterward attempted to explain in a letter to the
Secretary of State : " Well weighing my peculiar
position, and well knowing that in shutting myself
up within the walls of the city, I should risk the
-whole stake in the chance of defending a wretched

fortification, which could not be lessened by an action in the field.''

On the morning of the 28th of April, Murray marched his wasted army out to the Plains of Abraham, with twenty pieces of artillery, and formed his line of battle. Riding out to observe the position of the enemy, he found that they were unprepared for action, and returning he gave orders for an immediate attack, and the army marched down the slope from the heights and into the plains near Sillery Wood.

Two companies of the French grenadiers advanced and met the vanguard of the British, and then drew back ; whereupon some of Murray's men pursued them, but were thus exposed to the fire of their own cannon, which obliged the gunners to cease firing, and they were repelled in turn by the French, who were now in battle array. The engagement immediately became general. The British left soon gave way, and drew back in confusion ; the right followed ; the artillery was lost ; and at length only two regiments held the forlorn hope, and Murray's men were forced to fly, leaving three hundred dead upon the field. The wounded amounted to about seven hundred, many of whom were left in the hands of the enemy. It is charged that only twenty-eight of these were sent to the hospitals, and the rest given

up to the Indians ; but the French accounts say
that the Indians, who had taken no part in the action, but had been skulking in the rear, came to the
field during the pursuit and killed many of the
wounded, while those that survived were protected
from the Indians, whom De Levis quickly dispersed,
and received the same treatment as the wounded
French.   The loss of De Levis has been variously
given at from four hundred to eighteen hundred.

The French made immediate preparations for a
siege by opening trenches.   The English garrison
was so reduced that not more than twenty-two hundred were fit for service ; but they all went to work
with alacrity, hoping to hold out until relief should
come.   Five hundred men who could not walk without crutches, made sand-bags and cartridges ; and
the women who were not employed in the care of
the wounded assisted in the light work of the garrison.   One hundred and thirty-two cannon were
mounted, and opened fire on the French lines.

On the 9th of May, a ship was seen turning the
bend below and advancing toward the city.   Both
armies were expecting relief, and their strength was
so nearly balanced that the turning of the scale
depended on the approaching ship.   '' Such was the
garrison's anxiety,'' wrote one of them, '' that we
remained some time in suspense, not having eyes

enough to look at it ; but we were soon convinced that she was British, although there were
some among us who, having their motives for ap-
pearing wise, sought to temper our joy by obsti-
nately insisting that she was French. But the vessel having saluted the fort with twenty-one guns,
and launched her small boat, all doubts vanished. It
is impossible to describe the gayety that seized upon
the garrison. Officers and men mounted the ramparts, mocked at the French, and for an hour raised
continual hurras, and threw their càps into the air.
The city, the enemy's camp, the harbor, and the
country around for miles in extent, reëchoed our
cries and the roar of our batteries.''

Other vessels arrived on the 15th, and on the following day they attacked and quickly destroyed the
little French fleet under Vauquelin. De Levis, having nothing more to hope for, raised the siege in
haste, abandoned his stores, and retreated to Montreal. A detachment of English troops pursued,
and brought back a few prisoners.

All this time, Amherst was ponderously preparing to go to the aid of Quebec, and early in May
he was ready to move from New York. Captain
Loring was sent to drive the French cruisers from
Lake Ontario, to prevent the French forces from
retiring to the west, and making another stand.

Amherst had chosen to reach Montreal by the roundabout way of Oswego and the St. Lawrence. Colonel Haviland was to take the direct route by way of Lake Champlain, with about thirty-five hundred men ; and Murray, aided by Lord Rollo and two battalions from Louisbourg, had been directed to ascend the river, and meet Amherst and Haviland before the doomed city.

It was the 9th of July when Amherst reached Oswego with part of his army ; Gage brought the rest on the 22d, and Johnson and his Indians joined the encampment the following day. There were over ten thousand soldiers and seven hundred Indians.

On the 7th of August, Amherst sent a detachment under Haldimand to take possession of the post at the head of the river, where Kingston now stands ; and by the 12th the last of the army were embarked, and an armed vessel was captured on the river by a detachment of men in barges, under Colonel Williamson.

On Isle Royale was a small work called Fort Levi, under the command of Pouchot, which the English expected to pass " like a beaver's hut." But learning that there were some skilful pilots there, Amherst determined to capture it. Batteries were therefore placed, and on the 23d the vessels opened

a vigorous fire, and were soon joined by the batteries.   Pouchot waited till the ships were within
pistol-shot, and then returned the fire with such
spirit that two of them were forced to run aground,
and one to strike her colors.

Many of the English ships bore Indian names—
the *Ottawa, Oneida, Onondaga,* etc.—and the Catholic Indians of Father Picquet's mission, who were
watching the contest from the fort, regarding the
ships as on their side on account of the names,
and because they carried Indians painted on their
flags, became very much excited at seeing them
faring badly, and especially when the *Ottawa* and
the *Oneida* drifted off and ran aground.

On the 25th, Pouchot, being nearly at the end of
his resources, surrendered to Amherst, with his
garrison of nearly three hundred men. Selecting
some guides for his ships down the dangerous course
of the river, Amherst despatched the remainder of
the garrison to New York by way of Oswego. The
Indians had secretly planned to destroy the garrison
when the fort should be given up ; but Amherst,
hearing of the plan, told Sir William Johnson to
dissuade them from it, promising them all the stores
in the fort, and threatening that his own soldiers
would turn upon them if they attempted a massacre.
The Indians submitted, but were sulky and dissatis-

fied, and Johnson told Amherst they would probably leave the army—as, indeed, most of them did. Amherst threatened them with vengeance on his return if they should commit any acts of violence on their way to their homes ; and they were forced to content themselves with a peaceable journey.

On the way through the rapids, sixty-four boats, eighty-eight men, and a quantity of stores were lost.   Amherst invested Montreal on the 6th of September, and was met by Murray, whose progress up the river had been a continual skirmish.   Nearly every village assailed him with a fire of musketry ; and he had taken vengeance on some by burning them.   Haviland, coming up from Crown Point, had forced Bougainville to draw off most of his men from Isle aux Noix, and received the surrender of the remainder, and reached Montreal a day later than Amherst.

Vaudreuil had resolved not to make any useless resistance, but to give up the city as soon as the English army should arrive ; and on the 8th of September, not only Montreal, but all Canada—from the fishing stations on the Gulf of St. Lawrence to the crest dividing the rivers that flow into lakes Erie and Michigan from those that find their way to the Mississippi and the Gulf of Mexico—was surrendered to England.

The provincial troops were to return to their homes, and the regulars to march out from their posts with all the honors of war, and be sent to France in British vessels, under pledges not to serve again before the conclusion of peace. The civil officers were also to be conveyed to France with their families and baggage ; and only such papers were to be retained as would be useful for the future regulation of the affairs of the colony. Religious liberty was granted, private property was to be respected, and the French colonists were to enjoy the same civil and commercial rights as the British.

An armament had been ordered from France to the aid of the French troops in Canada, consisting of a thirty-gun frigate, two large supply-ships, and nineteen smaller vessels ; but, learning that British ships were in the St. Lawrence, the officers thought best to put into the Bay of Chaleurs, whither Captain Byron, in command at Louisbourg, sailed with five vessels and destroyed the entire fleet, together with two batteries and two hundred houses.

After long negotiations, the preliminaries of peace were signed on the 3d of November, 1762, and ratified February 10th, 1763. By this, called the Treaty of Paris, Canada, Nova Scotia, and Cape Breton were ceded to Great Britain. France reserved New Orleans and the territory west of the

Mississippi, but immediately afterward ceded them to Spain. They did not, however, remain long in Spanish possession, but were returned to France, and finally conveyed to the United States in 1803.

Thus Great Britain gained possession of nearly all the inhabited portion of North America. The struggle to found a French empire in the west was over, and New France disappeared from the map, while the boundary of British America was moved northward to the Polar Sea. It looked as if the lines of British territory were definitely settled. But already there were predictions that the power of England on the western continent was soon to be assailed by her own children in the colonies that she herself had planted ; that the spirit of independence which had been growing up among them would break into open rebellion against the arbitrary exactions of the old country and the repressions imposed on the growth of trade and manufactures, so soon as the fear of French aggression from the north and Indian hostilities on the frontier should be removed.

Writing after the fall of Canada, a French diplomatist said : '' The colonies will no longer need' the protection of England. She will call on them to contribute toward supporting the burdens they have helped to bring on her, and they will answer by striking off all dependence." And in the letter before alluded to, said to have been written by Montcalm in 1759, when he knew that the surrender of Quebec was only a question of time, he said : " If they must have masters, they prefer their countrymen to strangers, taking care, however, to yield as little obedience as possible ; but, Canada once conquered, and the Canadians one people with those colonists, let the first occasion come when England seems to interfere with their interests, and do you believe, my dear cousin, that the colonies will obey ? And what would they have to fear in revolting ? "

Some English statesmen also saw the danger, and wished to take it into consideration in arranging the terms of the peace. " If the people of our colonies find no check from Canada," said one of them, " they will extend themselves almost without bound into the inland parts. They will increase infinitely, from all causes. What the consequence will be, to have a numerous, hardy, independent people, possessed of a strong country, communicating little or not at all with England, I leave to your own reflections. By eagerly grasping at extensive territory, we may run the risk, and in no very distant period, of losing what we now possess. A neighbor that keeps us in some awe is not always

the worst of neighbors.   So that, far from sacrific-
ing Guadaloupe to Canada, perhaps if we might
have Canada without any sacrifice at all, we ought
not to desire it.   There should be a balance of
power in America."

INDEX.

Lightning Source UK Ltd.
Milton Keynes UK
UKHW020754211118
332720UK00012B/1017/P